As I flew in from the east to the west, I stayed to the north of the treeline, just out in front of our pinned-down troops. My port-side M-60 machine gun was blasting away at the treeline as the other gunner threw out a red smoke grenade while we passed above the hedgerow at about a hundred feet. As I pulled right, my wingman came in from the west in the opposite direction, dropped his red smoke grenade, while firing, and we joined up over the friendly LZ to the north at three thousand feet.

"Do you have our red smoke, Rooster?"

"That's affirmative. We have a good sighting of the treeline, but can't make out the friendlies in the paddies."

"Okay, Rooster, on your next orbit you are cleared to commence attack on the treeline. Drop on the treeline between the two red smokes: drop first pair closest to the western smoke. We'll then walk up the treeline eastward."

"Roger Eagle, Rooster One rolling in hot, I have the treeline."

"Continue Rooster One."

"Okay Rooster One, I have your wings level, lined up. You are cleared hot."

The Special Warfare Series
from St. Martin's Paperbacks

NAKED WARRIORS by Cdr. Francis Douglas Fane,
USNR (Ret.) and Don Moore

AIR COMMANDO by Philip D. Chinnery

MOBILE GUERRILLA FORCE by James C. Donahue

PROJECT ALPHA by Sedgwick Tourison

CHOPPERS by J. D. Coleman

COVERT OPS by James E. Parker, Jr.

CLEARED HOT!

A Marine Combat Pilot's Vietnam Diary

COL. BOB STOFFEY

St. Martin's Paperbacks

AUTHOR'S NOTE: This is a personal narrative of what I saw in Vietnam. The events all happened. The chronology and geography are correct. The names of the characters, other than those of presidents, generals, and admirals, have been changed and bear no resemblance to the names of any of the actual people in order to preserve their privacy and anonymity. Any resemblance to other actual persons, living or dead, is entirely coincidental. Nothing is intended or should be interpreted as expressing or representing the views of the U.S. Marine Corps or any other government department or agency.

CLEARED HOT!

Copyright © 1992 by Col. Bob Stoffey.

Cover photograph from Wide World Photos, Inc.

All rights reserved. No part of this book may be used or reproduced in any manner whatsoever without written permission except in the case of brief quotations embodied in critical articles or reviews. For information address St. Martin's Press, 175 Fifth Avenue, New York, N.Y. 10010.

ISBN: 0-312-92941-2

Printed in the United States of America

St. Martin's Press hardcover edition/March 1992
St. Martin's Paperbacks edition/April 1999

10 9 8 7 6 5

This book is dedicated to all the brave wives, sons, and daughters who have suffered the loss of their husband or father in Vietnam, Cambodia, and Laos, and to those who still suffer the unknown of the MIA.

Contents

Preface

I have had the privilege of serving my country as a Marine Corps pilot for a quarter of a century. During those exciting years of my life, I had the additional experience of serving as a combat pilot during our nation's longest and most frustrating war—the Vietnam War.

For the Americans, this war covered a period from 1962, with the introduction of advisors and support helicopters, to 1973, when the last of the U.S. combat units were retrograded out of that country in accordance with the Paris Peace Talks Agreement and the release of our POWs.

During this nine-year period, 440,000 American marines served in the Republic of Vietnam and 58,000 Americans died there. I strongly suspect that there still are some MIAs somewhere in Laos and Cambodia. I was only one of those marine pilots who served there. Each Vietnam veteran has his own story and own perspective of that long-term, limited war.

I had the unusual experience of spending three combat tours in Vietnam—more than four years away from my family. I saw three separate phases of this Vietnam debacle and political—not military—defeat. My three combat tours covered the years 1965 to 1966, 1969 to 1970 and 1971 to 1973.

I flew 440 combat missions as a helicopter pilot in the UH-34D transport, UH-1E and AH-1G Cobra gunship helicopters and also as a forward air controller airborne (FACA) in a twin-turboprop-engine OV-10A armed reconnaissance airplane. All missions were at very low altitudes over the battlefields. Additionally, I spent a tour of combat duty as the Marine Corps aviation officer and amphibious warfare officer on the staff of the commander, Seventh Fleet, on board the fleet's flagship, the guided-missile cruiser USS *Oklahoma City,* off of North and South Vietnam.

I saw a lot, but can convey only a small portion of it in a book. I tell it as I saw it. I hope that those who enjoy flying will like it. For those who wish to catch up on some of the history of that war, I have included a small portion of that. However, the entire content is one fighting man's perspective. If you were there with me and saw it differently, write your own story.

The quotes throughout the book reflect my best recollection of what was conveyed in conversations, but are usually not exact, verbatim quotes, due to the passage of time.

During my military flying career, I had the opportunity to fly twenty-four types of single-engine prop and jet airplanes, and multiengine prop and turboprop airplanes along with numerous types of helicopters. The airplanes were the T-34 Beech Mentor; the North American SNJ, T-28, and T-33 trainers; the F-9F

Cougar swept-wing fighter; the twin-engine prop SNB, US-2A, C-45J, and C-117 transports; the single-engine prop Cessna Bird Dogs OE-1 and OE-2; the Learjet aircraft; the single-engine jet Douglas attack bomber A-4; the AD-1 Skyraider single-engine prop attack bomber; and the North American twin-turboprop OV-10A Bronco. The helicopters I piloted were the Bell HTL-6 and the Piaseki twin-rotor HUP-2 trainers; the Kaman HOK-1; the Sikorsky HRS-3, HUS, and UH-34D; the Boeing CH-46 assault transport; and the Bell UH-1E Huey and AH-1G and AH-1J Cobra attack helicopters.

Since this is primarily a flying story, I would like to list, in fond memory, those Marine Corps pilots who were close personal friends and who died while flying. I list not only those who died in Vietnam, but also those who died in aircraft accidents in other parts of the world. They are very few compared to the total number of those who died in their beloved flying machines in the service of their country, but they were sad losses to me, and many also to my wife, Eleanor, who knew some of them from our various Stateside tours of duty that we shared.

NAME	RANK	AIRCRAFT	PLACE WHERE DIED
John Hannah	First Lieutenant	HOK-1	Okinawa
"Bo" Barkley	First Lieutenant	OE-1	New River, NC
Paul McNally	Captain	UH-34D	Vietnam
James Magel	First Lieutenant	UH-34D	Vietnam
Lee Gingras	First Lieutenant	OV-10A	Korea
Wiley Cable	Major	CH-46	Monterey, CA
Bernie Terhorst	Major	CH-46	Vietnam
Leroy Blankenship	Major	CH-46	Vietnam
Charles Rogers	Major	F-4	El Toro, CA
Bill Tepo	Major	F-4	Vietnam
Don Berger	Captain	C-117	Vietnam
Bob Norton	Captain	OV-10A	Vietnam
Hank Henry	Major	AH-1G	Vietnam

Ken Pennington	First Lieutenant	AH-1G	Vietnam
Tom Diefenbach	Air America	O-2	Laos
Darrel Tipples	First Lieutenant	OV-10A	Camp Pendleton, CA
John McCammon	Major (ret.)	Learjet	San Clemente Island, CA
Tom Guerinot	Major	OV-10A	Camp Pendleton, CA

Additionally, navy chief Bill Hunter, corpsman serving in VMO-2 and killed in action near Da Nang, will never be forgotten by the Huey medevac pilots for his continual heroism.

Finally, among the first Americans shot down over Kuwait in January 1991 and held as POWs in Iraq were VMO-2 flyers in an OV-10B Bronco: Lt. Col. Cliff Acree, commanding officer, VMO-2, and CWO-4 Guy Hunter, chief aerial observer, VMO-2. Our prayers were answered when they were released by Iraq on March 7, 1991.

I did not write this book to change anyone's feelings regarding the Vietnam War. I may have written it because ten years ago nobody would listen to a Vietnam veteran and possibly some history may have been lost of what happened there. Possibly, I wrote it because I kept seeing actor Tom Selleck, in *Magnum P.I.*, every Thursday evening on TV wearing a baseball cap with "VMO-2, DANANG" on it. I flew in VMO-2 for many years, in several places including Da Nang, Republic of Vietnam, and wore that same kind of hat on occasions. I was the commanding officer of VMO-2 for eighteen months. When finished reading this book, you'll know what "VMO-2, DANANG," is all about. But I'll still wonder why Tom Selleck was wearing my old hat.

Maybe another reason that I wrote the book is that back in October 1976 I visited the National Air and Space Museum in the Smithsonian Institution, in Washington, D.C. There I was surprised to see, in the Vietnam section, the very same helicopter (identical serial number as logged in my flight book) that I had flown on combat missions in Vietnam. It now is a shiny, clean helicopter, minus the numerous patches we had on it covering bullet holes. Therefore, after reading this book, the reader will know exactly how that helicopter was used in Vietnam.

Or, quite simply, the answer to why I wrote this can be found in the last sentence of the book.

Acknowledgments

I wish to thank my wife, Eleanor, for her many hours proofreading the manuscript. Without her painstaking work, the manuscript would never have gotten past the rough-notes stage. I would like also to cite my son, Bob, who typed much of the initial draft, and Mike Friedman, who provided new concepts and assistance.

CLEARED HOT!

chapter 1

Vietnam, 1965

The steady drone of the four turboprop engines of the Marine
Corps KC-130 transport aircraft from VMGR-152 abruptly
changed. The drone shifted to a high-pitched whine as the plane
started a descent. Lieutenant Colonel Duphey, the KC-130 aircraft commander, could be heard on the Mickey Mouse headset,
saying, "Okay, fellas, to our right is Vietnam. We'll make a
descending right turn to intercept the Da Nang one-eight-zero
radial for a straight-in to runway three-six. I'll keep it high until
final approach. Some of our other transports have received hits

from Viet Cong guerrillas. Some when they were as close as five miles to Da Nang Airfield. That city ahead, for those who can see it, is Da Nang. Not too long ago, it used to be called Tourane, under the French rule."

I leaned to the right, twisting my neck to try to see through the small porthole window. I was just another passenger in the cold, large, metallic fuselage of this marine cargo and passenger aircraft. As I peered out of the right side of the aircraft, I saw a very green countryside. There were large brown and black mountains that appeared to be about fifteen to twenty miles inland from the expansive, golden beaches that merged with the white surf of the ever-so-green, calm-appearing South China Sea.

All the officers and troops, about 150 of them, were straining to look out over the countryside that none of them had been to before. Only two KC-130 crew members in the cargo compartment and I wore earphones that allowed us to hear the in-cockpit chatter of Colonel Duphey, his copilot, and the flight engineer.

I had known Duphey for several years. Therefore, when we and the other marines boarded the KC-130 at the Marine Air Base, Futema, Okinawa, Colonel Duphey had given me a plug-in-type crew member's headset. This enabled me to listen to the crew talk as they flew all the way down to Vietnam from Okinawa.

The KC-130 had, besides the troops, about twenty officers of varying ranks traveling on individual orders. Most were coming from the States; the others had joined up at Futema on Okinawa. The enlisted men, in dark green utilities, had their M-14 rifles lying under their cloth seats. Each had been issued one clip of ammunition. The officers had no weapons. They would draw their pistols from the unit that they reported to. There were only a handful of Americans in Vietnam. It was spring 1965.

Inside the aircraft, there were four jeeps and two "water buffalo," or water trailers, along with one 105-mm howitzer artillery piece. All equipment was strapped down to the center passageway of the troop/cargo hold.

The flight had been long and very boring. Most of the passengers had slept and now had awakened because of the change in the sound of the engines for the descent into Da Nang Airfield.

Curiosity had half of the marines up from their webbed seats and standing around the small portholes of the fuselage.

Colonel Duphey's voice came over my headset, "Crew chief, tell all the passengers to sit down and strap in. We're approaching for a landing." I saw the two crewmen going up and down the aisles, telling the marines to strap in for the landing. I tightened my seat belt and continued to peer out of the nearby porthole. As the plane rolled out of the turn, the noise of the landing gear coming down convinced all the passengers that indeed they were landing in Vietnam. I saw the green beauty of thousands of rice paddies with dikes built around each paddy plot. There were hundreds of tree-lined villages with grass-roofed huts. I saw people in black pajamas wearing golden-colored, straw, conical hats. Most of the people were out in the rice paddies working. Along the paddy dikes were caribou, or water buffalo, similar to the type I had seen in the Philippines some years back. The country, green and lush, was simply beautiful.

I looked about the semidark passenger compartment. I could see the excitement with very little apprehension on the faces of the young enlisted men and the similar expressions on the faces of the slightly older officers. I knew that they all had some feelings of approaching the unknown. Yet, I thought, they probably felt like I felt. War is why I'm in this Marine Corps uniform. This may only be a small communist guerrilla revolutionary war, but if we don't stop the communist guerrillas here, I thought, where will we stop them? Along the Mexican Border? The Vietnamese in the South have asked for our help, and as usual, we Americans are here to assist. As a professional marine, this is where I should be. I leaned back into the cold, webbed seat and turned away from the small porthole. I closed my eyes and thought. All of us aboard were on individual orders to replace some marines who had completed their thirteen months' tour of combat, assisting the Republic of Vietnam in fighting off communist guerrilla attacks in the farming countryside. The Russians, and to a limited degree the Chinese, were supplying arms and equipment to the Viet Minh, now called the Viet Cong, or VC. Unlike the internationally supported direct invasion thrust of the North Koreans into South Korea just six years after World War II, this war was different.

I reflected on the history of Vietnam, which I had researched after receiving my orders while stationed in Hawaii. In Hawaii I had been a pilot in Marine Aircraft Group 13 and a platoon commander in the 1st Air and Naval Gunfire Liaison Company—1st ANGLICO.

Leaning relaxed against the webbed seat-backing, I thought about how well I had been trained for all these years. I had eight years of Marine Corps training and was now a captain. I had flown fixed-wing aircraft (airplanes), both prop and jet, and helicopters for over two thousand hours in many parts of the world: Korea, Japan, Okinawa, Cuba, Puerto Rico, and the USA. I was ready; I was well trained no matter what the size of the war. I had a small exposure to combat conditions in '62 in Cuba as a search-and-rescue-helicopter pilot flying off the USS *Boxer* supporting the Marine Corps low-altitude photo missions flown over the Cuban missile sites. These photo flights were flown by VMCJ-2 of Cherry Point, North Carolina, and were flown from Key West, Florida. I flew along the Cuban coast, close in, as the marine jet photo-birds came in low over the missile sites. In the event one was shot down, my mission was to go in and get the pilot of the recce-bird. Therefore, this going into a hostile environment in Vietnam was not a completely new experience. The same feelings of the unknown were present.

As the KC-130 squeaked onto the runway at Da Nang Airfield, the warm air of Vietnam filled the aircraft. The lumbering transport rolled out and taxied to the west side of the field, where the U.S. Marine Corps helicopter squadrons were located. I saw Vietnamese air force T-28 aircraft loaded with bombs on the east side of the runway. There were also eight A-1 Skyraiders (also called ADs or SPADs). I had flown this aircraft out of Iwakuni, Japan, back in 1958 for a very short period, as they were being phased out of service. That was shortly after I had flown the T-28 aircraft in the Naval Flight Training Command. The AD was a very large, single-engine aircraft that could carry the bombload of a WWII four-engine B-17 bomber. I loved flying it, but it was unbelievably slow. Next to those Vietnamese aircraft were parked five U.S. Air Force F-102 jet fighter-interceptors. The F-102 Delta Dagger could climb to sixty thousand feet in about five minutes. The rest of the east side had a mixture of Vietnamese civilian transports, including vintage U.S.-made C-47 Gooneybirds and DC-3 prop transports of the 1941 pioneer airline era.

After parking, we quickly exited the KC-130, and I was directed to the headquarters of detachment Marine Aircraft Group 16, called SHUFLY. I walked past the CH-34 helicopters of HMM-162 and of HMM-163, my very first assigned squadron of "Ridgerunners" in Japan in 1958. The dusty tents of their flight line indicated that it was a dirty and hot job for the mechanics. Looking over the helicopters, I saw that they were filled with dirt and sand. All of the Plexiglas windows were removed from the pilot's and passengers' compartments. M-60 machine guns, one on each side, hung out the open windows in the belly of the aircraft. The choppers did not resemble the slick, shiny, clean CH-34 helos that I had flown for three years in HMM-161 in Kaneohe, Hawaii. The CH-34 choppers had been redesignated UH-34D, meaning utility transport helicopter. Pilots and crews continued to use the two terms interchangeably. A few hundred feet behind the flight line of dusty tents, I saw several rows of brown stucco buildings with dark brown tile roofs. One of those buildings was the location of the group headquarters. The rest appeared to be the officers' living quarters. I stopped a second and thought. So this is home for the next thirteen months, away from my wife and children. Upon checking into the S-1, personnel, the major said to me, "Captain, General McCutcheon, the assistant wing commander, is now down here for a while. He plans to expand our operations. He read your background and told me to tell you to report to him upon your arrival."

"Where's the general?" I asked.

"He's in the officers' club. But first go ahead and get your living area. It's in building 3, across from here. After you drop your B-4 clothing bag, you can chase down the general."

I asked, "Major, why would the general want to see a lowly captain?"

The major replied, "As I said, the general read a copy of your officer's qualifications jacket. He reads the OQJs of all the pilots coming into the country to see their backgrounds. He saw that you had attended both the navy and Marine Corps supply schools, plus he saw that you had been an engineer as a civilian.

He said he wants to talk to you about his plans to build a new airfield."

I thought, Hell, I came here to fly, not play engineer or supply officer.

I walked over to the rather nice, but dusty, row of stucco buildings and entered building 3. It must have been 120 degrees inside. The walls had green open shutters, but no breeze came through.

A young corporal wearing wrinkled, green utilities greeted me. I told him my name and he led me down the dark hallway to a small room. There were four folding cots with mosquito nets draped over them.

"Well, Captain, this is your new home, sir. As you've probably heard, this is an old French officers' living area. One night during the French Indochina War, every French officer sleeping here had his throat cut by the Viet Minh . . . about forty officers died that night."

"Thanks a lot, corporal. You made my night. I'm sure I'll get a good night's sleep in that cot."

I dropped my B-4 bag and walked over to another, similar building, which had a sign over the double doorway that read "DETACHMENT MAG-16 FAR EAST JUNGLE FIGHTER OFFICERS' CLUB."

As I walked into what was obviously the officers' messing area for dining, combined with a bar, I couldn't miss the Southeast Asia overhead ceiling fans slowly turning the hot air around. It was like a scene from the old movies in the thirties with Peter Lorre and Sydney Greenstreet, in a sweating bar in Singapore or some other exotic place. It was extraordinary—bamboo chairs included.

The general was a thin, short man with piercing blue eyes. He had been a pioneer in helicopters with HMR-163, the "Ridge-runners," the first and only Marine Corps transport helicopter squadron in the Korean War. He was a lieutenant colonel during that so-called police action. They were the very first choppers to move combat troops in action and to fly day and night missions in combat. Their sister squadron, VMO-2, had light, fixed-wing Cessna observation aircraft, "Bird Dogs," for forward air control (FAC) for controlling attack bombers and also had a handful of HO4S choppers for medical evacuations. Not many years later, the army began using helicopters for troop transportation and assault.

The general was seated at the bamboo bar with two colonels. His neatly starched utility cap, with its single brigadier general's star, sat to the side of his mixed drink.

As I approached the only three men in the bar, since it was only about 1500 in the afternoon, one of the colonels turned around and said, "What is it, Captain?"

"Sir, Major Plum in S-1 told me to report to the general right now."

The general swirled on his barstool and said, "Can I help you, Captain?"

"Well, sir, Major Plum said that you wanted to see me when I checked in from Hawaii. Because of my supply and engineering background."

"Yes, I sure do. Join us and have a drink—but mix your own. The bartender doesn't come aboard until 1600."

I went behind the bar and mixed a rum and Coke, while looking for ice cubes.

"Captain, we're lucky we flew in a small amount of booze and beer. But there is no ice here. There isn't ice anywhere in Da Nang that we know of yet," said the other colonel.

So I sat down with a warm rum and Coke in a room of about 120-degree heat, next to two colonels and a brigadier general, thinking, This sure is a strange way to get introduced to combat.

The general looked me in the eye and said, "We are planning to bring in our fighter and attack aircraft shortly to support our grunts, who will be coming in at that time. With the jets here, there simply will not be enough room here at Da Nang for our helicopters and eventual three jet squadrons. Therefore, we plan to build another airfield three miles east of here on China Beach, next to the South China Sea."

He got up, walked to the open window area facing east and pointed. "The airstrip will be located somewhere between that large green mountain on the north called Monkey Mountain and that solid brown-gray mountain called Marble Mountain on the south."

"Sir, with all due respect, what does this have to do with a captain who's a helicopter pilot?"

"Well, Captain, you have a supply background, and as a helicopter pilot you fully understand chopper operations, plus you have an engineering background. All of this is important to order supplies and coordinate with the Seabees to help me get that helicopter field built fast. Therefore, I had Major Plum assign you to Lt. Col. Tom Vaile's squadron, Marine Air Base Squadron 16. MABS-16 will have the task of working closely with Naval Construction Battalion 8—NCB-8—the Seabees who will build the actual cantonment and runway before we move three helicopter squadrons there."

"But General, I came down from the Air Naval Gunfire Liaison Company, 1st ANGLICO, in Hawaii where due to my grunting duties I only flew a couple of hops a month in a T-33 jet. I came down here expecting to fly a lot. If I get tied up with building an air base, I'll get very little combat flight experience. I need a flying billet in a flying squadron, not a base-support squadron, sir."

"I understand, Captain. But we're a small informal group here and we all must do what each of us knows best. In a few days the full MAG-16 group will be flown in here from Futema, Okinawa. We won't be a mere detachment of MAG-16 anymore. Included will be the group supply department and group supply officer. That supply department will handle the standard aviation and ground supply needs for all of the squadron. You will continue to draw on them for normal squadron supplies. But what I want you to do is to personally handle the unique requirements of supplies and materials to build a base. None of those supplies are in a normal air group supply system. The Seabees will do the actual construction, but I'll rely on your innovative capabilities to ensure that they get what they need and build what you, Lieutenant Colonel Vaile, and I feel is required for a full MAG helicopter airfield."

"But General, what about my flying?"

The general leaned downward to his flight equipment strewn on the floor. He reached for his flight helmet and handed it to me.

"Captain, due to my job these days, I don't have much time to fly. But a couple of times a week I go out on a routine helicopter resupply mission to carry ammunition to the ARVNs and bring back their wounded. Today was a routine flight, but coming back along the coast, in fact over Marble Mountain, some Viet Cong gave me a few bursts of AK-47 fire. I really didn't know it until something hit my helmet."

I looked at his helmet. A perfect round hole went through one side near the top and exited the opposite side. I looked in amazement at the helmet and then automatically at the general's sweating forehead and matted hair.

He laughed and said. "See, you'll get your flying along with combat experience."

Now I knew why he was having a warm drink before the end of the normal working day—if there was really going to be a normal working day here in this blast furnace of a country.

The general took back his helmet and said, "Captain, do your primary job first and fly anytime you want. I'll tell each squadron CO you can fly anytime you wish, in their aircraft. Fair enough?"

"Sir, I really want to go to a flying squadron, but what can I do?"

"Captain, if those pussyfootin' congressmen back in Washington run this war like they did in Korea, instead of allowing the military to do their thing, we'll be down here for years—and you'll have more flying than you'll really want. Now, go check in with Colonel Vaile, your new boss. He's been expecting you."

To say I was pissed off would be putting it mildly. I drifted across the compound to a cinder-block shed with a corrugated sheet-tin roof. The sign on the door read "CO, MABS-16." The tin roof amplified the heat in the room. But it did not dampen the enthusiasm of Lieutenant Colonel Vaile. He greeted me and briefed me in much more detail about my assignment.

That night I didn't sleep a wink—between the ARVN artillery shooting to the west of Da Nang firing flares to light up the rural areas, mosquitoes buzzing all around outside my mosquito netting, tremendous heat with humidity, not being assigned to a flying squadron and the story that forty French officers died from having their throats slit right here where I was sleeping . . .

The next morning the compound was alive. Helicopters were lifting off, dust flew about the area, and a mixture of marines in marine utility uniforms, Australian bush hats, flight suits and an array of different shoulder-worn weapons greeted me in the mess hall. It really did look like a Far East jungle fighter group, rather than a U.S. Marine Corps air group. Most of the officers had grown fancy handlebar moustaches to add to the color of this strange, active group.

I started the day off conducting an in-depth inventory of the supply files with my four assigned supply personnel. This would lead to an actual physical sighting and counting of everything that MABS-16 rated. I had to determine what we actually had on hand by Table of Organization (T/O), or number of people, and the Table of Equipment (T/E), or actual items rated. What complicated it was that my SNCO (staff noncommissioned officer) Gunnery Sergeant Frey kept telling me that many of the items were still in Okinawa and were to be shipped to Vietnam. But exactly what was here and en route was not recorded precisely. I rated thousands of items, large and small. I rated 660 general-purpose personnel living and office tents. Records indicated that somewhere in the RVN there were 420. MABS-16 rated sixteen M-60 machine guns for perimeter defense. Only eight were recorded to be at Da Nang. Were the rest in Okinawa? I rated, and was told we had in the field here, six tactical-aircraft fuel-dispensing-system (TAFDS) units, to fuel the choppers at remote landing zones. I rated numerous mess-hall reefers (walk-in refrigerators for the mess halls), ice-flake machines, personnel shower units, Bay City cranes, trucks, jeeps, bulldozers, and 640 rifles and six hand-held .45-caliber machine guns—"grease guns."

It was so hot, about 125 degrees in the shade, that I could hardly think straight, let alone work. Like everyone else, I had to get five more shots in addition to the four given to me by medical in Hawaii. The plague was common. So they had one shot that they gave you in the ass cheek, just for the plague. The big decision was into which cheek did you want it? It was a large quantity of liquid antibiotics dispensed through a horrifyingly large needle and container. And the corpsman was right—you couldn't sit down for three days. So naturally, you couldn't fly for several days. The rule of thumb was that you needed five days in the country to acclimate to the weather and shots before climbing into a cockpit. But by the second day, I was down at the squadrons telling them to schedule me for my area familiarization flights and missions to start after my five-day "grounding" time. The acclimation to a hot, humid climate was no fun. *Everybody,* all ranks, got the Da Nang "two trot." That is, by your second, third and fourth days in Nam, you frequently, throughout the day, took two steps and crapped in your pants. None of us knew if the runs were from the intense heat or the drinking water. Everybody suffered through the two or three days of accomplishing very little and staying fairly close to the latrines. According to my T/E, I rated eight portable four-hole latrines. I didn't relish the thought of having to walk around inventorying them, but I would have to, like every other piece of equipment that I owned.

I figured the first five days I'd inventory the records of supplies on paper. I then could get my first familiarization (FAM) flight of the combat area. After that, I could fly out to conduct the actual inventories of my TAFDS units, which were spread all over the I Corps area, plus my reefers, cooking equipment and tents up north at the Phu Bai Airfield. This would give me excuses for more flying—both normal supply missions for supporting the ARVN and my required inventory flights, including having to count weapons and sight weapons by serial numbers of our MABS-16 troops displaced at the Tam Ky city TAFDS landing zone (LZ) and Phu Bai.

On the fifth day I called operations at HMM-162 and was assured that I was indeed scheduled to fly as a copilot the next day. This would count as my area FAM flight. I had a 0500 brief and a launch time of 0615.

I was in the briefing tent at 0445 to make sure I had everything required for the early-morning launch. I drew my armor vest and armor torso girdle from the ready room tent, and produced my nice, clean, red and white helmet. The other pilots were quick to tell me that I should get my bright helmet painted green or black later that day, that it was too easy a target to sight in on. I carried, along with my other flight equipment from Hawaii, my normal orange flight suit. The other pilots were quick to point out that there was a small aviation supply section, separate from my own MABS supply, that carried a small amount of flight equipment, including flight suits that had originally been orange but had been dyed green. Apparently the local Da Nang Buddhist monks had been angry about American pilots wearing flight suits the same color as their orange religious robes, plus common sense of escape and evasion dictated green or brown flight suits in the event of being shot down in this jungle and rice paddie country.

I thought that my first FAM hop would be an area fly-around, like we did anywhere else in the world when we checked into a new geographical area. Not so here. Promptly at 0500, Captain May began briefing the four of us, two pilots and two copilots, for a two-plane mission.

"Gents, we start engines and engage rotor blades at 0605 and we launch at 0615 for a resupply flight to an ARVN-protected village very close in to Da Nang. The village of Quang Dai is located at coordinates nine-zero-one, five-nine-nine. Keep in mind that your current maps are French-made and the coordinates differ due to our shifting over period to developing our own maps. Every map is figured from Paris, not Greenwich, England. Study the terrain closely so we land at the correct village. The ninety-degree bend in the Song Vu Gia River is straight east from the vil we want to land in.

"I'll carry an internal load of medical supplies and an external hook load of concertina wire for compound security. Dash Two, you'll carry an internal load of M-14 carbine ammo, grenades, and mortar shells.

"We'll climb out on normal VFR"—visual flight rules—"to three thousand feet and remain en route at angels three. Directly over the village, I'll kiss you off and start a spiral descent straight down into the center of the village, hovering next to the vil water well in an opening big enough for only one chopper. You stay in orbit. I'll hover and release the barbed wire, then after they roll it out of the way, I'll land and my crew chief will kick out the medical supplies. Dash Two, your gunners cover me on my descent. When I climb back up in a spiral over the vil to three thousand feet, Dash Two, you leave your orbit and drop your load in the same zone. We're supposed to have a green smoke grenade go off at that landing zone as we fly over it, so it should be a piece of cake finding the landing zone.

"Weather is not a factor. It's clear as a bell. The LZ is considered secure. So we may only get some distant small-arms fire from around the vil.

"No matter what the mission develops into, bingo"—go home—"fuel state is 400 pounds.

"Emergencies are to be executed as per squadron standard operating procedures.

"Let's go to S-2 to get the intelligence briefing for the day."

At S-2 we received the codes to use for communications, codes which changed daily, and a briefing on what they thought was the ground-action situation of friendlies and bad guys.

Captain May then said, "Let's preflight the birds, kick the tires, and light the fires."

The pilots signed the "yellow sheet" maintenance forms to assume responsibility for the aircraft, as the copilots, myself included, began preflight inspections of the birds.

At exactly 0615, after Da Nang Airfield tower cleared us, we climbed north into the prevailing wind, turned right and then south along the "rivière de Tourane," or Da Nang River. As we continued our climb over Hoa Khue Dong village, I had a good look at the exact terrain where we were to soon build Da Nang East Airfield, just north of Marble Mountain. It was a vast stretch of sand. We leveled at three thousand feet and moved along at 120 knots, passing over Hill 55 toward our LZ. The countryside was beautiful. An occasional fire burned here and there, but generally it was a very peaceful scene. The terrain was flat and dotted with hundreds of villages and rice paddies. To our left was the blue-green South China Sea. To our right, or west, were small hills and then large dark purple mountains toward Laos. The pilot, in the left, or command, seat, pointed out to our left and said, "That is the city of Hoi An. We have a TAFDS fueling farm and fairly large LZ there. Highway 14, which we are about to cross, comes out of the western valleys and goes past Highway 1 right into Hoi An near the Song Cua Dai outlet, where these rivers spill into the South China Sea." We crossed Highway 14 and the lead chopper turned inland. We could see our objective, Quang Dai. Off to our left, at the village of Ky Lam, the only railroad ended abruptly due to a destroyed structural steel bridge. The railroad ran north and south along Highway 1, but trains no longer ran in this embattled area. The VC destroyed all bridges and mined key road areas.

As we approached the vil, a green smoke grenade went off in the center of town and we saw that the wind blew from west to east, so we would land into the western breeze. No radio transmissions were exchanged, as my leader, Captain May, threw me a kiss and abruptly turned downward into a tight, descending spiral with his large, awkward external load hanging in trail. We orbited and it was quiet except for the *wop-wop* of the rotor blades.

Shortly, Dash One was back up in orbit and we went into a deep nose-down attitude, picking up 150 knots of speed, and spiraled to earth. I could see the ARVN troops around the outside of the village and about twenty of them below awaiting our delivery of ammo. At about fifty feet before touchdown the pilot in command quickly but smoothly pulled back on the cyclic, or stick, and pulled up on the collective as he opened his motorcyclelike throttle to increase engine RPM as the rotor blades began to slow. We went straight on in with a hard thud, no hovering like back in the States. Our gunners and crew chief passed the ammo to the small-statured ARVN troops. In a short few minutes, the crew chief said, "All clear; take 'er off, sir."

We climbed back up slowly, at ninety knots, in a similar spiral pattern, staying over the friendly-held village. That was it. My FAM hop and first mission. There was nothing to it—no firing at us, nothing. After we rendezvoused with Dash One, the command pilot said, "Here you are. You take us home on Dash One's wing."

I took the controls for the first time on this flight. It sure felt great to fly the machine again. We landed at Da Nang and debriefed the rather routine, uneventful flight. Since we did not get any hits on either chopper, nor did the ARVN ground forces report any hostile fire at us, operations did not give us credit for a combat mission. But it was a good FAM hop and I felt ready to be the command pilot on my next scheduled mission.

I returned in time for a late breakfast. I then went to my supply office and worked until 1930, going over the matériel and supply lists. The next morning, while standing outside my office and looking across the sandbagged wall through the barbed-wire fence, I watched the nearby Da Nang civilian residents going about their normal activities. As I stood there, just getting acquainted with their way of life, I noticed that at the end of one narrow alley, a small, frail Vietnamese woman stood against a building holding a large piece of wood, like a club. Gunnery Sergeant Frey came out of our hut and said, "Sir, I see you've spotted 'Whack 'em.' "

"Whack 'em?" I asked.

"Just watch the little old lady—give her some time. Pretty soon a dog or two will wander down that alley towards her."

Sure enough. It took about ten minutes of patience and a lone black mongrel came meandering down the alley. The little lady, peering around the corner of the end building, waited. As the dog came up to the corner, little ole Whack 'em whacked the hell out of the mutt with her club. The dog never knew what hit him.

Gunnery Sergeant Frey said, "Whack 'em just caught dinner. Dog is a Vietnamese delicacy. She averages about one dog every third day."

I realized then that we were indeed in a different country and had to learn a lot about the inhabitants' ways of doing things. That afternoon I got a haircut at a Vietnamese barber in a small screened-in porch. Sam, my barber, did a good job for my Marine Corps crewcut, but cut my neck too closely in the shave. It burned for the rest of the day as my sweat ran over the injured skin.

The next morning, while eating breakfast, I got the word going around that the ARVN artillery caught a group of Viet Cong in the open to our west last night. Included with the twenty dead, armed VC was our own officers' barber, Sam. I thought, That son of a bitch shaved me yesterday with a straightedge. I never fully trusted a Vietnamese from that day on, particularly the barbers. How could one know who was VC; who was truly anticommunist?

Two days later I was able to get on the flight schedule again. I was assigned as an aircraft commander, but as a wingman in another two-plane supply mission. It was another routine mission, good weather all the way. The LZ was an old, triangular, French-built outpost, now run by the ARVN. It was just twelve miles northwest of Da Nang Airfield on a three-thousand-meter-high hill overlooking the Ca De Song River and a long valley called Elephant Valley.

We both landed on the outside of the fortress and as close to it as possible. We each had twenty ARVN troops and ammunition, and all was unloaded rapidly. As soon as we simultaneously lifted off, we began taking intense small-arms fire from our north, across the river. Our gunners on the north side, our right side of the chopper, began responding with their M-60s. The VC fire appeared to be coming from a small village, called Loc My, near a large sandbar. We quickly exited around the fortress and headed south, then climbed eastward for Da Nang.

We headed home, asking each other if anyone got hit or if the helo had any visible damage. I mentioned to my combat-experienced copilot, Lieutenant Carter, "I didn't see any ARVNs returning fire or giving us a base of fire on our climb out. Did you?"

"No, Captain. It's common for these guys way out in the defensive outposts not to fire at the VC. I think they don't want to get the VC pissed at them. Since the ARVN stay buttoned up and don't patrol from these outposts, they don't endanger the VC. The VC, on the other hand, don't bother the fortresses. We're the only guys who get shot at when we deliver supplies."

Upon our return to Da Nang, we could find only six bullet holes in the aft end of the starboard tail section.

The metal shop would put metal patches on the holes. No control surfaces or control cables were damaged. The second flight of mine in Nam was more than just flight time. It counted as a combat mission. It was logged as such in my flight logbook by the squadron's operations clerk.

The days ran by rapidly, each day warmer than the last. Things were happening quickly. I began flying to places like Tam Ky and Phu Bai, conducting inventories of my responsible equipment. I continued flying regular combat sorties as big events were forming. The 1st LAAM Battalion, a light-antiaircraft-missile battalion supplied with HAWK (homing-all-the-way kill) missiles was already located in the Da Nang area. The 9th Marine Expeditionary Brigade, which included two battalion landing teams, BLT 1/9 and 3/9, had been afloat in the vicinity of Da Nang. Since January 1965, the 9th MEB had been aboard the Amphibious Task Force 76 flagship, the *Mount McKinley,* and aboard APA-45, the USS *Henrico;* AKA-106, the USS *Union;* and on LPD-2, the USS *Vancouver*. On March 8, 1965, they were ordered ashore. They landed at Red Beach, northwest of Da Nang. BLT 1/3 was flown in from Okinawa and joined the rest of the 9th MEB. Twenty-three additional helicopters were flown in from LPH-5, the USS *Princeton,* to add to the SHUFLY capabilities. We now had five thousand marines in the Da Nang area.

Most of our chopper missions, at this time, continued to be ammunition resupply and food for the ARVN outposts. The ARVN did not eat rations like us. Their food was live—so we flew chickens, ducks, pigs and even cows to their tightened-up enclaves of defense. We then began airlifting ARVN assault troops in company- and even battalion-size helo lifts. On one such ARVN operation, Quyet Thang, much resistance by the VC was encountered. It was an airlift using a total mix of twenty-six helos to lift 465 ARVN troops of the 5th Airborne Battalion. The lift was from Tam Ky in Quang Tin Province to an LZ twenty-five miles south of Da Nang.

The antiaircraft fire was intense. One UH-34D chopper was shot down. The pilot was wounded and the copilot died of wounds. The crew chief was also wounded. Five other choppers were damaged and limped back to Da Nang. Three lifts continued into the LZ, despite intense VC fire. Total Marine Corps casualties in this assault were two killed and nineteen wounded. My UH-34 chopper had twenty-two bullet holes to be patched. This alerted us to the fact that the VC were now heading for Da Nang in numbers. More marines were arriving, as I continued my flying of supply missions and organizing to assist in building an air group helicopter airfield near Marble Mountain.

President Johnson gave the go-ahead for a very limited series of air strikes against very selected targets in North Vietnam. The air campaign was called "Rolling Thunder." To offer the pilots of the air strikes into North Vietnam some search-and-rescue (SAR) helicopter support, our two squadrons at Da Nang ran SAR missions into North Vietnam. I volunteered for several of the night SAR missions so that I could get my daytime logistics work done. On one of these several trips up north, this is the way we did it.

As the pilot in command of a two-plane SAR flight, I briefed my other plane commander and our two copilots at 1600 in Da Nang. We launched northward, climbing out over the Da Nang Bay and the Hai Van Pass to Hue Phu Bai, our base south of the DMZ, 17th parallel, where HMM-161, the "Pineapple Squadron," from Hawaii was now stationed. We were briefed at Phu Bai by the HMM-161 crews that flew the daytime SAR missions across the DMZ. I knew most of the pilots, since that had been my last flying squadron in Hawaii in 1962 to 1964. One of my best friends, Capt. Bill Morse, had been killed in his UH-34 during the first night launch from an LPH off the shore of the city of Hue, during the Pineapple Squadron's movement into Vietnam from Hawaii.

We flew to a small city to the northwest, Quang Tri, near the DMZ or 17th parallel. There was a small airstrip near Quang Tri that had a few HMM-161 choppers and a couple of VMO-2 UH-1E gunships located in support of an ARVN operation going on. We refueled and then sat in the ready tent as it grew dark outside. At 2015, there was to be an air force strike against aircraft hangars at an airfield located to the west of the city of Vinh in North Vietnam. At 1915 we took off from Quang Tri and stayed on the deck at about three hundred feet of altitude, using slow cruise speed to minimize fuel consumption. At the low altitude, the radar-controlled antiaircraft guns in North Vietnam, above the Cau Viet River boundary, could not track us. We flew with running lights on dim, so only our wingman could make out the fuselage shape. I led the flight section out to the middle of the river. I then turned down the river to the east toward the South China Sea. If the North Vietnamese saw us, they would think we were patrolling the south side of the Cau Viet River or DMZ. When about eight miles east along the river, I abruptly turned north across the DMZ into North Vietnam, with my wingman stepped up above my port side. Heading 030 degrees, we increased our speed, remaining three hundred feet above the ground level (AGL). We maintained radio silence. It was a moonless night and I could not see any hills or mountains. The sparse number of villages in the area did have some fires inside and outside of their thatched-roof huts. This gave me a rough feel for the terrain. At exactly twenty minutes after takeoff, I climbed to two thousand feet indicated altitude, which according to my map and flight planning should have placed us at five hundred feet AGL over some mountains en route to the east coast. In ten minutes I turned to a heading of 360 degrees, since we should be crossing the beach, feet wet. This placed us in a position over the water in North Vietnamese territory ready for any aircraft limping homeward bound that might have to ditch up here. The flight path to get up there gave me maximum fuel time for loitering in the area.

At this time, both my wingman and I switched over to "Joy Ride" frequency, a newly established air-control coordinator. However, we maintained radio silence. I entered a holding orbit at two thousand feet with my wingman in a comfortable position, but at a distance far enough back to still allow him to see my dim fuselage running lights. We anchored there in a very dark, very quiet night, listening only to our flapping rotor blades. I could see the numerous villages lit up, forming the beachline. Unlike South Vietnam, the North had no enemy invaders, or so-called guerrillas, fighting there. After all, they were the invaders to the South. So the countryside was calm and dark without battle fires, in contrast to the night scenes in the South, where firefights and artillery glowed nightly.

Sure the limited air raids caused a little excitement in the North. But it's on the ground, face-to-face with your enemy, that you know you're really at war. Simply bombing without ground assault would not end this continual North Vietnamese attack against the South, I thought. Then, as an hour dragged by, in orbit, a loud clear voice over the earphones was heard, "This is Joy Ride, mission accomplished, you are clear to RTB. Thanks, out." *RTB* meant "return to base."

I clicked my UHF radio button on my cyclic twice. This indicated to Joy Ride that I heard his message and was complying. My wingman clicked his UHF radio transmitter, alerting me that he heard that we were cleared of our "SAR ANGEL" mission. Apparently the air force bombers did not receive any serious hits over Vinh. I maintained a low, 2,300 engine RPM and descended with my wingman in the chase position, leveling off at five hundred feet out over the water. Making sure that my radar altimeter was accurately measuring five hundred feet, I stayed feet-wet, or over the water, until I came across the large outlet of the Cau Viet River in the DMZ. I headed west up the river, staying in the middle of the river to minimize being shot .at. I then turned southwest, went about eight miles up the river and picked up a TACAN (tactical air navigation) radial out of Phu Bai to help me locate Quang Tri Airfield in the dark night. I turned southwest toward Quang Tri. Just as I rolled level, with my wingman following, large bright green-orange balls of fire, in a steady stream, began crossing my helo nose about three hundred meters in front of me—pretty far ahead. Then a second string of a similar heavy line of tracers joined the first lethal line of fire. It was big stuff; not AK-47 or .50-caliber. It must have been 57-mm or 14.5 guns, coming from our right rear on the north side of the Cau Viet River.

Automatically, I dove for the deck and to the south side of the river. I glanced back to see if my wingman was still with me. He was. The steady stream of light continued to light up the darkness ahead.

"Lead, that's heavy fire out front. What the hell is it?" asked my wingman.

"Dash Two, it's the big antiaircraft stuff they throw up at our jet jocks. It's probably 57 Mike-Mike. We probably screwed them up. They saw our lights, dim as we have turned them down, and they thought we were jet aircraft. Good thing: they sure gave us a lotta lead time shooting way out in front. Now let's really fake 'em out. We'll slow to fifty knots and get on the deck, then we'll increase speed when very low. They won't be able to figure us out in the dark like this." I answered as my altimeter radar light warning came on to indicate I was now at fifty feet above the river.

As I leveled and was about to increase my airspeed, the large, glowing tracers quickly adjusted and moved directly in front of my Plexiglas windscreen. I abruptly turned left, away from the deadly fire.

"I'm hit . . . hit hard, lead," my wingman shouted into my earphones. I kicked left rudder and looked to my port side. He wasn't shitting. The aft end of his chopper was fully ablaze.

"Okay, Dash Two, we're just about feet-dry on the south side of the river. Put your landing lights on and find an open spot to land. I'm easing back and doing the same. Landing lights coming on."

As I slowed to forty knots in a nose-high landing attitude and pulled back beside my burning wingman, I also watched the greenish tracers from the two firing guns falling well short of our rear now. We were safe from the big guns, but we had a hell of a problem with Dash Two.

Right in front of us was a large open area with tall elephant grass surrounded by thick tall trees.

"Dash Two, take it straight in ahead. I'll land to your right. Get your crew the hell out of it. Your whole rear fuselage is burning like hell."

"Roger, One. I'm landing. My crew chief says nobody is hurt in my belly, but he can't get the fire out with the extinguisher."

We both touched down simultaneously. I watched my wingman reach up and throw his rotor-brake handle on. The whole grassy field area was lit up from his burning chopper. The large white word "MARINES" stood out against the green fuselage in the brightened area as the flames and sparks ate at the fuselage from tail pylon to mid-aircraft. The two gunners and crew chief were out and running toward my aircraft's left troop compartment doorway. The copilot was now on the ground, as the pilot was climbing down the left side of the chopper. There was no time for the gunners to unhook their M-60 machine guns.

While I waited and watched for my wingman and his crew to run from their burning helicopter, I called Joy Ride and Phu Bai DASC (direct air support center) to keep them informed of our situation, in the event that we all needed help.

In what seemed like an eternity, the pilot finally jumped into our belly.

"Lift off, sir," shouted my crew chief down below me.

I twisted on the throttle, pulled up on the collective and pushed forward on the cyclic. My chopper rose and nosed forward. As we cleared the tall thick trees to our south, we were again in total blackness with the burning helo well behind us. My eyes adjusted to the total darkness of the night as I scanned my instruments. The aircraft increased speed past 120 knots. My readjusted night vision was interrupted by a flash of brightness from our rear. Dash Two's aircraft had blown up and lit up the sky. It sure didn't take long for the magnesium tail section to burn to the fuel tanks located under the center of the fuselage.

As I kept the collective full up, increasing the rotor blades' pitch, with maximum throttle, I climbed at a two-thousand-foot-per-minute rate of climb, as shown on the indicator. Passing through 1,500 feet of altitude, reddish orange glowing streaks arched through the black night from directly under my nose. I felt three distinctive hits somewhere in the aircraft.

"How you doing down there, Sarge?" I asked my crew chief.

"We got a couple of rounds, but I don't see any internal damage down here. Nobody is hit, sir."

As we passed through 2,500 feet, the green, glowing tracers arched and fell behind and below us. We were out of small-arms-fire range.

I switched from the Phu Bai TACAN channel to the Quang Tri TACAN frequency, and my TACAN needle swung immediately to Quang Tri. I turned twenty degrees right, putting the TACAN needle on the nose of my aircraft.

"Okay, guys, we're heading for Quang Tri to refuel and look over the bird for battle damage. Anybody hurt down below?"

"No sir. Everybody is fine down here," replied my crew chief.

"I don't know if those were VC shots at us on this side of the river, or ARVN shots. Possibly the ARVN thought we were North Vietnamese in Russian Hound helicopters crossing south of the DMZ. I guess we'll never know who fired those small arms," I spoke to all listening on my intercom in my aircraft.

"Captain, it doesn't matter who the hell fired them if you get one in the head," replied my salty copilot.

"You bet. I have Quang Tri in sight now. Let's get Dash Two's people checked over carefully by the Quang Tri flight surgeon, as we refuel the bird before heading to Da Nang," I responded for all to hear.

We landed and refueled, and the flight surgeon at Quang Tri determined that all five crew members of my downed wingman's aircraft were in good condition to return to Da Nang base.

The two-hour flight back to Da Nang went swiftly and soon we crossed the Hai Van mountain pass and peninsula. We saw the lights of Da Nang city, northeast of the field, and I switched to Da Nang DASC which was located on the top of Monkey

Mountain. DASC responded to our check-in with, "Good job, choppers. We thought both of you were shot down just south of the DMZ. Good to see you make it back. The air force Thuds out of Ubon, Thailand, did their thing up there and fortunately didn't need you tonight. Sorry you lost a bird. But we're sure glad you're bringing the crew back with you."

"Good night, DASC," I responded and switched to Da Nang tower, as I started our descent over the blackened Vung Da Nang, or Bay of Da Nang.

"Da Nang tower, this is Smokey One at five hundred feet due north, feet wet, for landing marine side. Over."

"Smokey One, understand single helo, cleared to land. Stay west of runway one-eight right, we have a Viet commercial inbound two miles behind you, over."

"Roger that, Smokey One out."

As we crossed Red Beach, I could make out the dimly lit rows of the notorious whorehouses along the dirt road, near the beach. The women working in these houses, we heard, were French women, blondes, redheads, and brunettes and some black French women; not Vietnamese women. I could now easily see all the people, including marines on liberty, walking the streets of downtown Da Nang, despite the late hour. We landed, switched to a ground-control frequency and taxied into the SHUFLY parking apron, where our other "Dogs" (our affectionate name for our UH-34 troop-carrying choppers) were parked. It had been a very long day—or rather, night. It had been eleven hours since we had taken off on this SAR mission. The tenseness of knowing we were flying into North Vietnam at low altitude gave way to the initial relief that none of the air force jets were hit in their raid. Now, complete relief, coupled with exhaustion, set in as I reached up to pull the rotor-brake handle, after disengaging the engine from the rotor-blade system by rapidly snapping the engine throttle to idle, thus disengaging the clutch. It was 0215. Da Nang city was still going full blast; Da Nang Airfield was dead silent. In just a few short hours, we all would be up again with the sun, doing normal jobs.

The next few days had us watching the 9th MEB move more marines ashore from ships that were anchored in the Da Nang Harbor. BLT 2/3 came across Red Beach, as we watched

VMFA-531, an all-weather jet fighter/attack squadron of F-4 Phantoms, arrive at Da Nang field. They flew in from Atsugi, Japan, and were the first fixed-wing marine squadron to arrive in 1965. With the arrival of the commanding general of the 9th MEB from off the flagship *Mount McKinley,* the headquarters of Regimental Landing Team 3—RLT 3—landed. The commander of RLT 3, with his BLTs 2/3 and 3/4, set up a defense perimeter around our Da Nang Airfield and around the airstrip way up north at Phu Bai. We now had a full marine air group, making us MAG-16—we were not simply a detachment of MAG-16 anymore. And soon, more jet fixed-wing aircraft would be coming to our crowded airbase at Da Nang.

The CGFMFPAC (commanding general, Fleet Marine Forces, Pacific), Gen. Victor Krulak, located in Hawaii, had recommended a Marine Corps expeditionary airfield be built about sixty miles south of Da Nang, on the coast. The communists had a buildup there. Their Viet Cong base at Do Xa was located in the Annamite Mountains about sixty miles inland. They had a supply route from those mountains, through the jungle eastward across some flat, sandy land, and across Route 1 to the beach in the vicinity of villages Am Son, Hai Ninh, and Long Binh, inland from Dung Quat Bay. The CGFMFPAC personally came out from Hawaii and selected the site for the airfield. Since there was no name for the specific sand dune area, he named it after his own name in Chinese mandarin characters: "Chu Lai."

Secretary of Defense Robert McNamara approved the building of Chu Lai Airfield, and the marines decided to send in three jet squadrons and three reinforced battalions.

ARVN 2nd Division units combined with Da Nang–based marines of K Company, 3/9, secured the area at Chu Lai, and on May 7, 1965, the elements of BLT 1/4 and BLT 2/4 landed across the beach. HMM-161, the Pineapple Squadron from Phu Bai, flew in many of the troops from the LPH USS *Princeton,* and other ships. HMM-161 had been flying all day and needed some help. Our SHUFLY operations section received the request for some additional choppers. So I flew a UH-34D Dog chopper in a four-plane division to Chu Lai to assist. It was a sixty-mile flight down to Chu Lai, passing Hoi An and Tam Ky cities en route. All day we flew uneventful short hops from Chu Lai to the ships, bringing in troops, ammunition, rations, and water.

We returned that night to Da Nang exhausted, sandy, and knowing where Chu Lai now was. It had been a full eight hours and fifteen minutes of actual helo flying time and hard work—a long, sweaty day. During the twenty or so sortie flights that day, none of us came under VC fire and therefore none of the flying that was recorded in our logbooks was logged as combat-missions. It was logged as just routine support flying. The 9th MEB was deactivated and the III Marine Amphibious Force (III MAF) was formed to absorb the full marine division and full marine air wing. The III MAF, with headquarters at Da Nang and under the command of marine general Lewis W. Walt, had to operate under a unique, touchy set of circumstances. Since the marines were only guests of the Vietnamese by request to be there, they could not command or direct ground or air operations against the VC. Coordinated advice is about what it amounted to. The initial ground activities primarily consisted of a perimeter of defense around Da Nang while we flew ARVN resupply missions out to the boondocks.

Then as our 2nd Battalion, 3rd Marines, expanded to the high ground to the northwest near Le My hamlet, the ground units began running into VC resistance. As the marines expanded, I flew many missions carrying external loads of concertina (i.e., barbed wire). On these flights, I could see the defensive wire going up over the nearby countryside to protect against VC night attacks, which had begun to increase. Despite intense heat and humidity, the Seabee construction crews of NMCB-10 and the marines of MABS-12 constructed the SATS (short airfield for tactical support) at Chu Lai. We pilots from MAG-16 at Da Nang continued to fly sorties in support of ground units at Chu Lai during this period. These eight-hour flying days in the heat and blowing sand put a maintenance strain on our ground crews and our beloved Dogs.

On June 1, 1965, the first flight of tactical fixed-wing aircraft arrived overhead at Chu Lai. A division of four A-4 Skyhawks from VMA-225 arrived from Cubi Point, Philippines. Several hours later, VMA-311, also with Douglas A-4s, arrived at Chu Lai. The ARVNs requested close-air-support strikes that very day. VMA-225, operating from the new aluminum runway and taxiway, and using catapults and arresting gear at Chu Lai Airfield, flew their first combat missions.

It was now mid-June 1965 and unbearably hot. My wife was writing letters telling me how the two children were doing and that our new '65 Mustang was running beautifully. I wrote her letters requesting cigars, since we had no post exchange yet, nor did the air force across the Da Nang Airfield from us. She wanted me to quit smoking, so I didn't get cigars in the mail. Instead, she sent me salami, which sweated wet in the over one-hundred-degree heat, but was a real treat at night with a warm can of beer. The warm beer was sure to get us "fighting mad."

We now had Marine Aircraft Group 12 (MAG-12) with five fixed-wing jet squadrons, and MAG-16 with five helicopter squadrons, in the Republic of Vietnam. As the summer heat intensified, so did the ground battles. The marines began to squeeze the Viet Cong and they were fighting back. Our 4th Marines had killed 147 VC, but sustained four marine KIAs and twenty-three wounded. The VC increased their nightly probes against the ARVN forces and our USMC outposts.

Since our airfield was considered secure and nothing unsafe had ever happened in the city of Da Nang from the time when the Americans arrived, liberty was still available for the marines in the city, if you had the strength after a long flight mission to go into town for the only cold beer around.

I was assigned to a two-plane VIP mission to fly General Thi, Vietnamese I Corps tactical zone commander, from his Da Nang headquarters, inside the city, to a meeting well south of Da Nang, near Hoi An. I was flying in the left seat of the UH-34 helo and Maj. Jerry Kitter was the pilot in the right copilot's seat. After picking up the general, we flew at a safe altitude to near Hoi An city and landed in a village which appeared to be heavily patrolled by ARVN troops. We dropped the general off and both choppers climbed northward, homeward bound.

Major Kitter relaxed as we climbed through one thousand feet of altitude for three thousand feet. Over the FM radio transmitter, I told our wingman, Dash Two, to take the flight lead home. I slid our chopper back and stepped up on Dash Two, as Dash Two accelerated and the pilot in its left seat lightly tapped his helmet to say that he had command of the two-plane formation. Just as we settled into the wingman's stepped-up formation slot, while still in a turning climb, I felt a breeze, or slight vibration, just below my nose. In fact, the breeze tickled my nostril hairs. Immediately, Major Kitter slumped forward onto the cyclic stick, causing the chopper to nose-dive. I pulled hard on the stick and kicked left rudder pedal to prevent our rotor blades from hitting the other helo's blades. I was still in a dive as I released the inertial reel of my shoulder straps and reached over to pull Jerry away from the stick. As I did so, I saw the blood rushing from his face—and there was a hell of a lot of blood. Just then Jerry shook his head, his eyes widened, and he put his left gloved hand up to touch his face. For a brief second, I thought he had been killed, until he moved. I thought he took one in the head. But apparently the round that zinged past my nose from the open cockpit window hit Jerry and had only stunned him. However, with all the blood gushing from the left side of his face, I couldn't tell how badly he was hurt.

"Major, you okay? Shall I put her down here?" He didn't answer me. He probably didn't know if he was okay or not. I leveled the helo as Major Kitter moved a little more, wiping some of the bright red blood from his face.

My headset earphones then crackled, "Dash One, where are you?" asked Dash Two, who had just taken the lead.

"I'm down behind you at seven o'clock. Jerry has been hit in the face. I'm trying to determine the seriousness of it, over."

"Roger that. I'm rejoining you as Dash Two and I'll follow along to see what happens."

At that moment, my crew chief, Corporal Feathers, poked his head up behind and below our copilot's seat. He crawled up a little more from the troop compartment.

"What should we do, Captain? Should we land and try to help him ourselves?" Corporal Feathers asked.

I responded, talking over the FM radio transmitter so that both my wingman and my internal crew could all hear at the same time, "We're coming up soon on Hill 55. We just crossed Highway 14. We could land at our arty site on 55 and hope that there's a medic near the LZ. Now, Corporal Feathers, try to get up here a little more. I'll unbuckle the major, you get his legs, and

I'll help with his upper body. As we lift, your two gunners can lift up on the seat and help pull the major down to the belly. He's starting to pass out from loss of blood. As soon as you get him into the belly, stuff your flight gloves into his facial wound and stop that fuckin' bleeding."

I was about three minutes out from Hill 55, and I hesitated. If Jerry bleeds to death because no medic is right close to the LZ at 55, or if I pass Hill 55 for Da Nang and he doesn't make it, I'll never forgive myself, either way.

"I'm heading straight for Charlie Med at Da Nang, Dash Two, we can't land anywhere around this badman's country other than Hill 55 and I'm not sure at this point if they have a medic near the LZ."

"Roger, One. I've looked your aircraft over for damage. Don't see any. That must have been a stray round that hit the major."

We quickly passed over Hill 55 and I motioned to Dash Two to switch UHF frequencies.

"Da Nang DASC, this is Carrier Pigeon One, inbound with two to Charlie Med with one WIA pilot in Dash One. Facial wound, heavy bleeding, three minutes out. Please tell Charlie Med. Over."

"Carrier Pigeon One, DASC reads you. We're calling Charlie Med now to have the meat wagon at their LZ for you. You are cleared down to three hundred feet west of Da Nang Airfield, inside of Freedom Hill. Call departing Charlie Med for pancake. Good luck with your crew member, over."

"Roger, DASC. Pigeon out."

I flew straight into Charlie Med, as my wingman orbited at three hundred feet. Charlie Med had an H-shaped grouping of old metal Quonset huts that had been shipped down from Okinawa with the medical battalion of the 3rd Marine Division. It was getting to be a busier and busier hospital every day. As the corpsmen approached my chopper on the ground from the right, I couldn't see them lifting Major Kitter into the litter. However, I vibrated on the ground long enough for me to see him hauled away from the chopper and out of the large white circled area which had a large red cross painted on it for the hospital LZ identification. When he was carried through the screened door of the emergency room Quonset hut, I lifted the chopper, trying to minimize blowing sand and dust over the tents of the corpsmen's and doctors' living cantonment.

I returned to the MAG-16 parking apron in about five minutes, still wondering how badly wounded Major Kitter had been. I planned to go visit him that night.

However, about five hours later, when leaving my logistics tent, guess who was heading my way? It was Major Kitter. I gave him a quick salute and a strong handshake.

"What the hell! I thought you bought the farm," I blurted happily.

"Are you kidding? And miss all of the fun in this tropical paradise?"

I looked over his face. He only had a patch on his left cheek, about a one inch square. Both eyes were puffed and black and blue.

"Bob, I sure as hell was lucky. The bullet just grazed me and cut out a curved chunk of cheek skin. But it felt like Joe Louis punched me out. They simply stitched me up and patched it. So I'm all ready for flight status again."

"If we can say getting hit in the face with a baseball bat is lucky, I suppose so."

Early that evening, I got word that more of my supplies had arrived by ship at Da Nang Harbor. So my troops and I set off with our six-by (six by six—six wheel and six-wheel drive) trucks and hauled boxes from the beach to the base that night.

More tents were in this shipment, and I really needed them badly. Several additional generators for our MABS engineer, Maj. Jack Bates, and water buffalo were included, along with boxes of that all-important toilet paper, helmets, canteens, pots and pans, and mobile, heated shower units.

On June 15, 1965, General Westmoreland, commander of the United States Military Assistance Command, Vietnam (COMUSMACV), in Saigon, gave our commanding general of III MAF, Maj. Gen. Lew Walt, permission to begin search-and-destroy operations near our defensive enclaves. He allowed this, provided that these ground operations assisted in the defense of the base. The 3rd Marine Division began aggressive patrolling, expanding the tactical area of responsibility (TAOR). They immediately found a VC camp just to the west of Da Nang. The camp was large enough to support about two hundred VC before the marines destroyed it. The VC—probably all local villagers nearby—could not be found. On June 21, squads of 2/3 were attacked by VC, and they killed four VC and captured two VC women. One marine was killed. The next day, just south of Da Nang Airfield, the VC attacked a small outpost of C Company, 1/3. The marines killed two VC without suffering any casualties. Each day activities of both VC and our marines escalated around Da Nang. The increased firefights and activities resulted in more medevacs flown by myself. Finally, the CG III MAF requested permission to bring in his remaining 3rd Marine Division battalions that still remained on Okinawa. The VC, at this time, were still concentrating attacks against the ARVN, not against us. The VC late-spring offensive against the 1st Battalion, 51st ARVN Regiment, near Ba Gai, twenty miles south from Chu Lai, resulted in 392 South Vietnamese deaths.

During this period, it was commonly observed that the Viet Cong were being reinforced by uniformed North Vietnamese regulars coming down through numerous branchings of the Ho Chi Minh Trail in Laos.

However, our patrols were really not going far enough south and east of the airfield. Our actual defensive position remained inside the airfield perimeter. CG III MAF had requested permission from General Thi, the I Corps Vietnamese commander, to establish some defensive positions to the south and east outside of the airfield perimeters. However, General Thi had responded by saying that he wanted the population of Da Nang to get used to seeing the marine presence in the area first, before moving the marines into the rural areas.

The heat made it difficult for the helicopters to lift heavy loads, due to what is called high-altitude density—thin air. I was scheduled to fly an assault lift coordinated by a ground sweep into the immediate valley to our southwest. The villages in this valley were fairly large, and there were about forty villages up the valley to the Song Thuy River outlet from the large western mountains towards Laos. The valley was called Happy Valley. I had flown over the villages here at a very low altitude at least twenty times. Each time the flight crew would discuss the simple fact that in all of these villages, Viet Cong flags, of red and blue with a gold star, fluttered over numerous thatched-roof houses. It was obvious that the VC had controlled this valley and all the villagers in it for some time before we ever arrived. Yet it was only six to ten miles away from Da Nang and very close to the ARVN I Corps command. Had the ARVN just ignored this controlled territory so close in to one of its major cities? Was it contested some years ago? Or was it an arrangement between VC leaders, General Thi of I Corps, and even the mayor of Da Nang? As a matter of fact, when we went on liberty nights to Da Nang, rumors were abundant that the VC from these villages in Happy Valley, villages such as Cam Ne, Phuc Thuan, Hoa Khuong, Phuc Hung and Vien Kien, were in on liberty right along with us in the same bars! Who knows? They possibly could have been there with us, especially Saturday nights, when Da Nang city was packed with ARVNs, civilians, U.S. Marines and U.S. Air Force personnel.

At dawn we loaded up the troops, and in three divisions of four choppers each, launched from the Da Nang Airfield in a straight shot to high ground just to the west of the village of Dong Lai, on the western end of Happy Valley. Simultaneously, ground-moving elements moved up the valley from the east near Xom Dao. This pincer movement trapped many hard-core Viet Cong throughout the numerous villages, and raging battles began almost instantly. As I shuttled more troops in over the valley, firefights were everywhere. On my fifth trip, I began bringing out wounded, and then more wounded. It was apparent that the Vietnamese I Corps commander did not tell us the extent of the large unit of VC in this valley. General Thi had to have known this. As the fighting raged on, our F-4 attack bombers were taking off beside us as we were loading troops at Da Nang, making a quick turn westward and dropping bombs almost immediately. Their ground crews and ours could easily see all the smoke of the battle, and the bombs falling from the Phantoms, so close to the airfield. At midafternoon, I was refueling at the fuel pits at the northeast corner of the airfield when a runner came up to the side of the aircraft.

"Captain, Colonel Vaile wants you at your supply office. The squadron here has a replacement pilot for you."

I saw the other pilot coming out of the helo. I had to go by the flight-line tent to fill in my flight time flown on that specific aircraft maintenance form, and then trudged up to meet with Lieutenant Colonel Vaile. When I arrived at my office area, my four personnel were scurrying about moving tents from my storage area to a truck.

"Captain, I pulled you off the flight because I need you to set up a small medical camp right here," said the calm Tom Vaile.

I responded, "What's going on, Colonel?"

"Hell, you ought to know. You've been flying up Happy Valley all morning. The battalions are getting so many casualties that Charlie Med can't house them all. So the III MAF told us to break out our extra tents."

So the rest of the afternoon we set up twelve general-purpose tents and I stood back and watched our choppers, including the same one that I flew that morning, serial number 148109, landing nearby with our wounded.

The message was brought home quickly: Charlie the Gooner will fight us and fight us nose to nose, when he has to.

The next morning I was scheduled to fly mortar rounds and small arms ammunition to a village called Phu Ha. It was a self-defense village with only the villagers and a handful of ARVNs defending themselves. The village had a large, deep moat around it. Inside the moat were hundreds of sharpened bamboo shoots called punji sticks. I landed inside the village with my wingman. The villagers clustered around unloading the ammo. There was some activity going on along the nearby river. I asked some villagers what was happening, but they couldn't understand English. An ARVN lieutenant came by and told me in rough English that the VC had somehow worked through the defense perimeter, captured the village chief and schoolteacher, and chopped their heads off beside the river. I walked farther over toward the river and sure enough there were two headless bodies lying in the weeds. The families wept beside them. This had been a common communist activity here for years. They killed the village elders, leaders or mayor, schoolteachers and Christian missionaries. Having eliminated the village's leadership, the Viet Cong then could better intimidate the villagers to gain their support. Ho Chi Minh's tactics followed age-old communist doctrines—just as the tactics of Che Guevara and Fidel

Castro had in Cuba not too many years before. Fish swim in the water; guerrillas live off the land with the rural inhabitants' forced support. The supply lines from North Vietnam were long. The VC needed the countryside's food and support. And I was convinced that at this point in history, the VC owned, by force, most of the countryside.

I flew back to Da Nang feeling that I had just witnessed a few more humans killed by the philosophy of communism exported by the Soviet Union. After all, Ho Chi Minh (Nguyen Ai Quoc) and Mao Tse-tung of China both attended revolutionary school training in Moscow in 1923. All of that seemed like distant history, but right now it was present-day, ruthless butchery and reality. These communists keep up with their motto: "The end justifies the means."

That night I sat in our officers' club drinking a warm mixed drink. (We still had not found out where to get ice.) I sat next to a Vietnamese major who had been invited into the bar after a nearby meeting. He and I talked a little and I asked him what the ARVN officers thought should be done now that the Americans were here?

He answered, "Most of us feel that you should supply us with the latest weapons, and train us to defend our homes and families. Then, as we better defend ourselves, use your airpower and amphibious capabilities to invade the North. With most of the North Vietnamese forces dispersed along the main supply channels to the South, you could capture Hanoi and Haiphong. Without the support of the North, the Viet Cong would wither on the vine, and we could reunite the country as a free country."

The next day, Capt. Walt Gilk, from HMM-161, flew in from Phu Bai and asked me for some dearly needed tents for their Phu Bai living cantonment. I had not received anywhere near my remaining required tents to build Marble Mountain Airfield. However, I couldn't let my old squadron down, so I gave him twenty general-purpose tents, while sweating out the shortages that I might confront in the near future.

That evening, I again sat down exhausted at the end of the officers' club bar. Shortly afterwards, two familiar lieutenants from 1st Air Naval Gunfire Liaison Company (ANGLICO) walked in. They immediately recognized me as the former commander of the 2nd Platoon, 1st ANGLICO, where I spent four-teen months in Hawaii, after my flying tour at HMM-161 in that state. They quickly told me that they had been sent down directly from Camp Smith in Hawaii to live in the villages south of Da Nang and offer U.S. naval gunfire control to the ARVNs and village self-defense forces. They had a real horror story to tell. Almost nightly, they said, the VC attacked their villages and killed women and children to impart fear upon the villagers. Captain Hayes, from their platoon, had been living in the house of the village elder, or chief, at Phu Ha. The other night the VC attacked the village, and while the siege took place, they got into the village elder's hut, shot the hell out of the captain and dragged off the village chief.

The last they heard was that the captain was so badly shot up he may lose the use of one arm. They didn't know what had happened to the village chief. Since this had been the same village I had been to just the morning before, I filled them in on the headless village chief and schoolteacher. We parted that evening. I never saw them again and later often wondered if they survived out there in those villages.

On the evening of June 30, 1965, six of us officers decided to go into the city of Da Nang for the purpose of having a sayonara party for two who had put their thirteen months "in country" and were leaving for the "real world" the next day. After we had our two jeep drivers drop us off in the middle of town, we proceeded first to dine in high fashion in a large Vietnamese boat restaurant on the Tourane River. Naturally, we drank French wines and ate long thin French bread, along with excellent French food. After that, we barhopped and expressed our envy of the two who were leaving MABS-16 for home. At around midnight, Steve Reno, Dutch Harris, Frank Brown and myself had a four-pedicab race home the three miles to Da Nang Air-field. The little, skinny Vietnamese pedaled the bicycle-borne rickshaws at a surprising speed as we laughed and drank beer, half in the bag. The fact that we were drunk dulled for us the rampant rumors in the Da Nang area that all of the pedicab pedalers were VC. I'm not sure if I pulled down my mosquito net when I hit that cot in our Da Nang French quarters—it was truly a crash landing.

It seemed like I had just passed out when I was awakened by a sickening *boomp, boomp, boomp*. I jumped up and looked eastward out of my open window area. There were mortars falling on the air force and Vietnamese side of the runway. I glanced at my wristwatch. It was 0130, exactly. I grabbed my pilot's .38-caliber pistol and bandolier of ammo, and ran out of the hut wearing only skivvy shorts. Many of us gathered, standing in awe as the unexpected took place—incoming tracer fire could be seen coming from the southeastern perimeter. This was the area on our south that the South Vietnamese were responsible for. Within minutes there was a small amount of small-arms gunfire on the airport parking apron. Seconds later explosions erupted. It was obvious that right across two taxiways and a runway from where we stood, our U.S. Air Force planes were exploding. Soon several more tracers were seen coming from the southeast, and all went quiet as six aircraft burned, lighting up the entire east side of the flight line. As I walked over toward the wing G-3 operations hut, I heard our artillery firing and then soon began seeing impacts out in the rice paddies southeast of the airfield. I again glanced at my watch—it was now 0200 on July 1, 1965. Maj. Sam Foss, who had flown with me in HMM-161 for two years in Hawaii, rushed by me. Major Foss had been assigned to G-3 and must have had some information.

"What happened, Major?" I asked

"The VC mortared the air force side, near the F-100s, and got through the wire and threw satchel charges at the aircraft. It looks like the F-102s and the C-130s got the satchel charges. That's all I know at the present."

Soon, all was quiet on the eastern front and I remembered to pull down my mosquito net. By evening of the next day, July 1, more information became available. A sweep by our marines did not find the so-called sappers. However, the ARVNs captured a North Vietnamese intelligence officer. He had been wounded during the sapper attack. He belonged to the 3rd Battalion, 18th Regiment of the North Vietnamese army. He filled them in on the details of the attack.

The attack force consisted of an eighty-five-man Viet Cong special operations company, reinforced by thirteen North Vietnamese sappers and a mortar company. The thirteen NVA sappers dug a tunnel under the South Vietnamese defensive wire, got inside, and ten of them reached the aircraft. They destroyed one F-102 and two C-130s and damaged two F-102s and one C-130. No South Vietnamese were reported injured, but two U.S. Marines were wounded responding to the action across the airfield.

Finally, on July 20, 1965, General Thi gave permission to General Walt to expand our defense boundary. Ocassionally, I received a newspaper from home. On the front page of the *Washington Post* was a U.S. Marine with a lighted cigarette lighter. The picture showed him holding the flame up to the edge of a grass shack, or "hootch," of a village. It mentioned that the marines had swept Cam Ne and the valley and had burned the village down. It sure made the U.S. Marines look bad. However, nowhere in the news article did it tell the whole story of the sweep up Happy Valley, the hundreds of VC who lived there, and the resistance and battles that gave our marines those heavy casualties that had me putting up tents for our wounded, or any perspective of the facts. I soon concluded our own "free press" was our enemy also.

Prior to this sighting of the news article, I would often succumb to the pleas of the AP and UPI news photographers to fly on combat missions. I often let them climb aboard my UH-34D, if there was room, and took one along. I never did that again. I simply hated them. I even kicked one physically from the belly of my helo one morning, after my crew chief twice told him to get off of my aircraft and the newsman insisted on going. More and more such false-impression stories were running off of our presses back Stateside, but even worse from UPI in Paris. The slanted news media gave a fine impression of the VC, never mentioned that the North Vietnamese were there in the South, and made the ARVNs and Americans look like the bad guys. Occasionally you would read that the North Vietnamese government denied that there were any North Vietnamese regular army units operating in South Vietnam. Some of the news correspondents saw NVA when I did. Why didn't they take pictures of that proof and get it published? Why wasn't there a newspaper picture showing that NVA intelligence officer that had been captured after that raid on our Da Nang Airfield on July 1? The many news reporters at Da Nang reported worldwide the damage we had received.

With the establishment of the III MAF command and the attack by the VC sappers on the air force inside of Da Nang Airfield, liberty in Da Nang was curtailed. Only people like myself, who conducted supply purchases, were allowed into Da Nang. Of course, there were many Americans right in the city, such as the Seabees, who had a compound there, an army logistics group, and the navy offloading their ships in the city.

On July 23, I was assigned to fly a two-plane mission to transport rations, water, and ammunition to a marine company that was conducting search-and-destroy operations well south of Da Nang, near Dong Ha. It was routine until I orbited at three thousand feet over the company.

"Red Goose, this is Bald Eagle approaching with two, over."

"Bald Eagle, this is Red Goose Actual." *Actual* meant that the speaker was not the radio operator, but the actual company commander. "We're pinned down here with most of my troopers caught in open rice paddies. It's a bad scene for choppers to land here. But I need the ammunition. I'm firing a green flare. Let me know if you sight me."

"Red Goose, I see your flare. Is that you up on that paddy dike north of the large rice paddies?"

"Eagle, that's affirmative. My men are laying out a red LZ panel for you to see where to land. Over."

"I've got the LZ panel on the top of the dike. I also see your men lying out in that paddy to the south. I see gun muzzle flashes from the treeline along the south end of the paddy. There's a village on the other side of the treeline. Looks empty, except for the VC firing from the treeline."

"Roger, Eagle. I've called my battalion for reinforcements and artillery support, but it'll be a while. Do you think you can land on this dike?"

"Red Goose, I don't know if I can fit my bird on that narrow dike. But right now, you need more ammo, Lieutenant. You've got to get those guys the hell out of that rice paddy. I'm calling Da Nang DASC to see if there's any attack aircraft in the area."

"Roger that, Eagle."

"Da Nang DASC, this is Bald Eagle on flight zero-five, over."

"Bald Eagle, go ahead, loud and clear. This is DASC."

"DASC, if you have some loaded fixed-wing within thirty miles of Da Nang, I have friendlies in contact and pinned down. I'm an experienced FAC and can run some close air support on the VC to even out the situation here."

"Bald Eagle, that is affirmative, we have a section of two F-8s with four five-hundred-pound bombs each, plus 20-Mike-Mike guns. Where are you from Da Nang TACAN?"

"I'm on the one-niner-zero at one-six miles from Da Nang."

"Roger. You will have a flight, 'Rooster,' checking in with you shortly. Go to TAC three."

On my radio, I called the lieutenant on the ground. "Red Goose, I've got some marine F-8s coming in shortly. Hang in there."

"Eagle, understood some stovepipes coming in. I'll notify my battalion so that they coordinate with the artillery we requested."

I switched my UHF radio to 275.5 megahertz, which was Tactical Air Control net three. I looked down, directly over the VC-held village. I couldn't see anyone in the hamlet. However, I could see crackles of muzzle flashes, looking like the Fourth of July fireworks going off along the darkened depths of a heavily vegetated treeline.

Just then I heard over my UHF receiver, "Bald Eagle, Rooster flight up."

"Roger Rooster, what is angels and ordnance lineup?"

"Rooster has flight of two F-8s with four Delta one Alpha and guns. We're at twenty thousand on the Da Nang one-four-zero for the one-niner-zero, sixteen. Ready to copy mission, over."

"Rooster, this is Eagle. I have a treeline with VC laying down a heavy base of fire at friendlies pinned down in open rice paddy. Enemy-held treeline is at coordinates Alpha Tango niner-eight and six-five-three. Treeline runs west to east for about thirty meters. I'll mark with hand-held red smoke grenade. Request two bombs each on first pass and we'll adjust from there. I want a zero-niner run-in with a right-hand pullout. Call rolling in hot. Give me a four-second interval between aircraft. Read back, over."

Rooster read back the specifics correctly and reported passing down through clouds at five thousand feet descending for an orbit at four thousand feet.

"Rooster, I'm with wingman in left-handed orbit at three thousand to the north of target. As soon as I sight you, I'll roll in from the east along the treeline and drop my smoke. My wingman will roll in from the west and we'll return to our orbit to the north."

"Eagle, Rooster at four. I don't see you yet."

"Rooster, I've got your smoke trail. Now I have you both. I'm at your four o'clock low. Keep your orbit to the right. We're going in with smoke mark now."

"Eagle Two, you swing around to the west and only come in after I make a smoke drop coming from the east. That'll have us coming in from two different directions with less exposure from the gooners."

"Roger that, Eagle One."

As I flew in from the east to the west, I stayed to the north of the treeline, just out in front of our pinned-down troops. My port-side M-60 machine gun was blasting away at the treeline as the other gunner threw out a red smoke grenade while we passed over the hedgerow at about a hundred feet. As I pulled right, my wingman came in from the west in the opposite direction, dropped his red smoke grenade, while firing, and we joined up over the friendly LZ to the north at three thousand feet.

"Do you have our red smoke, Rooster?"

"That's affirmative. We have a good sighting of the treeline, but can't make out the friendlies in the paddies."

"Okay, Rooster, on your next orbit you are cleared to commence attack on the treeline. Drop on the treeline between the two red smokes: drop first pair closest to the western smoke. We'll then walk up the treeline eastward."

"Roger Eagle, Rooster One rolling in hot, I have the treeline."

"Continue Rooster One."

"Okay Rooster One, I have you wings level, lined up. You are cleared hot."

"I have two away, Rooster One. Rooster Two, cleared for roll-in. Make your drop thirty meters at twelve o'clock from Dash One's hits."

"Eagle, Rooster One off target."

"Rooster Two, I have you lined up. You are cleared hot."

"Roger Eagle, Rooster Two, cleared hot."

"Rooster Two, I have two drops."

"Eagle, Rooster Two off."

"Rooster One. Move your drops up about another fifty meters twelve o'clock from Dash Two's hits. You're cleared hot."

"Roger Eagle, Rooster One, cleared hot."

Rooster One dropped perfectly on the hedgerow, followed by his wingman. All bombs were gone.

"Okay, Rooster One, you are cleared for two runs each with your 20-Mike guns, over."

"Roger Eagle, I'm in hot."

"Eagle Dash Two, this is Eagle. Remain at three thousand feet, I'm going into the LZ. As soon as I lift off, commence your approach on the same LZ panel on the dike."

"Roger Eagle."

I descended in a dive and flared nose-high near the bottom. As I approached I realized that I could not fit the whole UH-34 chopper on the dike. I chose to place the right tire on the LZ panel, leaving the right side with its doorway on the dike and the rest of the chopper hovering out over the paddy. It was a hover with one wheel down, as my crew chief kicked out the ammo. As they were unloading, I looked across the flat rice paddy as the marine F-8 Crusaders were still strafing the treeline with their guns blazing. The marines who were pinned down were now charging, with fixed bayonets, across the last quarter of the distance from paddy to hedgerow.

"Eagle, this is Rooster One flight off target, winchester. Can you give me a BDA?"

"Rooster. Thanks a lot. You sure helped the lieutenant down here. Our grunts are now taking that treeline. I can't see anything from here on the ground, but I'm sure you killed a few. The only BDA I can give you is fifty meters of treeline destroyed with undetermined enemy in it."

"Roger, Eagle. Will you give that BDA to Da Nang DASC on your way home?"

"I sure will, Rooster. See you at the bar later. Out."

I lifted off and my wingman repeated the one-wheel landing on the LZ cloth panel. The company commander thanked us a few times over the Fox Mike radio and we climbed for home. After landing and while postflighting the aircraft, we counted only three small-caliber hits in the lower aft part of the fuselage. The metal shop would quickly put a metal patch on the holes and the bird would be ready for a night mission.

The next day, I took a jeep and drove from Da Nang Airfield through the southern edges of Da Nang city, across the Da Nang River bridge at Binh Thuan to the sandy beach area across a dog-patch hamlet of Hoa Khue Dong. The Seabees were already out on the sand under the burning sun, with their surveying equipment. This is where the Da Nang East Airfield would be built.

Marble Mountain, to our immediate south, rose much taller than what it appeared to be from Da Nang and from the air. Working with the Seabees as they laid in a pierced-steel runway, I began to work on the layout of the base. I drove back and forth the eight miles through the outskirts of Da Nang daily, passing villages that were rumored to be under Viet Cong control. The U.S. 9th Marines were now moving about in this area from Monkey Mountain south to Marble Mountain. Our grunts of the 9th Marines had pushed southwest of the perimeter of Da Nang Airfield, running into heavy VC resistance at Duong Son and Cam Ne. The 3rd Marines conducted Operation Blastout south of Cam Ne. The marines, for the first time, came across fortified VC villages in several hamlets. They learned the dangers of the VC punji sticks, Malayan whips, fighting spider holes and mazes of interconnecting tunnels between the hootches, as well as between villages. A CBS television crew was along at Cam Ne, and despite the viciousness of the Viet Cong defensive booby traps, CBS reported in its Stateside news that there was practically no resistance. Yet notwithstanding this statement, four U.S. Marines had somehow been wounded.

In the meantime, restraint directives continued to pass down to CG III MAF from Washington, and Saigon, and from the local ARVN command. As a result of restraint pressure, rules of engagement were published and posted in our pilots' ready tents. "Do not fire unless fired upon," and so forth. I initially thought that was a logical approach to the unknown, until one day one of my gunners was killed while we were in an approach to what was known as a hot zone. After we received a hail of Russian AK-47 incoming, my remaining gunner fired back as I touched down in a cloud of dust. I believe that might have been the turning point of my perspective of this unknown war lost in the jungles of Southeast Asia. From then on, I realized that the only good communist is a dead communist. I swore that if I ever had to return to this battleground again, it would be with my own fingers on a gun trigger, not sitting elevated in an assault transport helicopter getting shot at.

Several days later, while on a routine resupply mission in the vicinity of Cam Ne village, we heard an urgent call for a medevac. Since we were right in the area, we called Da Nang DASC and told them that we would pick up the wounded. This freed DASC from having to dispatch UH-1E medevac helos from VMO-2 at Da Nang. As I landed next to the Yen River, I saw several wounded being hauled out to my chopper. Leaning out my window, I noticed two marines who appeared dead. To my shock, one of the dead was Master Sergeant Navine, my old platoon sergeant from my Naval Aviation Flight School days in Pensacola, Florida. His open utility jacket exposed a gaping wound in the middle of his chest. His piercing blue eyes, which once stared me to the dirt on the old grinder drill field, stared straight upward to the blue sky. He appeared tranquil—as if all of this turmoil was now over. It was—for him. The Navine Machine had stopped. I flew the wounded to Charlie Med and then flew the two KIA to the morgue located in the northeast corner of Da Nang Airfield. It was a large, morbid-looking, sheet-metal building with large refrigerators. Here they kept the bodies of the Americans prior to flying them home. Two morgue workers carried body bags out to my aircraft and I bade good-bye to a "real marine" who once taught me my left foot from my right. I muttered, "Semper Fi, Sarge."

My crew chief in the belly of my UH-34 chopper asked, "What was that, Captain?"

"Nothing, Corporal, nothing. I just hate to see good marines die when our congressmen don't understand what really is happening in the world and therefore never support our president's stand against communism. I guess they are waiting for these guys to start working over Central America and Mexico."

"Roger that, sir."

The next morning I got the word that my TAFDS units at Tam Ky had been blown up by sappers. So I had to break out a new fueling system and we flew it down to Tam Ky. This attack upon our choppers' refueling station indicated for the first time that the helicopters were beginning to get to the Viet Cong.

The 7th Marines now arrived. I was flying a mission in support of the 4th Marines in a two-day operation called Operation Thunderbolt. It was a battalion operation about twenty miles south of Chu Lai. Most of our lifts consisted of delivering cans of water and lifting our U.S. Marine heat casualties. It must have been 120 degrees with high humidity. I emptied my own two canteens of water early in my flight sorties. I returned to my Da Nang parking apron late in the afternoon. As I disengaged the clutch, shut down my engine, and applied the rotor brake, I saw our Catholic chaplain, Father Roland, waiting for us. He was always asking for chopper rides into the heat of battle, so I thought that he would be asking for a flight to the action down at Chu Lai. However, he called me aside from the rest of my crew as we were kicking off our heavy, totally sweated armor suits.

"What can I do for you, Chaplain?" I asked above the noise of the airfield. He looked serious, as he put his hand on my drenched shoulder. "We just got a message from the Red Cross. Your father died. I'm sorry. Your family has requested you return for the funeral."

I stood there in the heat, with dirt and dust flying about me from a taxiing helo and a thunderous roar in my ears as two MAG-11 F-4Bs climbed out to the north.

Above all the noise and turmoil of this busy airfield, the chaplain shouted, "We have your emergency-leave orders cut. You're scheduled on a C-130 flight out to Okinawa at 1800 tonight."

At 1700 I was standing at the C-130 flight line with B-4 bag in hand. The C-130 was not going to take off until 1830. I stood there watching the mechanics working hard at preparing Col. John Bing's MAG-16 helicopters of HMM-261 and HMM-361 squadrons for the next day. Col. Tom O'Donnel was to take command of MAG-16 from Colonel Bing, first thing in the morning. It was quiet at Da Nang Airfield now, as the sun set just above the dark, tall mountains to our west near Laos. Too many thoughts passed through my mind to convey. I wondered how my mother was taking my father's death. I wondered what exact day my dad died. I wondered what my father had thought of my being here in some small war in a country that he never heard of, a country that was eleven thousand miles away from the coal mines of Pennsylvania. I thought of some of his World War I stories from his experiences in battles, such as the battle of Argonne in France. Was there a thread of relationship from his war forty-seven years ago? Was there a link of rationalization between these conflicts so many years apart? Or was it simply man's continual survival among man, generation after generation? My deep inner reflection and simple question—what am I doing here?—gave way to the barking of the crew chief of the C-130 from VMGR-152, the marine transport refueler squadron.

"Load 'em up. We're going home," he shouted.

The flight to Okinawa seemed long in the darkness. This was a free, space-available flight for me on emergency orders. I would have to pay my own commercial flight passage from Okinawa to Pennsylvania. Or I could try to catch an emergency flight seat on any military plane, if there were any going back east. We landed at Kadena Air Force Base and I soon found out that there were no military flights to Japan that night. I barely had time to purchase a commercial ticket on Japan Airlines and a change over to Pan Am for San Francisco. We were soon en route to Japan. While in the rear of the aircraft drinking a cup of water, the pilot of the JAL aircraft slapped me on the back. To my amazement, it was Kugo Setsuo. Kugo, while an ensign in the Japanese navy, had gone through the Pensacola, Florida, U.S. Naval Aviation Flight School course with me. Additionally, I had once in 1958 flown across Tokyo Bay to visit him. He had been serving as a helicopter pilot for the Japanese navy at Kizarazu.

Kugo asked me where I was going, and I told him. He gave me his condolences and we discussed our various career paths and families, before he returned to his pilot's compartment.

Hours later I felt that we had entered a holding pattern and figured we must be holding at altitude near Tokyo. The weather looked bad outside, so I assumed that there were delays at Tokyo International. Moments later Kugo came back, found me belted in and said, "What flight do you have a ticket on out of Tokyo International?"

"Pan Am flight 075."

"I will call my JAL dispatcher on our company frequency and check 075's departure status. We are held up here due to showers that are slowing departures and arrivals."

"Thanks, Kugo."

Moments later, Kugo was back telling me that all was cleared as requested.

After a bumpy, rain-swept approach, the lights of Tokyo International runway could be seen as we made a gentle descending turn inbound westward across the bay, and the large cities of Tokyo and Yokohama merged ahead.

While taxing in, the stewardess came to me to tell me that the captain said that I should get up and make my way to the rear door with my hand-carry. I glanced out the window and the large Pan Am 707 was parked ahead, lights flashing in the rainswept taxiway. I saw a ground handling truck parked next to the 707. As our JAL plane stopped, the stewardess opened the door, and Flight Captain Kugo shook my hand amidst the noise and pelting rain. He shouted, "Sayonara." To my surprise, the efficient Japanese ground handlers had somehow found my B-4 bag, which fortunately had my name stenciled on it in a large Marine Corps traditional manner. They had opened our JAL baggage compartment and using flashlights they dug through tons of bags to find mine. In the rain the broadly smiling Japanese gave me my bag, and I ran the one hundred feet to PA075 and up the step ladder that they gladly extended. I was shown to an empty seat, as the other passengers were wondering what was going on.

Hours later, at twenty-nine thousand feet over the blue Pacific Ocean, I thought: I still don't know what date my father died. Can I beat the race with the sun on time to make his burial?

Arriving at San Francisco International, I promptly called my wife.

"Eleanor, I'm in San Francisco, I'll be home in hours. When is the funeral?"

She responded, "It was yesterday."

Dejectedly, I said, "I'll call you from wherever I land on the East Coast. Give my love to the children and tell my mother I'm on my way home."

I went into the airport bar and had a few drinks. I missed the burial and that was what the race against time had been all about. It occurred to me that I might as well call Travis Air Force Base, about sixty miles north of San Francisco, to see if they had any space-available flights bound for the East Coast.

It turned out that Travis AFB had a C-121 going to McGuire AFB, New Jersey. Now that time was no longer of the essence, why pay for an airline ticket? I caught a bus to Travis and checked in with the navy air traffic coordinating officer in the air force terminal. The plane was scheduled for McGuire Air Force Base, but had to fly diagonally across the country down to Little Rock, Arkansas, to drop off four air force colonels. Then it would head directly for Jersey, after refueling.

We arrived at Little Rock Air Force Base at 0730. I was in the small terminal coffee shop sipping a coffee when all hell broke loose. A muffled explosion sounded somewhere on the base and people soon were scurrying about—outside and inside the terminal. Air police (AP) vans and jeeps were flashing their lights as they scurried by from the main gate. Nobody inside the terminal seemed to know what was going on.

Then the terminal loudspeaker announced, "There has been a serious accident in one of the intercontinental ballistic missile silos. All personnel are immediately restricted to the base. No person is allowed to leave by surface or air. There does not appear to be a fear of any nuclear detonation. Please keep calm as the investigation proceeds. We will keep you posted. Stay in the vicinity of the terminal. Please do not call out this classified information over the phones."

There was dead silence inside the terminal. Outside, sirens screamed, vehicles sped by. I walked out the front door and saw some black smoke rising about a half mile away. Many vehicles were heading in that direction. There was nothing else to see. I walked back into the terminal and called Eleanor. As the long-distance connection system took time, I thought: If I were an irresponsible news reporter, I'd now be calling this sensational, but dangerously confidential, information in to my editor to get a scoop—regardless of what it meant for national security. I told my wife that I was stuck in Little Rock due to transportation problems and that I would call her later.

About four hours later, while sitting in the terminal, I witnessed numerous air force small Learjet-type aircraft arriving, one after the other. I never saw so many generals, air force or otherwise, anywhere. I suppose they were a mixture of missile men and Washington brass. We heard in the terminal that the explosion of the missile in the silo threw the nuclear warhead across the base, with no nuclear detonation, of course. Two hours later, the loudspeaker announced, "All personnel are free to continue on your way. Travel off the base is now permitted. Do not approach the out-of-bounds areas marked by the AP."

I checked with the air force transport section, and the C-121 crew that I had flown in with had canceled the flight to McGuire AFB. I caught a cab to Little Rock National and flew to Newark, New Jersey, commercially.

The next day, under the humid heat of Pennsylvania's August, I stood next to my father's grave. An American Legion stand stood in the fresh soil, holding a fluttering American flag. I felt badly about missing his burial by a day and a half.

Later that day, I felt worse. My brother Bill related to me that he had called the duty officer in Headquarters Marine Corps on the previous Friday night to inform him of my father's death and ascertain how I could get home from Vietnam. The duty officer said that he would send a message out to my unit in Vietnam. However, it was the responsibility of the American Red Cross to send authenticated requests to the military command of military relatives' deceased immediate family members. Since it was after 1700 on Friday evening in Washington, D.C., and since the Red Cross was not the military, the Red Cross did not work weekends. Accordingly, the Red Cross would not verify, nor would it send an authenticating message through the Red Cross network to the Da Nang Red Cross unit, until Monday morning. The two days lost in the Red Cross passing the information that ultimately was handed to me by our chaplain at Da Nang were the two days that I needed to make the burial. The funeral director had told my family that the heat of the summer precluded keeping the body more than the extra day he already had retained it while awaiting my arrival.

My other brother then related his experience with the Red Cross. He bitterly told me how they operated at his airfield, sixty miles outside of London during WWII. He said that as they returned in their battered B-17s to the airfield, and as the flight crews walked en route to their debriefings, three mobile stands operated along the taxiway. One stand had tea and crumpets. It was the British RAF support kitchen. The tea and crumpets were free, paid for by the British government. The second stand was the American Red Cross. It served coffee and doughnuts to the exhausted flyers. The coffee cost a nickel and so did the doughnuts. The third service stand was another coffee and doughnut mobile kitchen. This stand also gave the coffee and doughnuts free. It was the Salvation Army's.

My next several days were a transition period to very peaceful life. The entire population around me did not know of the violence that I had experienced just hours ago, nor did they care. I really wondered if it was worth going back to the war zone for these people. Nobody seemed interested, except my close relatives and family.

My wife and two children had moved not long before from an apartment to a home in North Plainfield, New Jersey. The new place kept me quite busy. I was glad to be there to help them get settled. It helped me block out the inevitable anguish that I knew would be upon us when, too soon, I would have to leave my family and return to my unit in Vietnam.

chapter 2

Return to Nam, 1965

The day came startlingly fast, and we all fought tears as I climbed aboard a commercial plane at Newark, New Jersey, en route to Hawaii. In Hawaii, I could catch a free military flight back to Vietnam via Japan.

As I flew across the United States, amazed as always by its vastness, I thought of how snug and serene the countryside looked—no firefights, no explosions or fires from warfare—but how naive its residents were. More than half of the civilized world was in the armed camp of the controlling entities of the

Kremlin. This summer of 1965 might be the midpoint in this battle between the two giants. But where and when in the future would this nation find the unity it needed for its future survival? It was a country without a national policy to fend off communism. Possibly, I thought, Russia will go broke someday supporting all of these national wars of liberation.

Upon returning to Da Nang Airfield, I was greeted first by the heat that was much more intense than the New Jersey muggy August weather that I had just left. I was then jovially greeted by Lieutenant Colonel Vaile, who quickly filled me in on how fast we would have to complete the new air base at Marble Mountain.

The next day I spent from dawn until dark working over at Marble Mountain in the blown sand and heat. The Seabees were constructing the runway by bulldozing the sand dunes and by hand-placing each pierced-steel plank, section by section, into place to form a five-thousand-foot runway fifty feet wide. This pierced-steel planking, or marsden matting, was the old World War II–and Korean War–type taxiway, parking apron, and runway matting. It was heavy steel, not the lighter, aluminum SATS (short airfield for tactical support) runway system that was installed by the Seabees at Chu Lai for the jet-aircraft operations.

As fast as the Seabees could cut wood, hammer nails, and build wooden frames called strongbacks, our MABS-16 utilities crews placed my supply section's large, general-purpose tents over the frames for housing twelve persons per tent. The 660-tent encampment began to rise rapidly in the sandy beach area along the South China Sea. The Seabees began building a large mess hall, while our utilities section built a motor transport office and sheds for large walk-in food-storage reefers and began construction of an enlisted club overlooking the surf of China Beach.

Late one evening, as I sat on my cot back at the Da Nang Hilton (which is what we called our French living quarters), a redheaded major came shuffling into my room. He had his B-4 bag and was wearing a sweated uniform of the day—obviously he had just arrived from Okinawa. He introduced himself as Maj. Cliff Rice. He then threw his bag down on the deck and left for the officers' club to find out if he knew anyone here in-country and what was going on.

The next several days Cliff Rice and I didn't see each other, except when he and the rest of us hit the rack nightly. He wanted to start flying badly, so he was gone daily getting through the bull at group to get into a flying squadron. I was gone before the crack of dawn, driving over to Marble Mountain Airfield.

Later on, about Major Rice's fifth day, I was sitting on my cot writing a letter home. A corporal came through the passageway and said, "Captain, which cot is Major Rice's?"

"That one over there that has most of his belongings still in the bag."

"With your permission, sir, I'll take Major Rice's personal belongings."

"Where is he going?" I asked.

"The major was shot early this evening in a chopper south of here. Apparently he got hit with a .50-caliber round in the thigh. It's pretty serious, I hear, and Charlie Med is having him evacuated right now to the hospital ship." The hospital ship was the USS *Repose,* which was located out in Da Nang Bay.

"Boy, he just arrived. That must have been one of his first or second flights in-country. . . . I hope he doesn't lose his leg," I responded.

The corporal left with the bag and I never saw Major Rice again. He was a roommate who came and left without my getting to know him personally.

A few days later all of MABS-16, about 550 people, moved to Marble Mountain Airfield to live in the first finished strongback tents. What none of us knew was that here we were building a base and living right in the middle of Viet Cong–controlled territory. We had not yet built any perimeter of defense; we had no wire at all around the construction site. Only sand dunes separated us from the five small villages to the east. So every night one or two snipers from the village areas would shoot directly into our tent area. We simply would come out of our tents and fire our own personal weapons back into the general village areas where we saw the sniper fire coming from. Since the mess hall was still under construction, plus the flying squadrons had not yet moved into the field complex, we had to eat C-rations. After a few weeks of heavily fortified C-rations, the so-called Da Nang two-trot never returned to most personnel. The utilities section, under Jack Bates, moved briskly despite the heat and blowing sand and built adequate numbers of large latrines and continued wiring all of the tents from the twelve motor-vehicle gasoline-driven generators that were going to be our source of living- and working-area electricity. RMK, a civilian American contractor, moved in. It used local Vietnamese civilian help. The workers began to build prefabricated sheet-metal hangars for the forth-coming helicopter squadrons. The Seabees, while drilling for water, broke several drill bits trying to get through the very hard marble flooring that lay under the sandy beaches at Marble Mountain. I had to fly to Taiwan to purchase drill bits, since I could not find any in Da Nang. Soon, the Seabees struck water. It was excellent soft water. Using our three-thousand-gallon col-lapsible rubber expeditionary water tanks, Major Bates estab-lished a potable-water station for drinking water. He also had built shower areas using my supply section's two available mo-bile shower units. I was short one shower unit. I ordered a shower unit from the 1st Marine Aircraft Wing supply at Iwakuni, Japan. Additionally, since we were getting sniper fire almost nightly into our living tent areas, we had placed our twelve M-60 machine guns out beyond the tents. I was short four M-60 machine guns, so I also ordered these four machine guns that we rated in MABS-16 along with the shower unit. I placed both items on what is called a Priority One requisition in my supply system. Priority One means ordering a supply inventory item while under combat conditions. Since we received normal marine air logistics (MARLOG) flights of a single C-130 from Japan and Okinawa once a week, I assumed that I would get those items next week, particularly since they were ordered Pri-One.

Major Bates set up the two available mobile shower units, one for the enlisted men and one for the staff non-commissioned officers (SNCOs). For the officers he hung up lister bags so that they could take a shipboard-type shower until the missing shower unit would arrive.

After getting a good handle on things in supplying MABS-16 in construction materials for a few days, I drove over to MAG-16 at Da Nang, where the helicopters remained with crews awaiting completion of the new base. Here I managed to get scheduled to fly the next day. I had some flying to catch up on. They sure could use the extra pilot. The whole air group was busily involved in a big operation called Starlite, about twelve miles south of Chu Lai.

The 1st VC Regiment, consisting of two battalions plus the 52nd VC Weapons Company, totaling about 1,500 men, was found to be located in the Van Tuong village area about twelve miles south of Chu Lai jet airfield. MAG-16, using twenty-four UH-34 choppers from HMM-261 and HMM-361, escorted by Huey gunships from the U.S. Army and by Marine Corps Hueys from VMO-2, had been carrying our 2nd Battalion, 4th Marines, into three LZs to the west of Highway 1, in the vicinity of Van Tuong. Simultaneously, the 3rd Battalion, 3rd Marines, landed ashore, to the east, from three amphibious ships, *Bayfield* (APA-33), *Cabildo* (LSD-16), and the *Vernon County* (LST-1161). A portion of 3/3 also set up a blocking position to the north of the assault area. The 4th Battalion, 12th Marines, artillery-prepped the area, and MAG-11 and MAG-12 jet bombers worked over the assault areas.

The first wave of choppers landed into LZ Blue near Nam Yen and were not shot at. However, the second wave took intensive fire. After moving all troops into the area, the eight helos from HMM-261 departed for Da Nang, and HMM-361 continued resupply and the medical evacuations. I was getting my flying in with HMM-361, so I got some good, action-packed flight time. Of HMM-361's sixteen helicopters, fourteen of them had received hits from enemy ground fire. Shortly afterward, HMM-163 helicopters arrived from off the LPH USS *Iwo Jima,* in the South China Sea, to assist in the airlift workload.

The battle raged for several days. The U.S. Marines had killed 614 Viet Cong, captured about 50, and obtained numerous weapons. The marines suffered 45 dead and 203 wounded and had one UH-1E gunship from VMO-2 shot down at An Cuong. The Viet Cong 60th and 80th battalions had their noses bloodied. This attack by the U.S. Marines had no doubt prevented a planned attack by the VC upon our airfield at Chu Lai.

One week later, the C-130 MARLOG flight from Japan and Okinawa arrived with some of my supplies that I had ordered through the normal supply system. The system was working so well that I couldn't believe it. A thermometer for daily temperature readings for our MABS-16 aerology (airfield weather forecasters) came in a soft paper envelope that was all sticky and gooey. I opened it to find that it had been broken and all of the liquid had leaked out of the fractured glass tube—obviously it should have been sent in a wooden box. Another item that was under a requisition calling for four front tires for the motor transport department's front-end loaders came in a six-inch-square wooden box. I opened the box in wonderment, thinking, *Imagine, four tires in a six-inch-square box!* Not surprised, I found four shiny brass door knobs. We didn't have a single door on the whole base—only 660 tents. Next, I looked over rejected requisitions to determine why I was turned down by wing supply in Japan. Two of the rejects stood out. The first and most important was my request for our additional four M-60 machine guns that I rated but did not have. Since we received sniper fire every night from the nearby villages, as well as automatic fire from a nearby Buddhist pagoda to our southwest, we needed those machine guns. The second item was important but not as critical. This was the shower unit for the officers' living area. I looked at the rejected supply requisitions. They had written across them "Priority One request rejected. Priority One is for combat action requests only. Please resubmit under request Priority Two, noncombat emergency. Pri-One is for combat conditions only." I couldn't believe my eyes. Here we are getting shot at every night, and my last chopper flight I returned with six bullet holes in the aircraft . . . and now some asshole in Iwakuni, Japan, is telling me we are not in combat. I had already waited two weeks for those machine guns. Now I'd have to reorder Pri-Two, and they'd be flown up on the C-130 MARLOG flight to Japan and come back the following week—I hoped with the guns. The idiots could have easily downgraded the requisition to a Pri-Two with a stroke of the pen and shipped the needed guns on this C-130 flight. I was so mad that I gave up on supply for the rest of the day and made a land-line phone call to Da Nang to get scheduled for a night mission. I was lucky to get scheduled for the night medevac standby flight in a UH-1E Huey Slick evac bird.

At about midnight, while sitting in the ready tent at Da Nang

Airfield, the phone rang and MAG-16 operations, Maj. Sam Foss, gave us a medevac mission. We were to pick up two seriously wounded marines near Chu Buai at grid coordinates AT 955620. Looking at the map, it obviously had to be reconnaissance personnel wounded to be that far out. The area was well to the south of our artillery base at Hill 55.

Bob Hill was our chief corpsman from the navy medical group assigned to our air group and always volunteered for the medevacs. So he was already strapped into the Huey when we got to fire up the single engine of the already preflighted bird. We climbed up southward with a UH-1E gunship escort at max speed and headed south at four thousand feet. The lights of Da Nang and the airfield faded rapidly as the black darkness of the overcast night enclosed us. Using our TACAN and heading for a TACAN radial from Da Nang at about 195 degrees and twelve miles, we soon were over the LZ's vicinity. Several small fires burned in the countryside as we looked for our LZ.

"Foxtrot Zero, this is Swift Six overhead for wounded. Do you see me?" I called over the FM radio at the unit somewhere below.

"Swift Six, this is Foxtrot Zero. We hear you but can't see you yet. We're setting off a green flare now."

"Foxtrot, I have the flare. Do you have any landing lights for us?"

"Negative landing lights. But we do have flashlights."

"Roger. Get two flashlights and place them two-zero meters to the north of the actual LZ and about one-zero meters apart, so that I can use them for night depth perception and closure rate, over."

"Roger that, Swift. We see you now. You're at our zero-niner-five from us."

"Foxtrot, we're turning inbound now. Turn on your flashlights. . . . Break, break; Dash Two, cover us, we're on final."

Just then all hell broke loose. Two steady streams of what looked like .50-caliber tracer fire came straight at us from in front of our approach.

"Dash Two, I'm breaking it off and will come in from the north instead. Take care of those bastards," I shouted to our escort gunship.

"Roger One, we'll work 'em over and watch out for you."

"Foxtrot, this is Swift One. Move the lights to the opposite south side, same distance from the LZ. I'll be on the deck from the north in three minutes, over."

"Swift, wilco."

As Swift Two worked over the two VC .50-cal guns, I approached from the north and straight into the hail of tracer from our three o'clock position.

"Foxtrot, we're taking heavy fire from your zero-niner-zero about three-zero meters. Hell, we're coming in. I have your lights."

At about fifty feet on my radar altimeter, I switched on my landing lights and saw the red panel marker and three marines with two wounded lying nearby.

"Swift One, this is Two, we shut one of these guns down. But there's another two to the west firing. I think these guys got gooners all around themselves."

"Roger, Swift Two . . . break . . . Foxtrot did you hear that information on Fox Mike?"

"We read that, Swift. This is Foxtrot Actual. I've decided to pull the whole team out now. We're of no value, since Charlie knows exactly where we are and they have us boxed in. Our information gathering is ended now. Can you get six plus two wounded out of here right now?"

"You betcha, Alpha . . . break . . . Two, did you read that?"

"Affirmative, One. I'll throw some 2.75-inch rockets into two more of these guns and then we're in for the remainder of their recon team."

As I was climbing out with two wounded and three team members, I could see Dash Two's gunners spraying the area. Soon I heard, "Dash Two out of the zone with three passengers."

"Roger, Two. Get the call sign from the recon leader in your aircraft for me. I can then call his operations center to tell them we had to extract the whole team and that they're inbound to Da Nang, after dropping their two WIA at Charlie Med."

We arrived at Da Nang after Charlie Med and postflighted our bird. It only had five big holes and three small .30-caliber holes. Not that bad with all the fireworks out there that night.

The following night I was scheduled to fly copilot with Maj. Sam Foss for a night hop. I went over to Da Nang to HMM-261 ready tent and Major Foss said, "The briefing simply is this: you and I are taking a single bird locally. The weather is CAVU." CAVU means clear, visability unlimited. "No enemy locations, no enemy fire, no nothing," Foss continued. "It'll simply be a three-hour night flight like back in the real world."

"What kind of flight is this, Major?" I quizzed.

"This, my friend, is a go-home flight. I'm leaving tomorrow for the real world. But I haven't done much night flying and I'm short on my annual nighttime minimums. So I don't want to do all the night flying catching-up in CONUS when I'm home with the family."

With that, we kicked the tire, lit the fire, and climbed to an orbit to the west of Da Nang Airfield, and flew in circles around Freedom Hill, Charlie Med, and just a little north, to the Da Nang Bay west. It was just like flying a night flight in the States to simply stay proficient on night flying and instrument flying. This was, without doubt, Sam's and my most boring hours of flight spent in Nam. But Sam got his night time, safely, and I was happy flying rather than sitting in the sand at Marble Mountain sipping warm beer. The most hazardous part of the night was the drive in my jeep alone from Da Nang Airfield across the old rusty, narrow Da Nang bridge east and through the four villages en route to Marble Mountain Airfield at about 2230.

A few days later I went over to Da Nang Airfield to see if any of the air force or Marine Corps units in the area had access to light switches. I needed about seven hundred light switches for the 660 tents, plus additional switches for the mess hall, enlisted club, and eventual SNCO club. I scrounged all over the base and nobody knew where I could beg, trade, or steal electrical light switches. When I was at the marine jet-fighter flight line, near the F-4s of VMFA-531, I noticed a small group of pilots and mechanics gathered in a circle. To see what was going on, I got closer to the Phantom jet that they were clustered about. It turned out that Col. (ret.) Gregory Boyington—"Pappy" Boyington, of WWII "Ba Ba Black Sheep" squadron fame—was visiting the jet flight line. He was employed by an electronics firm that supplied a part to the F-4 maze of electronics. So it was a business trip for him, but also an opportunity to talk with current combat pilots. I eased on into the conversation, and it was interesting to hear what this Congressional Medal of Honor winner had to say about flying. Additionally, he said better what most of us had reluctantly said about how spineless congressmen were, preventing us from fighting a war the way it should be fought, the way it was fought in WWII. We all concluded that it was amazing how all of our presidents from Truman to Johnson had wanted to contain communism, but congressional wimps had invented the term of limited war.

From the airfield, I reluctantly went down to see my Da Nang city source of hard-to-get items. I had to visit Lily Ann. She was a Chinese merchant dealing in hardware and anything else that she could manipulate in the black market of Da Nang. I previously had purchased corrugated tin sheets from her that Major Bates needed for the roofs over his precious electrical generators, to prevent the blowing sand and forthcoming monsoon rains from damaging the only electrical sources we had.

Her Chinese name was not Lily Ann, of course. But that is the name she used to deal with the Americans who needed things that were upstairs in her large, warehouselike hardware store located in the middle of downtown Da Nang. We sat on the matted floor, Japanese style, and sipped hot tea.

"Lily Ann, I need about seven hundred electrical light switches for my base. I will place one switch in each tent to operate two single light bulbs per tent. Can you get me seven hundred switches cheaply and rapidly?"

"Captain, I can get anything you need. Didn't I get you tin sheets from Korea?"

"Yes. But my budget is very limited. Can you get me a good price?"

"Captain, I do not have light switches here in Da Nang. I do not know where I will get them and I do not know what they will cost me. Seven hundred light switches may be quite a problem to obtain. How soon do you need?"

"Yesterday," I responded.

Lily Ann had a cute, young Vietnamese girl wearing a flowering au dai, or split, long, flowing dress, pour more tea for us. Lily Ann then called her Vietnamese store manager upstairs by shouting, *"Bui Q tren lau."* As I sipped tea, the two of them haggled back and forth in Vietnamese. Then she turned to me and said, "Captain, I can get you light switches in one week. Is okay?"

"Okay. I will visit you next week and see if you have the switches. Keep the price down," I responded.

I jumped into my jeep and drove south of the city to Da Nang bridge, crossed the rusty structure with its military communications land wires hung all along it, and then turned right at the small village on the east side of the bridge. I headed south toward Marble Mountain Airfield thinking, I suppose she'll get el cheapo wares from Hong Kong and charge me a small fortune for unreliable junk switches. But where the hell else can I get light switches in this semiprimitive country? There simply are none in the navy or Marine Corps supply systems.

As I drove along the dusty, bumpy road next to the several villages located directly across from where we were building Marble Mountain Airfield, some of the villagers were smiling and waving at me. I waved back knowing that this is exactly from where the VC fire at our tents each night. As I turned left into a small ravine cut through a sand dune and onto our sandy road which would eventually be inside of the base fenceline, I glanced at the several young Vietnamese girls who were smiling and waving in their black pajamas and dark yellow conical hats. They were calling me to join them for a romp in the straw and sand. They were standing directly next to a straw hut that had one wall covered with hammered-out soda pop cans forming a tin wall for rain protection. As I whisked by, I could see the numerous bullet holes punched through the tin multicolored wall. Those holes were from us firing this way in return fire at the VC nightly. Many of those holes were mine, from my .45-caliber grease gun. I had heard from the Seabees that some of these gals were crawling into our machine-gun nests at night and selling themselves to our gunners out there in the sandy gun emplacements. So far, our defense perimeter officer, Lieutenant Grinder, had not yet caught any of that going on in his machine-gun nests. But he was checking for it each night.

The Southeast Asia monsoon season soon approaching was anticipated with hopes of a cooling off from the unbearable heat of summer. I continued to fly normal resupply missions throughout the I Corps area.

Soon, another full-scale operation was planned and we were ready to attack the remainder of the VC regiment from the Starlite operation. The operation was to be twenty-two miles south of Chu Lai and to move north toward the Batangan Peninsula. On September 7, 1965, naval gunfire ships—the cruiser *Oklahoma City* (CLG-5) and two destroyers, *Orleck* and *Prichett,* along with the APD *Diachenko*—provided naval fire support for this new operation, called Piranha. The marines of the 1st Battalion, 7th Regiment, and the 3rd Battalion, 3rd Regiment, aboard the Seventh Fleet ships *Bayfield, Belle Grove,* and *Cabildo,* came ashore early in the morning on White Beach by LVTs. In the meantime, forty UH-34D choppers from MAG-16 lifted 3rd Battalion into the LZ Oak four miles inland from the beach landing.

We received only small-arms fire from the VC as the marines poured into the area. After helo-lifting the 3rd Battalion, we began lifting two South Vietnamese battalions into LZs Birch and Pine from Quang Ngai city. Again, only light enemy fire was directed at us in these LZs. The enemy could not be found in large numbers. Very little naval gunfire was needed. After three days, the operation was terminated. The U.S. Marines and the ARVN jointly killed only 178 VC, captured 360 with weapons. The ARVN had 5 KIA and 33 WIA; the U.S. Marines suffered 2 killed and 14 wounded. During the operation, I had an opportunity to hear my old outfit, 1st ANGLICO, attached to the South Vietnamese battalions, call in naval gunfire support.

The days and nights drifted by as we progressed in building the new base. The tents were up. The mess hall, a wooden-framed building with Lily Ann's Korean tin roof, was soon to be completed. The MAG-16 group commander and headquarters staff moved into the new base. My tent, which had Major Bates, our utilities officer, and three others, soon filled. One of the officers to move into my tent was a very active, congenial Catholic chaplain, Father Paul Roland. This memorable navy lieutenant was everywhere, and wanted and needed everything. I always felt that he had moved in with me because he knew that I had access to building materials and jeeps and trucks. Father Roland daily wanted to see our MABS-16 priority list of construction. He talked us into adding a chapel to the list and he badgered us daily to increase the building priority. He couldn't understand why I always had his wooden chapel listed as number ten. The number ten, or as stated in Vietnamese, *muoi,* was driving him crazy. To sedate Chaplain Roland, I gave him a large general-purpose tent, and we erected it in the center of the living areas, near headquarters. This was to be used as an interim chapel until we could, some months down the road, build him a nice wooden chapel. Father Roland was soon out looking for cloth materials, parachute silks, and so forth, to decorate the inside of the drab green tent.

As the rest of the air group ground crews and maintenance people moved from Da Nang, the helicopters were flown over to their new home. We now had our own chopper base of UH-1Es (Hueys), HR-2Ss (heavy haulers), and UH-34Ds (transports). We immediately strung concertina wire around a four-mile perimeter and set up the only twelve M-60 machine guns that I had in my inventory. We placed the machine guns out near the newly laid wire fencing; right across from the several questionable villages to our west.

Lieutenant Grinder, in charge of airfield defense, obtained land mines from the grunts and set them in the sand around the wire defense line. I was still waiting for my reordered additional four M-60 machine guns to give to Lieutenant Grinder for expanding his cross-fire posture. I was then assigned an additional duty as the MABS officer in charge of the mobile alert platoon, or reaction platoon. This was our second line of defense to back up Lieutenant Grinder's defense setup in the event the VC got over the wires into the airfield.

During this period, marine ground units had indicated that nightly, large numbers of VC traveled an area located about twelve miles northwest of Da Nang. The area was located up what we called Elephant Valley along the Ca De Song River on a flat rice-paddy area near Hoi An Thong village complex. A small operation was planned for a midnight helo assault into that area in hopes of catching a fair amount of active VC at night. The operation was suitably called Operation Midnight.

At 2330, with troops already aboard, twenty UH-34s and four

UH-1E gunships started engines, engaged transmissions, taxied out in divisions of four each and climbed out, heading south from Marble Mountain. I was in the second four-plane division and thought, With all those engines and rotors turning at near midnight, the VC across the street from us in those villages have already passed the word to their units in the field that a big helo lift is going somewhere. We went about five miles south then came back to the northwest, passing west of Freedom Hill heading straight for the LZ and a night assault. In minutes, the first troops were on the deck running all over the village complex. We, in our choppers, returned to Marble Mountain Airfield (now designated MMAF) to pick up more assault troops and to drop them into the same LZ. I heard the next day that there were only two VC killed in the area. Either the local VC got the word out to all area VC that there was a large night helo lift, or intelligence via other VC means gave the attack away. Possibly, just by coincidence, there was no infiltration by VC from the mountains through this flat land that very night we dropped troops there. The other possibility was the VC simply went underground into their numerous tunnels in the villages.

The first tactical helo lift at night had been performed by HMR-163 Ridgerunners during the Korean War, and VMO-6 routinely flew night medevac missions in Korea. Additionally, during 1962 the marine squadron HMM-362 flew night missions carrying ARVN troops in the Mekong Delta area of Vietnam. However, historically, this large-scale night lift was the first full marine helo lift of this war. It did prove to the VC that we could strike at night with large numbers of helicopter-borne troops. The night had belonged to the VC as they moved freely across the rural countryside. This was no longer a sure bet for them.

Various small-scale operations continued placing a heavy burden upon the ground and air crews of our helicopters. The helicopters were beginning to show wear. On one such helo lift, called Gibraltar, HMM-161 carried a battalion of the U.S. Army 101st Brigade into an area near An Khe with only seven choppers, and all choppers got hit with ground fire. One of them was shot down. This operation involved helo-lifting ARVN, U.S. Army, and the 2nd Battalion, 7th Marines. The operation resulted in killing 226 VC with our total losses at 13 killed and 44 wounded.

On one of my routine two-plane resupply missions, I was assigned to fly down to a South Vietnamese outpost called Hiep Duc, about forty-five miles southwest of Marble Mountain and twenty-five miles west of Tam Ky. It was located about two miles from the rising mountains to the west and along the Son Thus Bon River at coordinates AT 925172. This entry to the rich farmlands was called the Que Son Valley by the marines. As I approached the city of Hiep Duc, which was the western district capital of Quang Tin Province, I looked over the old French-built triangular fortress that was occupied by a small regional force unit. It was truly serene down there with the running river, rice paddies, treelines and people walking around the town to the east.

I descended with my wingman in our usual straight-down-spiral approach and we landed unmolested just outside of the fortress. It was a nice Sunday morning and it almost felt like a quiet Sunday back home. Our crew members helped the Vietnamese troops unload some pigs, ducks and ammunition. I lifted up with my wingman tucked in closely and we started our slow, spiral climb directly over the outpost. As we crossed the western side of the fortress, the hills to our west came alive with flashes. These flashes against the dense greenery indicated that we were taking heavy fire from the hills above us, and some just at our climbing altitude. I kicked hard left rudder, pushed the cyclic far to the left and pulled harder upward on my collective, while twisting my throttle increasing engine RPM to 3,200. This put me and the wingman passing directly over the fortress and away from the fire. Just then the whole collective stick came off in my left hand and I had neither collective rotor-blade pitch control nor engine power control. I shouted to my copilot, "You got it, Lieutenant!"

"Roger, Captain. I have it. What's wrong?"

"Look at this. The whole control shaft came uncoupled," I responded as I held up the collective, which had wires running down through it. We couldn't believe our eyes at this rare situation. The copilot flew the plane home without incident. But we never heard of a helicopter rotor-blade pitch control collective handle ever coming loose. It wasn't the best time to have a mechanical malfunction, but better than having it happen during a flare to a landing, or just at lift-off.

Back in my tent that night, my good friend Chaplain Roland was at it again. "Bob, I need some help in getting some things for the chapel."

"What kind of things do you need, Padre?"

"I need kneelers and a crucifix. Something nice that will be good for the chapel tent now, but then fit nicely into the wooden chapel MABS utilities will eventually build."

"How can I get that for you?" I asked.

"I don't want that from you. I simply want you to drive me to downtown Da Nang and I'll visit the bishop of Da Nang. He'll help me."

"Fine. We'll go down tomorrow afternoon in my jeep," I answered.

The next afternoon we drove down to the main street in Da Nang city. I drove into the large open gateway of a white-painted wall and into the courtyard of a beautiful old European, Gothic-style, single-spire church. The church organization obviously ran a school for girls, as numerous white-clad young girls scurried about the large yard. Chaplain Roland asked a few Vietnamese where he could find the bishop, and due to the language barrier, it took some time to get the location of the bishop's office. When we finally found it, we both went in.

Since Chaplain Roland didn't know the Vietnamese language, and the Vietnamese bishop didn't know English, they both talked to each other in the Roman Catholic church Latin. I didn't understand a word and therefore sat there bored to death. When they finished, the bishop called for a priest to come into the office. The priest was a Caucasian and it turned out that he was a French priest still there from when France was trying to run the country. The French priest knew Vietnamese but couldn't speak English. Chaplain Roland didn't know French. So, as before, the chaplain and the French priest spoke Latin. They started walking from the bishop's office, so I tagged along asking, "Where are we going, Chaplain?"

"We're going all the way back over to China Beach. There's a large village on the north end of the beach, near Monkey Mountain. That entire village consists of Catholics who came down with this French priest from Hanoi when Ho Chi Minh allowed a million Catholics to leave North Vietnam after the French left Indochina. The priest says that there are several good workers in that village who can build church kneelers. He'll also look for a wood-carver to carve a large crucifix for us."

We drove back across the Da Nang bridge and headed north past about five villages. Then the French priest pointed to the right at a very large fishing village on China Beach. I drove into the village and the priest gave me hand directions to locate the village chief's hut. We got out of the jeep and entered the hut. The priest spoke Vietnamese to the chief and the chief ordered all of us tea, as we sat on the sandy floor. Soon another Vietnamese man came in and got involved with the discussion. Chaplain Roland spoke Latin to the French priest; the French priest spoke Vietnamese to the chief. Apparently the other Vietnamese was a good carpenter and he began making hand signals in the shape of church kneelers and seeking approval for sizing of the kneelers. Soon an order was apparently concluded for some fifty wooden kneelers. Just as I thought the deal was over and I began rising, the chief put his hand on my shoulder to sit back down. He pointed out toward the beach. I peered through the open window and saw five Vietnamese running along the edge of the village with Russian AK-47 assault rifles. They were only about thirty yards from where we sat and they were heading south. They apparently were VC forming up for the night. They could not see my jeep inside the village among the grass shacks, or we might have had some complications. I reached up and unsnapped the leather stay strap over my shoulder holster to free my aviator's .38 pistol, just in case they saw my jeep. I deeply regretted not having my trusty grease gun along. I'm not sure what the hell I could have done with that .38 pistol against five automatic rifles. But soon they vanished into the village immediately to our south. Chaplain Roland said, "We're all done here. I have my kneelers ordered. They'll be ready for pickup in two weeks. But nobody here feels qualified to carve a Christ on a crucifix."

"We'd better get out of here, Chaplain. It'll soon be evening and the VC activity will pick up," I told him.

With that, the three of us drove off and we dropped the French priest off at Da Nang city and returned to our airfield. Halfway down the road to our airfield from the Da Nang bridge was a Catholic orphanage. Naturally, Chaplain Roland wanted to visit there. So in we went. It was a nice, clean area with a lot of Vietnamese children. Whether those children had lost their parents to the war or just were abandoned, I didn't know. As the orphanage director introduced the chaplain to a crowd of youngsters in one of the classrooms, the children began to cry out *"Wo, wo, wo, wo,"* patting their mouths open and closed with the palms of their hands, American Indian style. I was amazed at this unconventional greeting. The last time that I had seen this noise-making was years ago while visiting a Cherokee Indian reservation in the mountains of North Carolina, as the Indians performed a dance for the tourists. The orphanage director, using broken English, explained to us that this is the way the locals cheer at a sporting event or welcome a good friend. After a lengthy conversation between the chaplain and the orphanage director, we headed for home base. As we rode the short two miles to the base, Chaplain Roland said, "Bob, the priest there told me that I'll be getting information from some of the Catholic villagers nearby. They hate the VC and will be providing information on them."

"Chaplain, you better tell Colonel O'Donnel, the group commander, about this intelligence source."

"I sure will, Bob," answered the chaplain, as we drove into our airbase compound and night fell upon the base.

Another routine mission that was interesting occurred on October 15. I was flying artillery rounds and small-arms ammunition to the ARVNs, located twelve miles east of Da Nang. The area was remarkable. It was an exceptionally beautiful former French villa consisting of six large European-style buildings located high on a mountain peak well into the jungle. This complex was the summer home, or getaway cool spot, for the top-level French colonialists years ago to beat the heat of Da Nang. It was simply beautiful; an aristocratic sight. As I flew over the triple-canopy jungle en route, periodically I could see an almost growth covered dirt road winding its way toward that mountain peak. It must have been some ride up through that thick jungle years ago, especially knowing that Bengal tigers roam that area of the country. As I approached the mountaintop from the east, I could look right into the hills of Laos. It must have been one of the best observation posts that the ARVNs had that was near the Ho Chi Minh Trail. The terrain was extremely steep, emerging from the thickly vegetated jungle floor below to the peak. There were eight 105-mm howitzer artillery pieces pointing in all directions and located around the outside of the clustered French buildings. The ARVNs had dug trenchlines between all of the buildings, and I saw four black, funny-looking French cars that had apparently been abandoned up there years ago.

My wingman and I landed without incident, except that there was not enough room for us to place the full helicopter down. We both placed only our nose and front landing gear on the ground, as our aft fuselage and tail wheel extended out over several hundred feet of nothing. The Vietnamese flag of yellow background and three horizontal red stripes fluttered in the mountain wind drafts as the Vietnamese unloaded their supplies. The area appeared calm on the mountaintop, with the ARVN and their families casually walking about the French buildings.

We both unloaded and leaped off of the hilltop with no need to climb for altitude. We already were at a safe altitude, or that's what I thought. Just then Corporal Thomas, one of my gunners, said, "Captain, we received a stray round up through the fuselage and the spent slug bounced about the inside of the passenger compartment."

"Dash Two, we got a round or two. Are you okay?" I quizzed my wingman.

"Everything appears A-OK in this bird, Dash One."

"We'll head straight for Da Nang field just in case one of us picked up a few rounds in the wrong place," I broadcasted.

We continued due east at six thousand feet and had passed about five miles east of Dong Son when my oil pressure started fluctuating, followed by the engine's running rough and a partial loss of power.

"Dash Two, I have engine oil pressure problems and a rough-running engine. I'm going to try to make Da Nang, over."

"Roger One. We don't see any damage or smoke; hang in there."

"Dash Two, I can't maintain altitude, and at full power I'm dropping about five hundred feet per minute. I may have to take it in. Stand by."

"Roger One. We'll follow you down and cover you, if you go in."

We skipped over a four-hundred-foot hilltop and were out over a valley that ran north and south. Up ahead I could see a narrow pass called Col De Dai La, and I knew the Khanh Son village complex lay directly on the other side and likewise the flatlands that lead to Da Nang Harbor. As I was still descending, I could see the 327-foot-tall Freedom Hill located near the Da Nang Airfield. But I wasn't going to make it near Da Nang. I was headed down toward a large open area of tall elephant grass.

"Dash Two, stay above me and cover me with your guns. We'll land and check the engine to see where we got hit and what we can do about it. Be ready to swoop in and get us if we have to get out of here in a hurry," I transmitted.

"Roger, Dash One. Be careful."

I landed in five-foot-tall elephant grass and quickly disengaged the clutch by snapping off my power throttle on the collective stick, slowing the rotor blades and then applying the overhead rotor-blades brake. I left the engine running. It snorted and missed roughly.

"Lieutenant, you stay strapped in and watch the gauges. The crew chief and I will get out and check the engine," I said to my copilot. I quickly climbed out the window and down the two steps of the fuselage and was almost shoulder deep in elephant grass. The crew chief came out of the belly of the aircraft, and we opened the clamshell doors of the nose of the helicopter. The crew chief took one look and said, "Captain, we've had it. We have a punctured oil line and a shattered oil filter. It's amazing that the engine is still running without any oil. Better have him shut it down, sir."

As I stepped backward to wave a cut-the-engine hand signal to the copilot, he was frantically waving his hands and pointed out in front of us. Then I saw a Vietnamese in customary black pajamas carrying an AK-47 rifle.

It was Charlie, but how many were there? Are they going to attack right now, or what? I thought. I quickly pointed up to the copilot and then pointed to my wingman flying a circle above us at about five hundred feet. I then pointed to the ground. The copilot got the idea fast, because he was seated about ten feet above the ground and could see VC starting to form a circle around us from the front of the aircraft. I could see the copilot talking on the lip mike, so I knew that he was calling our wingman down to get us the hell out of there.

I then gave the copilot the engine-cut signal again, and he shut the noisy engine down. Except for the flapping of the wingman's chopper descending, the field became quiet. I ordered both gunners to pull out the M-60 machine guns from the crew compartment and to set up a defensive position on either side of the helicopter. I rapidly climbed back up to my pilot-seat area. I quickly looked around and saw about twenty gooners starting to surround us. I reached into the aircraft and grabbed my trusty grease gun (M3A1 submachine gun) that I always had lying between the seat and center console. As I leapt from the side of the aircraft, the VC all stopped moving and went down into the deep elephant grass, as Dash Two flared to a touchdown beside us. I didn't have to tell the four other crew members to run to Dash Two. The two gunners with M-60s and the crew chief with his .45 pistol were in front of me as we practically dove into the belly of the helicopter, which immediately lifted up, flying directly over the gooners. While crossing directly over about twenty Charlies, I expected all hell to let loose. But they simply all looked up at us without raising their rifles. As best we could figure it, we had unexpectedly dropped out of the sky within a few feet of a group of local VC, who either didn't know what to do because of the lack of a leader, or thought more helicopters were inbound for an attack on them and did not know what to do yet. Or they were expecting our low-flying wingman to fire upon them as he orbited them. Since his gunners didn't fire upon them, they might have been confused as to what to do.

En route to Marble Mountain Airfield, Dash Two called group operations requesting a HR-2S (Sikorsky CH-37C) heavy hauler from HMH-462 to come out and airlift our disabled

UH-34D chopper back to base. He advised operations of the approximately twenty VC around the aircraft.

As Dash Two landed and taxied into his parking revetment at MMAF, looking out, I saw an HR-2S cranking up its two engines and loading about fifteen security troopers aboard, apparently to get my downed helicopter. That night in the mess hall I heard that when the HR-2S arrived over the scene to externally load my helicopter, there was nothing there but charred wreckage. The gooners apparently torched it off with an incendiary grenade, or got it burning some other way.

For months I had been unable to buy any cigars, since there was not a base exchange or store at Da Nang Airfield for the armed forces. Occasionally, I could find a few cigars in the Da Nang bars, but that was rare. Since my wife wanted me to stop smoking, she didn't mail me any cigars.

Finally, we heard that the air force was going to open a base exchange. I eagerly watched it being constructed. It was located just off the air base property and on the north edge of the city. It was a large, metal prefabricated building. Several weeks later the opening date was announced. That day I got up at 0500 and drove from Marble Mountain to the new store area and parked out front. There were about three hundred military in a long line waiting for the 0800 grand opening. About two hours later I ran frantically up and down the aisle of the large exchange. I found cigars and then saw a large, startling sign: "One pack per customer"—the same with cigarettes. I couldn't believe my eyes. As I grabbed my one pack of cigars and headed toward the main office to find the exchange manager and raise hell, I walked by one aisle that was full of Kotex sanitary napkins. I stopped in shock. I thought, What the hell is this doing here? We don't have females here in our combat units. There aren't even any nurses here.

I found the manager, an air force major. He was beaming and thrilled that he had warm six-packs of soda pop, beer, cigarettes, and even potato chips for the troops.

"Can't I buy more than one pack of cigars?" I asked.

"Sorry, Captain. This is our first day of operation and I want to spread the goodies around a little. Once we get fully operating, there will be no limits on anything you wish to purchase."

"Major, why are all those Kotex boxes along the wall? Hell, there isn't anyone here that can use them."

"Captain, when I flew to Bangkok to order my stock, the stock had come in a block configuration for Thailand where the embassy and other U.S. government employees include women. So they shipped the whole block of stores to me. I had it all put out on the shelves. Who knows, maybe it'll sell. If not, I'll remove it and ship it back to Thailand."

I left the exchange confused, but with my one pack of precious cigars.

I returned to the exchange the next morning for another pack of cigars. To my amazement, the line was three times longer. Our grunts were somehow managing to get guys back from the field to buy some goodies. I was thrilled to see these dirty, tired marines out there in the long line in front of me. If anybody could use a can of soda pop, a bar of soap, or what have you, they could—and they sure deserved it. Once I got inside the building, I headed for the cigars. The sign regarding one to a customer still stood there. But to my surprise, most of the boxes of Kotex were gone from the shelves. I saw the store manager walking nearby.

"Major, who the hell is buying the Kotex boxes?" I asked.

"Captain, you won't believe this. The field marines have discovered that the Kotexes are the perfect size and material to clean out their mortar tubes. They're buying Kotex like nuts and taking them back to the field of combat. I guess I better keep stocking it," he chuckled.

I left the exchange and returned to my base and tent area to enjoy a cigar.

My living-area tent was located in the northeastern corner of our base, with the defensive wire only about thirty yards away. Besides myself, Maj. Jack Bates and Chaplain Roland, we had Curt "Smokey" Cassen, our MABS control-tower and crash-crew officer, plus several other MABS officers in this tent. Since I was the supply officer, naturally I had the only machine gun, the .45-caliber grease gun. All the other officers had pistols like the officers in the other tents. The residents in my tent were afforded some level of comfort knowing that we had that extra automatic weapon to defend ourselves with each night.

In the next tent to my south were some headquarters-staff pilots, including my closest friend over the years, Capt. George Gross. Across from my tent were some more MABS officers, including Lieutenant Grinder and Sgt. Khoa Nguyen (pronounced *win*), who was our local Vietnamese interpreter assigned to us from downtown Da Nang. Since we were located on the northern extremity of the base, we all had to walk through the other living areas for about a half mile to the mess hall and the headquarters area. It was another quarter of a mile across the runway to the helicopter flight line on the west side. Behind and to the west of the flight-line tents was our wire perimeter fence line and a dirt road outside our western perimeter that ran north and south and separated us from the Seabee tents. The Seabees had just started construction of a naval hospital to their immediate south, located on the Da Nang River as it winds its way southward from the Da Nang Harbor and city of Da Nang. Directly south of the construction site was the Buddhist temple from which we received nightly gunfire at our living area. We never fired back at the temple area so as not to disturb the local Buddhists.

During early October 1965, we began getting ground-assault probes by the VC. At about midnight they would charge our wire along the north corner, near where we lived, and fire automatic weapons and throw a few grenades, then withdraw as our machine gunners on the defense wire fired at them. This would have all of us running and diving out of our tents and crawling into deep foxholes that we had dug next to our tents. Each night the VC attacked a slightly different area of the fence line, working their way southward along the western wire perimeter, probing for a weak area.

Each night about five of us would gather in my tent at a table that we made, and would drink and talk over the events of each day until 2200. We made sure that our two bulbs in the tent were off no later than 2300, since about 2400, or midnight, we could expect random firing from the villages to our west, or a small VC probe on the wire.

On one such evening, as we drank and talked and wrote letters home while clustered around our gathering table, Sergeant Nguyen came in and told Chaplain Roland that some local villager had approached the northeast wire near one of our machine-gun emplacements and that he wanted to talk to the Catholic priest. Chaplain Roland said, *"Di thi di"*—Let's go. At about 2230 the chaplain returned.

Major Bates said, "Well, Chaplain, what was all that about?"

"A local villager wanted to tell me that the VC are planning a big attack upon our base here during the very next moonless period. I had to run down and report this to the group commander."

Jack Bates said, "Did you hear that, Bob? You better not be night flying or staying overnight somewhere else until after this next moonless period. We need that grease gun here in the event that Charlie comes over the wire."

Our MABS established a personnel hiring department and began hiring local civilian men and women to work on the now fairly large base. Each Vietnamese was screened in downtown Da Nang by I Corps personnel to assure us that none were VC. But who really knew? Our flight surgeon gave each a physical exam and did find several who had TB and were therefore not hired. Those hired were employed to assist the messmen in the large mess hall with such duties as cleaning up the tables, washing the dishes, and taking out the garbage. Some were employed to load garbage on our marine dump truck as it went around the camp daily. Others were hired to be house women to be paid individually by the officers to keep their tents clean of the piles of sand that blew inside daily and to wash their clothing. So during the day, the base appeared just like any busy U.S. military base in Japan, Okinawa, Korea, or Gitmo, Cuba, where the locals work all day on the base and then leave. At night the atmosphere changed to one of watchfulness, as we could see numerous firefights and flares going off all over the countryside, particularly to the south.

Since we had only tents with us as an amphibious force tasked with the projection of seapower ashore, we normally lacked covered storage facilities. Since it became apparent to us that we were going to stay a while, like during the Korean War after the Inchon landing and recapture of Seoul, we started thinking that we needed more than tents for day-to-day, long-duration operations. This was not a WWII island-hopping campaign. In looking around, I found that the army had been pouring hundreds of conex boxes into the RVN via the piers of downtown Da Nang. A conex box is a structurally strong steel box about seven feet high, six feet wide, and five feet deep, with a strong steel security door on the front. The boxes are normally used for overseas shipments. The more I looked at these conex boxes, the more I knew that we had many uses for them. We could use them for aviation parts security, avionics equipment, weapons storage, supplies storage, food-service's nonrefrigerated storage, and so forth. Since they were not in our supply system, there was only one way to obtain them—take them, as was done in WWII scrounging activities.

So I talked to a Seabee unit that was located in the middle of Da Nang city. I asked them if, on occasion, I could use one of their forklifts and operators to load equipment from the Da Nang docks. They complied. So the next day I had my cooperative air force sergeant from our base, with his truck, drive me down to the piers, where stacks of conex boxes were unloaded from shipping. I had explained to this sergeant my need for conex boxes for our base, and he of course responded that he could use one or two for his radio equipment. I called the Seabee unit and asked them to have their forklift and operator meet me with the air force truck at the piers. As the air force sergeant drove up to the middle of the many piers, the Seabee forklift showed up magically. I told the forklift operator to load up three conex boxes, and we were all out of there in five minutes. After I had about twenty conex boxes well distributed throughout our base over a three-week period, the group commander asked me, "Where the hell are you getting these good conex boxes?"

"Colonel, you never ask a supply man the source of his hard-to-get items."

He never did ask again. But he did come up with suggestions as to where he could well use the boxes. By the end of a four-week period, the army got wise and put an armed guard on the pier.

One day we slowly drove by the pier looking over conex boxes as the Seabee forklift operator followed us. We went by the army guard and continued north, past the piers. At the end of the road we turned left and were thrilled to see about twenty conex boxes. So, without words exchanged, the air force sergeant backed up the truck. I opened the rear swing-door and the forklift operator moved rapidly in and loaded a conex box. As he lifted a second box, an old army master sergeant came running out from an old French building.

"Captain, what are you doing with my conex boxes?"

"Sarge, don't worry about them. The air force general at the Da Nang Airfield sent us down to pick up a few. You don't mind us taking a few for the general, do you?" I asked.

"No sir. As a matter of fact you can have half of them. I only need ten. But why I'm upset is that this conex box that the forklift operator has up in the air is my staff NCO club's month's supply of liquor."

"You're kidding," I laughed.

"No sir. Have him put it down and I'll show you."

After the forklift placed the conex box down on the ground, the sergeant got his keys out. It was only then that the rest of us noticed that there was a lock on the steel door. The sergeant opened the lock and door. We were astonished. There were thousands of dollars worth of cases of the world's finest liquors. The forklift operator had the forklift gently nudge the box back into its original position, after the army sergeant locked the door. The sergeant then said, "Thanks, Captain. I sure as hell would have been out a lot of the club's money if you had accidentally taken that liquor locker of mine. As you probably have guessed, these are not really my conex boxes. I simply took them off the piers down the street. But I do really need ten to operate this club, once I get it going here. So tell that air force general if he needs more than ten, I can get him some more, if you give me a week's notice."

My air force sergeant and I drove off, after the forklift loaded the truck, and we laughed all the way through Da Nang, as the forklift slowly followed us until midtown, where it disappeared into the Seabee compound. We figured that this joint air force, Marine Corps and navy Seabee operation was too much for the old army sergeant to figure out and challenge.

On the drive back through our Marble Mountain Airfield, we

dropped off two of the conex boxes. One box was set up to store laundry overnight for our new on-base Vietnamese-operated laundry firm. The second box was given to the MABS-16 military police unit to use to lock up a badass at night. Since they didn't have a brig but did have a problem marine on their hands, they couldn't keep him in this steel room during the day, because of the intense heat. During the day he could be seen walking around inside a concertina wire yard big enough for him to exercise in. He was soon evacuated back to Okinawa to stand trial for some serious violations of the Uniform Code of Military Justice.

Another day, another typical mission. I was scheduled to fly number-six plane, or tail-end-charlie, in a flight led by Don Lark. This flight of six UH-34s was scheduled for a routine ARVN resupply to move troops and ammo from Hoi An on the coast to An Hoa located west and in the base of the hills. We were the second flight of the day for our air group, so we would be called flight two, mission 968, and would be coded 1R9 for a transport mission. Therefore our lead plane, with Don Lark as the flight leader, was designated Two One. Two Two had a pilot by the name of Kirk in command, Two Three was commanded by Green, Spook piloted Two Four, and Bob Lock flew in command of Two Five. I flew with a pilot named Andrews in the last aircraft, called Two Six. Since we were flying supplies from one secure area to another secure area, we had no requirement for a Huey gunship escort. The load to move was about ten thousand pounds of supplies and fifty pax (passengers). Our assigned common squadron frequency on FM radios was 38.4 megahertz. At Hoi An, the LZ call sign was Alpha Bravo Truce on frequency 42.4 megahertz and at An Hoa the LZ called Joie on frequency 38.8 megahertz. Our bingo fuel was three hundred pounds. After unloading all ARVN troops, we would then bring our ground loadmaster back from An Hoa. The mission was humdrum routine until the end of the second sortie, or trip, going into An Hoa. We received fire from all quadrants going in and coming out. Two Two, with Kirk in command, got hit, and so did Bob Lock's Two Five. No serious damage was sustained by any aircraft, and no personnel were injured. It was a fast three hours and fifteen minutes of flight time of two sorties for each aircraft and return to base.

I debriefed and walked across the runway to my office tent where I ran my supply system. As I entered the dusty, hot tent, Gunnery Sergeant Frey said, "Sir, believe it or not, our long-awaited four M-60 machine guns arrived. Lieutenant Grinder will be thrilled to hear this."

"I'm sure glad to see those M-60 machine guns," I happily said.

"Captain, the shower unit arrived also, but it can't be used."

"Can't be used. Why not?"

Gunny Frey took me to the backside of the tent and pointed through the open tent flap to a very damaged shower unit.

"An ARVN truck hit the shower unit while it was being towed across the Da Nang bridge."

I said, "Gunny, do you realize how long it will take to get another shower unit from the wing in Japan?"

Lieutenant Grinder was in our supply tent in minutes to pick up his new M-60s and was off to build four new sandbagged gun emplacements. He installed two on the beach and two on the western perimeter; one just across from a village called dog patch by the marines and one across from the notorious Buddhist temple from which we received fire nightly.

That evening at about 2000, I was seated at our table with the glaring single light bulb hanging above. I had totally dismantled my machine gun and had parts lying out on the table. I also had taken six of my .45-caliber bullet clips apart. Each clip holds twenty .45 slugs. The clips frequently got full of sand here and needed cleaning to ensure that they would feed into the chamber. Jack Bates was sitting there smoking his usual cigar, and I was trying to bum a cigar from him. George Gross from the next tent dropped in with a bottle of rum. I had several canned Cokes that a friend of mine had flown in from the Philippines. So we proceeded to drink rum and Coke. Then Smokey Cassen drifted in and joined us. Finally, Chaplain Roland sat down. Everybody was involved in normal evening chatter as I continued to clean my trusty grease gun. Smokey said to me, "Why the hell are you tearing down your gun now? It's already dark out there. Why didn't you clean it at high noon?"

"Hell, it's only 2200. We've never been attacked before midnight. I have plenty of time to clean it up and put it back together."

My trusty M3A1 submachine gun was called a grease gun because of its resemblance to a hand-held grease gun used for lubricating automobiles. The M3A1 was built by a division of General Motors for the production of cheap submachine guns during WWII. Only 700,000 were manufactured, and they were used during WWII, during the Korean "police action," and by marine Corps tank crews and marine air base squadrons for aviation units to defend themselves on the base.

Jack Bates broke down and gave me a nice big cigar. I had several neat lines of .45-caliber slugs in rows of twenty standing in the center of the table, as I continued cleaning the metal loading clips.

Chaplain Roland made a statement, "If I get out of this place alive next year, I'm going to buy myself a brand new 1966 Plymouth convertible. It'll be painted black on the outside and the inside will be pure white for purity."

We all chuckled at the purity line. At that moment, automatic-weapons fire started sounding off loudly just outside our tent area. It was coming from outside our northeast defense perimeter. Then our M-60 gunner, located about thirty yards from our tent, began returning fire, as more bursts of automatic-weapons fire were incoming. Then several rounds ripped through our tent and our light bulb above us smashed into pieces. We all hit the wooden deck and began crawling toward the tent exit, then down the three wooden steps to the sand outside. As we all wildly crawled, more incoming began splintering our plyboard floor. As we struggled single file into our deep trench, a hole behind sandbags, Smokey said, "Goddamn it. The gooners are early tonight."

"Do not take the name of the Lord in vain," smilingly responded the chaplain.

"Chaplain, maybe you better say a fast prayer for us right now," said a chuckling Jack Bates.

George Gross turned to me in the crowded foxhole, as the firefight on the defense wire continued blazing away. He said, "Bob, do you have your grease gun?"

Despite all the flares and tracers lighting up the area about thirty yards in front of us, it was dark in our hole behind the sandbags. So I raised the grease gun and said, "Yep, George. I have the gun. But the clips and ammo are up above us on the table."

"Oh shit. We may need that gun tonight. We don't know how many gooners are trying to break through out there," said George.

I said, "George, did you bring your rum bottle?"

"No. It's also still up on the table."

"George, you owe me rum from when you crashed the OE aircraft into the Atlantic from off of the USS *Boxer* in 1959, with two cases of my St. Croix rum aboard. So how about you going back up for that rum bottle of yours?"

"Bob, I'll make a deal with you. You crawl back up into the tent and get the bullets and clips. I'll crawl up behind you to get the rum bottle."

As VC bullets flew overhead, ripping into our tent, George snaked up behind me as we crawled up the steps to the plyboard floor and toward the table. While lying down next to the table, I reached up and grabbed a handful of clips. But the bullets were lying all over the floor and table. By the time I grabbed enough bullets to stuff my numerous zippered pockets of my flight suit, George was gone and back in our foxhole with the rum. Under the night flares, I crawled back down into the hole and began putting slugs into the clips.

As I loaded the first clip, the others in the foxhole were filling up the additional clips. George then said, "I have the rum and a glass to pass around, but no canned Coke."

"No sweat," I said. "You don't think that I quit digging when finished with this foxhole. Feel way back under the flooring of the tent and reach over the sandbags. See? I have another hole. It's what I call my cowering hole. What if a hundred thousand Chinese poured down here like they crossed the Yalu River during the Korean War? I figured that I better have a hiding hole behind our fighting hole, just in case the numbers get out of hand."

"So what does that have to do with canned Coke?" asked Bates.

"Well, Jack, crawl back there and bring out a six-pack of Coke. I have a month's rations of Coke hidden under the decking."

Jack got us a six-pack and George poured the rum. I watched the fence-line action closely with my trusty machine gun loaded. With an increase of our night flares, the whole area beyond us was now like day, and the VC withdrew, firing as they fled. I didn't get my drink until the last firing ended from our gun emplacement on the perimeter. Chaplain Roland spoke up, "This rum and Coke isn't as good as church wine, but it does the job on a noisy night."

As we dusted the sand from our sweated bodies and reentered our tent, Bates said, "Don't put your finger in that light socket. The tents are all hot-wired to the light bulbs because Bob hasn't gotten me those damn light switches I need."

I said, "Jack, there's been a delay, but I'm going down to get them tomorrow from Lily Ann in Da Nang."

The next morning I drove to Da Nang city, with the chaplain coming along to do some searching for someone to make him a crucifix. I dropped the chaplain at a men's old-age home on the northern end of the city. The French priest had told Father Roland that there was a well-known wood-carver living there. I proceeded downtown to Lily Ann's warehouse.

Again, it was upstairs, tea provided by a lovely Vietnamese girl, and Lily Ann all businesslike.

"Well Lily Ann, did you get me my seven hundred light switches?"

"Ah. Yes, I did. It was not an easy task. But, as always, I get what you need."

She clapped her hands and her store manager arrived from downstairs. A few directions by her and he was back downstairs getting some samples of light switches for me to look at.

"So how much are the light switches going to cost me, Lily Ann?"

"Very reasonable cost, Captain. Only four American dollars per switch."

I jumped from the floor shouting, "Four dollars! That's twenty-eight hundred dollars just for the light switches. Where did you get these switches? From Europe somewhere? I'll give you only two dollars per switch and that's it."

"Captain, I can sell these light switches for four dollars each to the air force and you know that."

"I don't think the air force needs any light switches. I'm leaving. If you can't sell them, call me with a two-dollar price."

"Captain, I have so many customers, but I will give you all seven hundred switches if you pay me three dollars each."

I sat down and sipped a little hot tea. "Lily Ann, I'll give you two dollars and that's all I can afford. Take it, or I leave."

"Bay io day?"—Right now?—she asked.

"No. Tomorrow. I'll come down with a pickup truck. I can't fit them all into my jeep. I'll pay you then."

"Duoc roi"—Agreed—she reluctantly grumbled.

Then the store manager came upstairs with a brown box and handed it to me. I couldn't believe my eyes. On the brown box was a label in the shape of a shield, colored red, white, and blue, like an American flag. Across the shield decal were two hands shaking depicting friendship.

"Lily Ann, this is a Handclasp, a friends-across-the-sea box. This is a U.S.-government giveaway gift to your government. You want me to pay for something that my government gave your government free?"

"Captain, I am not the Vietnamese government. I paid for these switches."

"But since your government got them free from the Americans, why are you charging me so much?"

"Captain, I had to pay politician in Saigon. Had to pay warehouse manager to tell guard to look other way. Does Vietnamese government control Highway 1? Do American troops control Highway 1 all the way from Saigon to Da Nang? No. VC control Highway 1 at three areas. Therefore, I must pay VC road taxes to have driver drive from Saigon to Da Nang with the switches. You understand. And then Lily Ann must make a little profit, no?"

"Okay. Okay. Lily Ann, I'm paying all the bad guys in the country, but it's cheaper for me than having to fly to Taiwan for the switches."

I walked out of her store very angry. I needed those switches.

I jumped into the jeep and shouted to her, *"Ngay mai"*—Tomorrow. I drove back down the crowded Da Nang streets with their fish and vegetable smells until I came to the old-age home where I had dropped off the chaplain. Chaplain Roland was inside waiting for me. "Bob, I found me a true artist. This old Vietnamese here spent a lifetime carving figurines. He used to own a shop downtown, until he and his wife got too old to take care of themselves. His wife is in a women's old-age home on the north side of town. I gave the old man an order to carve me a large crucifix."

"Chaplain, has he made any crucifixes before?"

"No. As a matter of fact, according to the building manager, he is Buddhist and has never even seen a figure of Christ on a crucifix."

"Well, then, how do you expect him to carve you one that meets your standards?"

"I gave him a holy picture from my prayer book. It's a very detailed picture. We'll just have to wait and see how he does. He'll have it ready in one week."

On the way back to our base, I kidded the chaplain that he'd have his first crucifix that reflects Christ as an Oriental instead of a Jew.

The next afternoon, I returned from Da Nang with an air force truck full of electrical light switches. We had a twenty-man U.S. Air Force communications group located on our base. We were a clear shot from our beach location to Clark Air Force Base in the Philippines. So the air force wanted their radio transmission and receiver antenna located right here on the South China Sea. Since this small air force group was eight miles from their supply source, they needed day-to-day support from my supply office. As part of my setting them up in tents and providing other goodies, the air force master sergeant in charge would drive me around Da Nang when I did some out-of-the-supply-system scrounging. This way the marines couldn't be blamed for something missing downtown. So, loaded with the switches, we parked the truck at Major Bates's office tent and delivered the switches to him. He immediately grumbled about how long it took. Then he said, "Where did you steal these?"

"Major, there was so much stealing involved in this that you wouldn't believe it. But believe me, I paid for these switches."

Just then a loud muffled explosion took place up the street near the officers' living-area tents. It didn't sound like incoming mortars. I had the air force truck run Major Bates and me up there to see what it was. A crowd had gathered around what had been the four-holer.

"What the hell happened?" I asked.

Someone answered, "It looks like a grenade blew up the shitter."

I quickly asked, "Was there anyone in it?"

"No. But sure could have been."

Lieutenant Grinder arrived. "Hmm, looks like the old trick used up at Phu Bai. Looks like one of our washy women who works for the VC probably pulled the pin of a grenade and then placed a rubber band around the handle to prevent it from goin' off. Then she placed it onto the crap can below the four-holer. The rubber band doesn't take too long to rot through and then breaks, allowing the handle to release open—and *boom*—there goes the latrine and anyone unfortunate to be sitting on it."

"We'll obviously have to watch the help here on the base more closely, particularly whoever goes near the latrines," I remarked.

"It could have been the garbage-pickup detail. They actually unload the cans daily," said Major Bates.

"I'll get talking it over with our interpreter and the people in downtown Da Nang. We have to find out who is working here that is sympathetic to the VC," said Lieutenant Grinder.

For the next few days, everybody was apprehensive about sitting and shitting in the latrines, day or night.

A few days later, the chaplain scrounged two trucks from motor transport to get his kneelers. They were beautiful kneelers and really dressed up the chapel tent.

It was mid-October and the heat was still there. The monsoons began in Southeast Asia. Several typhoons had swept up toward Hong Kong, but none had struck our area yet. However, small amounts of rain began and the sand now stuck to our flight boots on the coastal areas, and it was very muddy inland at most of our LZs. The rain did nothing to cool it off—in fact, the air seemed even more muggy.

I continued to fly every chance that I could. I took off one midmorning on a resupply mission to the U.S. Marines conducting an operation called Red Snapper. It was a joint USMC and ARVN search-and-clear operation on the Phu Gia Peninsula. It was a well-planned beach assault, coordinated with a motorized column from Da Nang, followed by a ground attack. However, the VC were gone, leaving a handful of weapons. My several sorties up there were routine, without any enemy action. My resupply flights up to the top of the Hai Van Pass just north of Da Nang Harbor were similar: no enemy resistance. It was an unusually quiet period and we began wondering where Charlie went.

One evening, while we were gathered as usual in our living tent shooting the breeze, Lt. Col. Tom Vaile came by to introduce his brother to us. His brother was a civilian who just happened to be the Esso oil company storage-facilities manager near Da Nang. The facility, with large fuel tanks, was located just north of the Da Nang Bay at the base of the Hai Van Pass; not far from the strategic Nam O Bridge. We all chattered about the VC and their activities, and drank. We were saying how lucky it was that the fuel-storage area had not been bothered by the VC. Two nights later it was attacked by the VC and badly damaged. We all kidded Tom Vaile that his brother apparently had not paid taxes to the VC and they had therefore struck his facility.

I flew various types of missions, mostly toward the southern areas from Da Nang. We also made extractions of marine reconnaissance units from the Happy Valley area, located southwest of Da Nang. Sometimes there were intense firefights and we would receive many hits. Sometimes it was just a quiet helicopter transport mission.

Marine Aircraft Group 36 was now well established down at Chu Lai, so we at MAG-16 now rarely flew support missions down that way from our Marble Mountain Airfield.

One gloomy, overcast day I flew in a two-plane resupply mission carrying rations and water to a marine supply company out in the flatlands near Bao An Tay, south of Highway 14. We were cleared into an LZ behind the grunts. It was a clear zone, with the grunts reporting no enemy. I asked for a green smoke grenade to be thrown to where they wanted me to land. I saw one, then two, and finally three green smoke grenades out in the tall elephant grass. All smoke grenades were quite a distance from each other. It was obvious that Charlie was up listening on our FM frequency and had thrown two additional green grenades out there along with our ground unit's grenade. It did confuse me, since it was the first time that I was exposed to the gooners throwing smoke to fake us out. After that incident, when the VC threw smoke out in various areas causing us to see several distant LZs, naturally we discussed the exact location of the LZ with the grunts a little more to make sure that we didn't land in a VC trap.

However, mistakes are made in any walk of life. An example of smoke being thrown into the wrong location by accident was as follows. I was leading a two-plane section of UH-34 helos on an ammunition resupply mission to one of our units that was in heavy contact with the enemy. This unit was sweeping westward up a valley that started just to the west of Dai Loc along the Song Vu Gia River and along the western extremities of Highway 14. As my wingman and I came over the village of Havi, I called the grunts below. "Zebra, this is Swift Four. I'm inbound to your LZ, passing over Dai Loc shortly. Over."

"Swift Four, this is Zebra. We see you. Continue inbound. We're throwing green smoke now. Be aware that our company is leaping off right now. So be careful. Over."

"Roger, Zebra. I'm just about over where I think you should be. I don't see any smoke."

"Swift, we have heavy contact and some problems here. But smoke is being thrown now."

"Zebra, I see smoke just to the east of that pagoda. Am I cleared to land?"

"Swift, I know they threw the smoke, but I can't see it from behind this hedgerow that I'm in back of. Also, I don't see a pagoda, or any other building."

"Zebra, am I cleared to land near the green smoke?"

"Affirmative, Swift. Cleared to land. But watch for moving troops."

"Roger, Zebra. Swift is cleared to land and is descending now."

I commenced the usual spiral, rapid descent to the smoke area, observing the smoke drifting from west to east. As I closed on the

LZ at a rapid rate while kicking my rudders around to ensure an approach into the west wind, I lined up with the Buddhist pagoda. The smoke was just this side of it and to my left. On final approach, I crossed a tall treeline and looking down saw numerous marines lined up along the treeline firing towards the area of the LZ, where the smoke had been thrown.

"Swift, this is Zebra. You're landing to our front. You just crossed me. I'm to your rear, behind a treeline."

"Zebra. It's too late. I'm on the deck with your ammo. I landed beside the smoke, where it was thrown. Send your troops out to get the ammo and water."

"Swift, stay put. You're just out in front of our assault platoon. We're attacking that village in front of you. Don't move or lift up now, or you'll get hits from front and rear."

At that moment, I looked in my rearview mirror and saw our grunts charging from my rear and shooting like hell. I glanced forward. The pagoda was straight in front of me, about twenty yards. The brush and smaller treeline along both sides of the pagoda that were in front of a small village came alive with sparkling flashes of return fire at the assaulting marines.

"Captain, we've landed right in front of an attack," shouted my crew chief over the intercom, as I saw my two belly gunners instinctively swing their M-60s forward, shooting into their left and right fronts at the treeline, respectively. Muzzle flashes now began going off in the two large open windows adjacent to the main entrance door of the pagoda, just in front of me. Since I was well elevated—about eight feet high in the seat of my UH-34D helicopter—I was looking straight eyeball-to-eyeball level with the VC gunners. There was no way that they could miss me, as they fired in my direction. However, they were concentrating on the marines attacking them and continued to ignore my gigantic obstruction in front of them. I wondered just how long both of them would continue to ignore my obtrusive presence. My copilot and I instinctively shrunk into our seats, trying to make ourselves small and hide behind the instrument panel. I thought, just one slight shift of either of those gunners out in front of me and I'm dead. All of a sudden an explosion took place in the middle of the pagoda and flames began shooting upward through the thatched roof. Apparently, our mortar men got a direct hit on the pagoda. Bullets were still flying in both directions. I still couldn't believe that neither I nor my chopper had been hit yet. Then the marines were on both sides of me and also along my wingman's aircraft. At my elevated eye level, I could see the pagoda's main temple door spring open and a Viet Cong come running out toward me on the elevated pagoda front porch. He was shirtless and his black pajamas were burning. His eyes were round with terror, as he kept coming and firing his AK-47. Then his knees crumbled as M-60 slugs tore into his chest. He toppled forward despite the impacts of the steel-jacketed slugs, and he fell right out in front of my helicopter. The grunts were now on the porch of the pagoda, throwing grenades inside. The flashes from the thick hedgerow on both sides of the pagoda ceased. The VC apparently were withdrawing as the marines charged the hedgerow. There now were only a few pops of gunfire here and there above the noises of my engine and turning rotor blades. The VC in front of me on the ground moved. To my amazement, he was still alive. He was too weak to reach his AK-47, which was lying next to him.

"Crew chief, go get that VC and weapon. We'll take him back to the ARVN POW camp, if our grunts don't want him for intelligence now. Make sure that his pants aren't still burning," I directed.

"Aye, aye, sir," responded the crew chief, as he unhooked his radio cord from his helmet and ran along the right of our chopper with his .45 pistol pointed at the severely wounded VC. The crew chief picked up the bloody VC, whose silk black pajamas had burned his legs charcoal black. He then grabbed the AK-47 and ran along the right nose of my aircraft to the large compartment-bay doorway. At that moment, I heard a thump and felt an actual impact upon my helicopter. I thought, *Hell, after all of that shooting right here in front of me and no hits, now I take an RPG round.* "RPG" stands for "rocket-propelled grenade."

"Crew chief, what was that? Did we get hit broadside?" I shouted over the intercom. There was no response. I stretched out and looked back to my right to see what was going on. The VC was lying on the ground and the crew chief was picking him up. I did not see any damage to that side of the aircraft. Then I heard the electrical noise in my earphones indicating that the crew chief was only now hooking his helmet back up to the intercom system.

"Captain, I never realized that these gooners were so damn light. When I threw this guy into the doorway, he flew so high that he missed the doorway and bounced off the upper part of the fuselage. I got him in on the deck now. We're ready to unload supplies."

"Shit, Sarge. I thought we got hit by a big round into the side of the aircraft, when you bounced him off the side of the chopper. It scared the hell out of me."

"No sir. It was only incoming VC," chuckled the crew chief.

The rear unit of the company of marines was now at the sides of both our helicopters and our gunners and crew chiefs were passing them the ammunition and water cans.

"Sir, I told the grunts down here that we'll take the VC back to the POW camp, if they don't need him. They said good. They can't handle any POWs at this moment," said the crew chief.

Soon we had unloaded our supplies and had lifted up, turning downwind, when airspeed allowed, to head east and away from the contested village below.

As we headed northwest toward Hill 55 at four thousand feet, the crew chief came up on the intercom. "Captain, the gooner just died down here."

"Are you sure that he's dead?" I asked.

"Yes sir. He's deader 'n a rock."

Later, I often imagined the sheer terror this Viet Cong lived through his last few minutes of life: he caught on fire inside the mortar-exploded pagoda; he ran out on the porch firing his AK-47, as he confronted hoards of attacking marines; he got shot badly; he was bounced off the side of a helicopter and then went for his first and last helicopter ride—all this to support Ho Chi Minh's dream of a unified Democratic Republic of Vietnam. I wondered, Will it be worth the efforts and the sacrifice? If they are successful, will the people here have it better? Or will they live like the Cubans, the Chinese, and the North Koreans in a free-domless and disastrous economy? Will there be an exodus of humanity from here like from Hungary and Cuba?

That night Chaplain Roland caught me and said, "Bob, the

crucifix is finished downtown. Let's go down to Da Nang tomorrow and pick it up."

So the next morning we rode down in my jeep and pulled up to the old-men's home. When we entered and saw the old man with the crucifix, we couldn't believe our eyes. It was a real work of art. It was three feet tall and carved so perfectly it was a masterpiece. The crown of thorns was realistic; blood vessels on the arms of the Christ figure stood out. There were wrinkles in the fingers as in an actual hand. The blood droplets from the wound in the side of the body appeared real in the wood.. The chest and rib cage was lifelike. We both were astounded with the craftmanship. Then to top off our amazement, the home supervisor conveyed to us that this old man had carved this body of Christ and crucifix by using a hammer and chisel; no knife or sandpaper. Chaplain Roland asked the supervisor how much would be appropriate to pay this talented wood-carver. The supervisor said to the old man, *"Baon hieu tien?"*

The old man answered in the monetary term of *"dong."*

The supervisor said to the chaplain, "Only one thousand piaster."

The chaplain said to me, "That's only about fourteen dollars. Not bad for all that detailed work."

The chaplain gave the old wood-carver that amount in Vietnamese piaster and the old man's eyes lit up with excitement and gratitude. I was so impressed with this art work that I wanted a crucifix also. So I ordered one and paid the old man in advance. I got the understanding that he could have one made for me within three days. This old man hadn't seen so much money come his way so fast and he expressed ambition immediately. I planned on returning at the end of the week to test his production capabilities.

Back at base, the word was out that due to the chaplain's intelligence information about an impending attack upon our airfield during the forthcoming moonless period, the group commander had requested from the III MAF commander a grunt company to beef up our defensive posture. Our defense consisted of our mechanics who worked all day on aircraft and then took turns manning the sixteen M-60s along the wire perimeter. Word was soon out that General Walt had reluctantly turned down our group commander's request for the grunt company because he felt that he was already too extended with his assets. So, naturally, the group commander was very concerned. He ordered all hands to dig slit trenches and fighting holes next to their tents, if they had not yet done so. Since we lived in the end tent near the extreme end of the base close to the defense wire, our fighting hole was not only finished weeks ago, but had of necessity been used on many occasions.

One evening at dusk, I had landed from a routine mission, after coming down through some patchy, low, thin clouds that were along the coast. It was a very thin layer at about 1,200 feet and it ran from the beach to about three miles inland. I debriefed with intelligence and walked back to my living-area tent. George Gross was sitting out in front of the tent on a lawn chair drinking a beer. So I got out my simulated lawn chair, which was made by a Vietnamese in Da Nang. It looked just like an American lawn chair of aluminum and webbing material, but the frame was heavy metal painted to look like aluminum. Lifting it was like picking up a refrigerator. In any case, we both relaxed and drank warm beer when directly overhead two marine F-4B Phantom jets punched out of the low, thin layer of clouds. It was now dark and the jets had their running lights on as they came out of the scud above at about 1,200 feet or so and leveled at about 1,000 feet for a downwind leg, heading north for an approach turn to Da Nang's runway 18.

"Bob, those guys are really wide on the downwind leg," said George.

"Yep, they'll probably turn left prior to the one-eighty turn in. They better," I answered.

"I don't think they can see Monkey Mountain straight ahead. The MACS radar site up there with its bright lights on top of Monkey Mountain can't be seen by these pilots below the low clouds. Holy shit, Bob, I don't think they're going to turn inbound. They're too wide," claimed George.

"By god, you're right, George. They don't see Monkey Mountain."

George got up from his chair and said, "I think they're going to fly straight into the mountain."

I got up and said, "They sure as hell are going to hit it."

They didn't turn. In seconds the first F-4B crashed and a split second later, his wingman impacted. The black mountain lit up; the overcast turned bright yellow and gray as the two aircraft burned brightly and ammunition began popping and exploding, streaking streams of red and yellow against the mountain background.

George and I stood in horror, shocked by what we saw. Within two to three minutes an air force SAR helicopter was en route from Da Nang to the crash site. In about five minutes one of our VMO-2 Huey choppers was climbing out from our airstrip, presumably dispatched by our tower. I imagine that the personnel in the radar dome control of the MACS (marine air control squadron) site up above the overcast not only heard the loud explosions, but felt the impact below them and wondered what was happening down there on the mountainside.

George and I sat down and discussed the tragedy. We asked each other if we could have had the time to take the few steps to our tent phone, call the control tower to broadcast on the guard (emergency) channel to the pilots downwind at Da Nang that they were too wide and that they were heading directly for Monkey Mountain? We both assumed that the pilots knew that they were wide, and also assumed that the pilots were more than aware of Monkey Mountain on the southern tip of Da Nang Harbor. We sat down feeling helpless as we watched four brave marine flyers unluckily perish before our eyes. We'll probably always vividly remember that accident. It occurred early in the evening on October 26, 1965.

The next morning, word got around that the possible reason that they were so wide on the downwind leg was that one of the F-4Bs had engine trouble and therefore they were probably extra cautious on their approach, causing them to concentrate on the airfield below, forgetting the exact location and nearness of Monkey Mountain. To add to my feelings over having watched it happen, I heard that an old friend, Maj. Bill Miller, was one of the pilots. Bill had been with me at MAG-16 in Oppama, Japan, in 1958 as a helicopter pilot.

The next morning I drove to Da Nang to pick up the crucifix that I had ordered from the old man. It was as beautiful as Chaplain Roland's. That evening some of the pilots from neighboring tents drifted by and saw the magnificent artwork of the crucifix. They each immediately wanted to buy one to send home. Chaplain Roland took their orders and their money. The next morning he gave the orders to the little old wood-carver in Da Nang.

As Chaplain Roland was down at DaNang ordering crucifixes, I was flying in a two-plane supply mission to an ARVN outpost on the top of a 660-foot sharp mountain peak. The area was called the Coal Mines. At the base of the mountain was an anthracite (hard coal) underground mine, similar to the mines in my hometown of Coaldale, Pennsylvania. The outpost and coal mine sat astride a snaking river, the Song Thi Bon. We approached from the east and could not land fully on the inclined mountain peak outside of the fortress. All we could do was place the main landing gear down on the edge of the triangularly shaped fortress outskirts. It was a real comedy as the ARVN troops tried to grab the loose geese, ducks and chickens that we had picked up at Hoi An city for them. The livestock ran around wildly in the belly compartment below me as the gunners and crew chief tried to grab them to hand out to the hungry ARVN troops. With the high power we had to maintain—since we were really more or less in a hover—the rotor blades really kicked up a dust storm. The ARVNs struggling to grab the livestock lost a few birds as the noise and rotor wind had the fowl flying around wildly. They caught most of them, and as my wingman and I climbed westward, I looked back and there still were some ARVNs chasing their meal around the outside of the old French fortress. Climbing northwest and then turning east, we began getting heavy fire. It appeared to be .50-caliber machine-gun fire. It was large and coming from directly west of the fortress, down in the jungle below. Our gunners returned fire, as we climbed out of the gunfire range. One of the big rounds tore through the left gunner's side of the fuselage, ripping through the gunner's left little finger. The gunner didn't know he had actually lost a finger until he ripped off his flight glove to try to stop the bleeding. I flew a short three miles to the airstrip at An Hoa. A marine jeep was dispatched with my wounded gunner to a nearby West German hospital. Two hours later we flew home with a gunner who had lost a finger for today's "day at the office."

That evening, the chaplain was telling us how excited the little old Vietnamese man was to get all those orders for crucifixes. He had several weeks of work now scheduled for making crucifixes.

Later, while sleeping soundly, I heard a loud explosion. Several of us ran out of the tent, and looking east, we saw a burning truck on the road between our western perimeter wire and the village just north of the Seabee camp. I knew immediately that it was our MABS two-thousand-gallon water truck, which had been hauling water day and night. It was now making a night run to Monkey Mountain for mountain water and returning to supplement our water supply, a trip made necessary by some well-water-pump problems. The VC, obviously, had laid a mine on the road and it blew up the truck. The VC probably had stolen the mine from outside of our perimeter fence, where we had mines buried in front of our defense wire. I stood there hoping that both MABS personnel in the water truck survived the mine explosion. Just then, we heard a bugle blow from the southwest area. We didn't have bugles, so it must have been a VC bugle. At that moment, all hell broke loose. I glanced at my watch. It was two minutes to midnight. A tremendous quantity of incoming mortar fire impacts began pounding the area up near our flight line. The sickening *woop, woop, woop* of mortar hits sounded like they were coming from across the street to the east near the Seabee camp. Then another heavy barrage sounded closer to the flight line. I ran to my tent. I jumped into my pants and tied up my flight boots. I grabbed my grease gun and threw two bands of .45 ammo clips over my shoulder. I had to get down to the command post in the center of the camp fast. I was the assigned officer in charge of the MABS mobile alert platoon. As I was driving my jeep south, past the SNCO living-area tents, I could see the explosions and fire behind and to the west of the flight line. Then I heard and saw our western-perimeter M-60 machine guns opening fire to the west. As I turned into the small open area in front of the group command bunker my thirty-man mobile alert team was just about all there and assembled. As I quickly quizzed them to make sure that they all had loaded weapons and spare ammo, the group operations officer came running out of the underground bunker to tell me that they got a phone call from across the runway and that VC had penetrated the wire: the VC were attacking through the ready tents en route to the parked aircraft on the parking apron. We then heard several loud explosions coming from the flight line. I had my troops spread out considerably so we could cover all the aircraft parking areas as we counterattacked. As we charged across the open runway, numerous helicopters were exploding and burning, particularly along the VMO-2 flight line. We now closed with the Viet Cong. The numerous burning choppers made daylight rapidly and we could see the VC running up and down the lines of parked aircraft. I knew that as we got closer and began firing, we could hit our own ready pilots and crews, which had been sleeping in the west-side ready tents, near the aircraft. But I didn't know if they were shooting at the VC in our direction, or if they were down in their bunkers due to the mortar incoming; or if they were dead and wounded. So I simply screamed, "Fire at will!"

As we closed with the VC, between the aircraft, some of the VC continued to try to drop satchel charges into the remaining VMO-2 UH-1E gunships and also down the exhaust stacks of the UH-34Ds and larger HR-2Ss. We now were all between the lines of parked aircraft, feeling the immense heat of the fires.

A lot of shouting and rifle fire was going on among the crackling flames of the damaged helicopters. Now the VC started firing back to stay alive and they stopped attempting to blow up any more helicopters. We were now shooting at them from very close range. As I ran along the taxiway that separated the VMO-2 Hueys from the UH-34Ds, two VC came directly in front of me from between two UH-34Ds. They were clad only in black shorts or swimsuits and were barefooted. Each had satchel charges, grenades and an AK-47 automatic assault rifle. They both raised their AK-47s while pushing their shoulder-hung satchel charges aside. Only one was fast enough to crank off some rounds in my direction. I gave them both a steady burst of grease gun and they both buckled to the steel matting. I felt a searing pain in my inside right wrist. The one bastard had hit me. I looked at my wrist and the flaming helicopter near me gave me ample light to show me that I was bleeding a fair amount, but the wound was simply a big scratch below the inside of my palm on the wrist.

Several more VC were now running back east through the tent area from where some of them had initially attacked. They were firing as they retreated. We charged up to the west wire and we spread out on both sides of the M-60 bunker position there. Out in front of that machine-gun bunker lay four dead VC. Apparently they were gunned down by the mechanic assigned there that night in that bunker gun position. He obviously killed them when they first came over the wire from the hospital construction site to the west. As the VC retreated across the street, the Seabees began firing at them, so they swung southwest, running through the burning construction site where the Seabees had been building a navy hospital.

As fast as it began, it was over. I turned to witness a ravished, burning flight line. The red crash truck was busy scurrying from burning helicopter to burning helicopter, showering the damaged aircraft with firefighting foam. We gathered our wounded and sent them to sickbay. The enemy hit us fast and hard and had probably inflicted more damage upon us than they had planned. One of my reaction force personnel told me that our machine-gun bunker just to the north of the VMO-2 flight line had killed nine VC when the VC first breached the wire. It was a new gun emplacement located up on a fairly high sand dune. Lieutenant Grinder had just had the emplacement built when he got his last four M-60s from me a few days before. It was apparent, with nine dead VC lying out in front of it, that the plan of attack did not include knowledge of that new gun emplacement. The gunner there told us that the VC had run straight at the sand mound and he simply shot them.

I walked over to where I had shot two VC, between the VMO-2 and UH-34D flight line. Both were dead. The one was almost cut in half from my burst of .45-caliber slugs. I grabbed them by their swimsuits and dragged them to the command bunker. At the command post we gathered to discuss the situation. My reaction team checked its amount of ammo. Some were sent to get more. In the center of the CP area we lined up seventeen dead Viet Cong, of the approximately one hundred enemy that attacked. Beside them we had four captured VC. Some were wounded. Lieutenant Grinder had placed concertina wire around the four prisoners. Our Vietnamese interpreter shouted to our group commander, "This one is a North Vietnamese. Look see. He have NVA belt buckle. Also look at hands: no have callus like local VC farmer hands with thick skin. Him city man from North Vietnam."

We all looked, and sure enough the so-called VC had smooth palms and he was wearing a black belt on his black bathing suit. The belt had a silver buckle with a communist star on it. He probably was an NVA officer. "Colonel, VC say five hundred more attack at 0500 hours," said our Vietnamese interpreter. I quickly went over to my troops and told them the news, hoping that the VC lied. I told them to make sure that they have plenty of ammo, drink a lot of water, and meet me here in ten minutes.

"We're going back over to the west wire and wait for them this time." I quickly ran to my tent, picked up several more loaded clips of ammo and returned. We then went through the rubble and smoldering aircraft. Cleanup crews were already established by the squadrons. I then heard that Chief Bob Hill, our chief navy corpsman, had been killed during the attack. He had been sleeping in a medical litter inside a VMO-2 Huey medevac chopper. He, as usual, had volunteered for the night ready medevac missions. Apparently, when the mortars began impacting, he had decided to stay in the chopper, probably thinking that the ready crew would be out rapidly to crank up the helo and to take wounded to Charlie Med. Instead of a flight crew, he was greeted by an attacking VC with a satchel charge of explosives that got him and destroyed the Huey.

Once we were along the west wire, I laid there in the sand only half-expecting more VC. Hell, they had accomplished their mission. VMO-2 was practically wiped out, and our transport helicopters were destroyed or damaged. In the darkness, with the cleanup crews noisily active to our rear, 0500 hours came and went and we waited. No VC came. Then slowly dawn peeked over the South China Sea, with the sun rising from over toward the Philippines. The acrid smoke blew toward us on the wire area, as the gentle morning breezes began to come in from our beach to our rear.

As I made my way back through the rubble and charred helicopters, I walked past the ready alert telephone located on the flight line in front of VMO-2. It had the wire cut. It was a neat shear job; not a cut from shrapnel of explosions or gunfire of the attack. I looked at it closely. It indicated to me that one of the VC attackers knew exactly where the phone was located on the flight line and took the time to snap it out of commission, while he was attacking at night. For the VC to know where that alert phone was located meant to me that a Vietnamese construction worker working for the American construction firm RMK must have been a VC or a spy for the VC. He must have given the VC planners of the attack more details of the inside of the aircraft parking area for their planning. That phone line was a direct line to our command bunker at group headquarters across the runway. I don't think my mobile alert company and myself could have gotten across the field any sooner even if someone had called the CP bunker on that phone because the VC were already inside the wire and on the parking apron in minutes. This cut phone line gave us some indication as to how well the VC had known our layout and how well they had rehearsed their plan of attack.

As I stood by the now worthless phone, Capt. Alan Pot came to me. Pot had been an OE-1 and HOK-1 helicopter pilot with me in VMO-1 in New River, North Carolina, back in 1960 to 1962. I had not seen him since 1962. I asked him when he had joined one of these squadrons here, since I had not seen him around the base. He replied that he was working over at wing headquarters at Da Nang and that he had come over here at dawn to get some flight time. As we stood there talking about how hard we'd been hit by the VC and North Vietnamese, someone yelled, "Hit the deck!" I thought, Damn it, here come some more incoming mortars. Lying on the deck, we both looked over to our immediate north. What had happened was that the crash truck that was parked in front of VMO-2 flight line had just had someone open its back doors. When the doors were swung open, a grenade had fallen out and it rolled about the steel parking apron. It laid there for a few minutes . . . we all watched and waited . . . it didn't go off. It must have been a dud. Obviously, last night during the attack, a VC had opened the back of the then-parked crash truck, pulled the pin from the grenade, tossed the grenade in the truck, and ran. Later, when it didn't explode, someone closed the door and drove the truck around for hours putting out fires, not realizing that the grenade with the pin pulled was in the back of his truck. Lieutenant Grinder disposed of the grenade. By 0800, I was down at the messhall eating breakfast and feeling very tired. We heard that there was a crowd of news reporters at the main entrance to our airfield, trying to get in to cover the devastating attack.

It had indeed been devastating. We had had nineteen helicopters totally destroyed and thirty-five damaged. Eleven of the damaged ones were so bad off that we had to ship them to Taiwan for extensive rebuilding. We suffered three marines killed and ninety-one wounded. One of our KIA was our MABS water truck driver that had run over a mine just minutes before the attack. The youngster riding shotgun with him was seriously wounded. We figured that the VC had placed a mine out there on the road, north of the field to prevent an immediate vehicular reinforcement to counter their attack upon us. Instead, the unfortunate water truck driver came by unexpectedly at midnight and ran over the mine just seconds before the VC attack time.

I finished breakfast and drifted over to the command bunker. The seventeen dead VC were still lying in the sand. The four captured VC had been taken to the Vietnamese I Corps headquarters in Da Nang for interrogation. The group commander said, "Let's get rid of these VC bodies."

"What should we do with them?" asked Lieutenant Grinder of our Vietnamese interpreter, who had just returned from delivering the POWs to Da Nang.

"Take them to Da Nang bridge area. Except for the North Vietnamese, they are local villagers. Their families will come and pick them up." I directed some of my men to take the tarpaulin off the nearby M-60 machine-gun bunker that was near the beach facing east. The tarp had been over the gun emplacement to shield the gunners from the sun, blowing sand, and rain. I then told the men to lay the tarp in a nearby dump truck. I didn't want the VC blood all over the dump truck. I then told them to throw the dead VC into the truck and drive to the Da Nang bridge and just dump them. As the truck drove off, the nearby M-60 emplacement started firing. We all turned to see what was going on from the beach area. We saw hundreds of long fishing boats extremely close in; just beyond the breakers. Were they VC picking up survivors? Were they curious local fishermen wanting to see what the VC did to us last night? Whatever the reason, they were too close in to our beach and there were too many. So Lieutenant Grinder told the gunner to chase them out to sea by shooting close to them. They quickly moved out to sea. But hundreds lingered in that area the rest of the day.

Late that day I wandered into sickbay to see about the burning gash in the inside of my wrist. The flight surgeon looked at it and was really angry at me for not coming in sooner.

"Captain, you know better than not get treatment for a wound down here in this moist, hot climate. Infection sets in fast and then it's difficult to heal down here."

"Honestly, doc, it's only a scratch," I responded.

"A scratch can become a problem in this climate. Besides, you have it full of sand and dirt," snapped the flight surgeon. "I'll have to list you on the wounded-in-action list report. You very obviously got shot here. Why the hell didn't you get in here right after the attack?"

"Doc, I was part of the reaction force and was tied up on the defense perimeter until dawn," I answered. The doc turned to a corpsman and said, "Put the captain on the wounded list with the others for the medical records." I said, "Like hell. No wounded list for me here. My wife in North Plainfield, New Jersey, just wrote me recently and in her last letter she mentioned that she was getting phone calls from crazy hippies. They have been saying terrible things to her that her husband, a marine, should not be in Vietnam. I sure as hell don't want my name on some WIA list published somewhere in the press back there to add to her heartaches and harassment."

"Okay. We'll just put in the record book that you have a wound and not say that it was from enemy action," said the flight surgeon. The corpsman wrote just that in my medical record, and it still is in there to this day. I left with my scratch cleaned and patched up.

I had to go to Da Nang that same day to pick up an order of nails that the utilities section needed for further construction. As I drove out of the base perimeter, I saw someone sitting on a bulldozer across the street from me. It was the commander of the

Seabee battalion. He was operating the dozer himself and he was knocking down the thatched huts of dog-patch village located immediately to the north of the base. I watched him knock down the hut that had some of its walls made from hammered out Coke and Pepsi cans; the one with many of my own bullet holes in it. He was rapidly clearing the area of huts. He was obviously very angry at the local VC sympathizers. Some of last night's attackers came through this village as the VC mortared the Seabee base. The mortars upon the Seabees caused them to stay down as the VC crossed the road to their east and attacked over our defense wire. The Seabee commander naturally was very angry because the Seabees had been building to their immediate south. (The commander was promptly relieved when the word of his bulldozing activity got around.)

Later that day I heard that Chu Lai Airfield had been attacked at the same time as we were attacked. The VC had destroyed two A-4 Skyhawks and had badly damaged six others. The MAG-12 marines killed fifteen of the attacking VC. There had also been an apparent coordinated, planned attack to take place at Da Nang Airfield. However, word was around that an artillery unit fired hundreds of rounds into an area to the east of Happy Valley where a group of VC had been reported. This probably messed up their attack capability. Additionally, a marine patrol led by Sgt. John Anderson had killed fifteen VC about five miles south of Da Nang Airfield. Intelligence figured this was part of an advance attack party.

The next day an annual inspection team from the Wing Supply Division (Rear) in Iwakuni, Japan, arrived and began inspecting my supply records and equipment. I received outstanding and excellent grades in everything except covered storage. They marked me below average for lack of covered storage for my supplies. The inspecting major said, "Captain, you've got to get some roofs or tents over this supply equipment located behind your supply tent."

"Sir, with all due respect, covered supply storage is pretty low on the priority list of our construction. The troops have to be fed under a roof and sleep under a cover and then we get to the other important items. However, eventually we'll get enough tents from *you,* or I'll buy lumber and build a covered shed for those supplies. You can't use wet toilet paper and I know that," I explained to the man who just flew in from Japan for a two-day inspection tour and really didn't know the problems we were living with in this hellhole.

That evening, Padre Roland told us that he had been to Da Nang. He said that the little old Vietnamese wood-carver was earning so much money making crucifixes, he now was able to afford to move out of the old-age home and get his wife out of a women's old-age home on the south side of Da Nang. They both now had a little apartment and shop in downtown Da Nang.

The following night I got scheduled for a night standby mission in a UH-34D squadron. About 0400 in the morning we launched to resupply a marine unit under heavy attack. It was a VC attack against Hill 22. Many months ago I had flown external loads of concertina to this twenty-two-meter-high mound located just south of Da Nang. It was now a hill held by A Company, 1st Battalion, 1st Marines. When we arrived in our helicopters, the scene looked like something from a World War I trench-warfare epic.

The VC had attacked well after midnight, breached the wire, and overrun a portion of the hill. VC were all over the place. They were right in the trenches and the defenders' tents. There was a pitched battle before the grunts were able to drive the VC out. The Viet Cong left forty-seven bodies behind. It had cost the marines sixteen killed and forty-one wounded. Only one VC was captured and he had informed intelligence that many of the new members of this Doc Lap Battalion were recruited right out of the city of Da Nang. Our air—both fixed- and rotary-wing aircraft—got more VC at daybreak. They were trying to get out of the area on boats on the Tuy Loan River.

Needless to say, we now knew we were in a real war. It was no longer a situation of supplying and supporting the ARVN. It was kill or be killed, and that's how I felt. Naturally, defensive measures were improved with more wire and minefields. More aggressive small-unit patrolling took place. Sniper teams were organized for night patrolling. Seismic noise detectors were emplaced in permanent defensive areas. Guard dogs were obtained.

We had several of the dogs assigned to our defense at Marble Mountain.

The monsoon rains began to fall in torrents. Our fixed-wing jets could not provide close air support, and only ground-controlled radar jet aircraft bombing missions—called TPQ missions—were being flown. We, in helicopters, continued our daily routines of flying supplies in to our troops and flying the wounded out. Additionally, our Huey gunship helicopters were providing limited, close, suppressive fire. We flew low—below the five-hundred-foot-high overcast. This made us very vulnerable to getting small-arms hits from the VC. So more and more patches became evident on the skins of the choppers, and our casualties began to increase.

One rainy night one of my tent mates, Smokey Cassen, asked me if I wished to fly with him on a Huey gunship escort mission up north of Phu Bai the next morning. Early the next morning, I was airborne in a UH-1E from the squadron VMO-2 heading for Phu Bai. We had four Hueys, and we flew up to Phu Bai, located just south of Hue. There, we briefed with HMM-161 transport-chopper pilots for a troop lift to an LZ Eagle, located twenty miles northwest of Phu Bai. Our Huey mission was to ace two Hueys, prep the LZ area and continue firing in the peripheral areas, as the other two UH-1Es escorted the assault-transport helos into the LZ.

As we approached the LZ, Smokey Cassen gave me control of the aircraft and said, "You've got the aircraft. This area has a lot of gooners up here so we'll probably run into a few today."

I pulled away from the rest of the choppers, and only my wingman followed me as we closed with the LZ. The LZ was a flat, open area surrounded by dense vegetation. The zone itself was clear; no people in it at all. I took the left side and my wingman took the right side and we dove downward. I fired my four M-60 forward-fixed machine guns and the port-side gunner raked the area to our left as I climbed back into a left attack pattern. My wingman worked over the dense brush on the right. We then began getting small-arms fire from the triple canopy jungle on both sides of the LZ. Our troop-carrying UH-34s were about four miles out for a landing. There didn't appear to be too many VC in the general area, or we would have been getting much more fire. So we cleared the inbound assault flight for a landing in the LZ. I warned them that they would be receiving light enemy fire. On one of my climbs from a gun run, I saw three gooners out of the edge of the western treeline.

"Watch this, Smokey. I'll vaporize them," I said as I turned on them. They were running so fast, one of them dropped his AK-47 rifle. I could have easily gunned them down with my machine guns. Instead, I reach up and flipped the number one rocket pod switch to "on." I rolled to the left and picked them on my cross hairs on the windscreen and then punched the red button on the cyclic stick with my right thumb. *Woomp!* Away went a single, spiraling 2.75-inch high-explosive rocket. It went right into the center of the three retreating Viet Cong. As I pulled left in a tight turn, we could see the cloud of dust where the VC had been. They were indeed vaporized. I drifted back to my orbit point and continued raking the jungle for the base of fire, as the UH-34s touched down on the ground in the LZ. Soon it was over and we refueled at Phu Bai and headed for home.

This UH-1E flight gave me my first KBA, or killed by air, that I actually was sure that I had killed the enemy. On previous flights, I had fired but never knew if I had hit VC. From then on, every time I had a bad day in a UH-34 transport helicopter mission, I would even up the score by getting scheduled in a Huey gunship with my guns and rockets.

The early winter rains increased in intensity. Although the ground action slowed due to the rains and mud, we were getting excessive hits in our low-flying helicopters. We could no longer fly from point to point at our former comfortable level of three thousand to four thousand feet. Below the five-hundred-foot cloud bottoms we were almost sitting ducks. As hits upon the helicopter increased, so did our flight-crew casualties. We had now flown many missions during numerous operations, such as Black Ferret, Blue Marlin, Golden Fleece, and Harvest Moon. The latter two were rice-harvesting and rice-protection operations of our ground forces that we supported. During September and October 1965, the marines protected the Vietnamese farmers harvesting their rice and then moved the rice from the fields in helicopters and LVTs. These operations denied tons of rice to the VC, who needed it to survive in the field of battle.

During these bad-weather, low-flying periods, the climbing air-crew casualties began affecting the helicopter crews. There was grumbling about the excessive risks. The general feeling was, Doesn't our government understand this is war? Why not bomb and invade the North and get it over with? Why are we sitting down here in an almost fixed position waiting for more and more gooners from the North? Our personal gamble was high; our government's risk-taking appeared low. The newspapers that were sent to us reflected more and more anti–Vietnam War sentiment Stateside and a total noncommitment from congressmen.

Brig. Gen. Marion Carl, who shot down eighteen Japanese aircraft during World War II and who now was our assistant wing commander, sensed this feeling among the helicopter community. So he gathered us all into our large MAG-16 mess hall and gave us a "fire and brimstone" lecture about having to fly at very low altitudes under the five-hundred-foot monsoon-season overcasts. His lecture was met with mixed emotions, and day and night missions continued through the winter.

The pressure of nonsupport back in the States, as reflected in letters of what the public expressed and what was written by our newspapers, not only affected the grunts in the field and the air crews, but also the support units, including nonflying maintenance crews and supply personnel. Drugs and alcohol began to seep into this stupid, unconventional war. As weak-hearted senators lost the will to stand up to the communist invasion from the North, their indecisiveness permeated the society back home and reached seven thousand miles across the world to those who had their ass on the line. For those of us who could close with the enemy and kill him, these feelings were somewhat relieved. But for the more numerous support personnel in the country, it became frustrating. We're not allowed to win this war? Why not? To know that we could drop two bombs, one on Hanoi and one on Haiphong, and then invade to end the war, as we had done in WWII, yet instead to sit here like ducks in a pond with no objective, no honorable military solution allowed by our national elected leaders, was beginning to gnaw at the souls of those who had to serve their thirteen months in hell.

Personally, I came to the conclusion that somewhere in the complex maze of Congress and the State Department a decision must have been made—maybe during the Korean War—that all our guided missiles and nuclear weapons had written on them "FOR DELIVERY TO USSR ONLY."

For years we had threatened the Soviet Union with our devastating arsenal in response to its own nuclear blackmail of us. But here, where American lives were immediately at stake, we didn't threaten Hanoi's government at all—a government that had no retaliation capability directly against us. Instead, we let them pour troops and equipment down the Ho Chi Minh Trail.

One example of this frustration and lowering morale for a noncombatant happened one early evening in December. Smokey Cassen, Chaplain Roland, George Gross, Jack Bates, and I were having our usual evening chat and letter-writing period in our tent. Several shots rang out. They were fairly loud and they sounded like they came from the center of the camp area. Several of us went down toward the group headquarters area to where the gunshots had sounded. As we approached, we saw a crowd around the chapel tent.

"What's going on in the chapel?" asked Chaplain Roland.

"Somebody is in there shooting up the chapel," someone answered.

Padre Roland and I walked into the chapel tent. Up front near the altar stood a young lance corporal with a smoking M-16 rifle. I noticed that the rifle was set for automatic firing.

"What's happening here, young man?" asked Chaplain Roland. A very angry and upset-looking young man of about twenty years of age shouted, "God put me here and it's hell. I want to shoot God."

It took the chaplain quite some time and some fast talking to calm the upset marine down. The marine then gave his weapon to the chaplain, who gave it to me. The chaplain had the young man sit down on the altar platform for a while and they talked. I just stood there holding the rifle and looking around the tent. The kneelers had been all shot up, and the splinters of wood were lying about. There were bullet holes in the altar. I then looked up to the crucifix. It had not been hit. Then the chaplain and the distraught young soldier left the tent. I followed, feeling very sorry for this emotionally injured man. Our flight surgeon had the young marine quickly flown out to the hospital ship *Repose* for evaluation by a psychiatrist.

During a large operation against a significant fixed Viet Cong unit, I was flying ammunition and water to a battalion near the village of Bich Tram. The LZ was about twelve miles south of Da Nang. Our grunts had apparently trapped this large VC unit between Hill 55 and an envelopment north and south towards the west and base of Charlie Ridge. The artillery from Hill 55 had been pounding the pajama-clad VC out in the open, flat land, as they tried to retreat to the hills at Charlie Ridge or the Nui Son Ga Ridgeline. As I was flying downwind at five hundred feet to set up for an approach from the west into the wind, I saw one of our VMO-2 UH-1E gunships landing right out in the middle of the battle. I extended my downwind leg so that I could see why the chopper was landing. I assumed that they had experienced engine failure and had to make an emergency landing. However, I did not hear anything on my radios indicating an emergency landing. I was getting ready to begin an approach to the Huey that landed amid all kinds of friendly incoming artillery explosions and in the middle of withdrawing VC. Then I saw someone run from the Huey. I watched very closely. That marine ran about twenty meters to open ground. I saw him reach down and lift up a VC "spider hole" cover, shoot his pistol into the hole, and drop the cover back down. I watched amazed as the marine Huey crew member returned to the UH-1E chopper. As he was crawling into the helicopter, he abruptly turned back around and ran back to the spider hole. He reached down into the hole and then I saw him pull out a light colored AK-47 assault rifle. He ran with it toward the waiting Huey gunship, as 105-mm howitzer shells exploded all around the area. He jumped into the chopper and it took off and climbed right out past me. I commenced my approach and landed way to the rear of those exploding shells and dropped off my load of ammo and cans of water.

That evening, while in the O club sucking up some beer suds and asking around who that VMO-2 pilot was, I got the full story. It had been our assistant wing commander, Brig. Gen. Marion Carl. He flew every type of aircraft, including helicopters, in our wing inventory. This day he was flying the VMO-2

UH-1E gunship to observe the close-air-support attack aircraft and the helicopter support of this entrapment operation. In the heat of the battle, as the marines were charging the fleeing VC and as our own artillery shells were falling on the VC, General Carl saw a single Viet Cong pop out from the common VC spider hole, fire at the advancing marines, and then drop back into his hiding hole, letting the cover fall back over him. The general decided to fly right down into the middle of the battlefield and land. He then ordered his crew chief to run out of the chopper and shoot that VC with his .45 pistol. The crew chief did so and returned to the Huey. But the general saw that the crew chief did not bring the VC weapon back with him. So he ordered the crew chief to go back and get the weapon. That is when I saw the crew chief returning the second time to the Huey with an AK-47 rifle in his hand.

Apparently, word got around about this over at wing, and I heard that it even got back to General Krulak at Fleet Marine Forces, Pacific, in Hawaii. We never saw General Carl flying our choppers as a pilot again. Rumors had it that General Krulak ordered him to quit flying as a pilot due to the possibility that the Viet Cong might shoot him down and capture one of our generals and make worldwide propaganda news of it. But that's the kind of gutsy generals the Corps has always had.

The monsoon winds and rain had their effect upon our beach on the South China Sea. Numerous living-area tents began to rot and tear in the wind and pelting rain. Many of these tents had been stored for years in Okinawa in warehouses. They apparently were never unfolded, aired out, and inspected for dry rot over the years. As a result, a tent's rated life expectancy of one year was, in reality, three months here in Vietnam because of the initial dry rot and the pounding rains and winds of winter.

Major Bates was responsible for providing dry living areas for the base inhabitants, and now the tents were leaking badly. Since we arrived as an expeditionary Marine Corps projection of sea power ashore, and didn't expect to stay for a long period of time, tents normally would have done it. However, the continual wet weather, plus the fact that it was beginning to appear that we all were going to stay here a while, caused us to decide to take the tents down from the strongback wooden frames and have utilities section hammer up sheet-tin sides and roofs. So it was back to see Lily Ann in Da Nang city for me. There I had to order loads of Korean corrugated sheet tin for Major Bates. His untiring work crews promptly replaced over six hundred tents with tin shed–like coverage. It was quite a relief to sleep in my folding cot without water dripping all over me each night. Another minor problem arose from the heavy rainstorms. The monsoon season caused hundreds of deadly sea serpents to get tumultuously washed ashore on all the beaches, including our beach. We began seeing these very venomous snakes in between our tents and we had to watch where we stepped during the aftermath of storms.

Then, one of the worst, and most embarrassing things that could happen to a supply officer happened to me. As I was driving to my supply tent one morning, an angry major shouted at me from one of our wooden latrines, "Hey Captain! Where the hell is the shit paper?"

"I'll get some toilet paper up to you right away, Major."

I got into my tent office and directed, "Sergeant Riley, run some toilet paper up to the northern end of the officers' country latrine."

"I can't sir. We ran out of toilet paper last night."

"Get me the gunny."

"Yes sir," said the gunny. "What do you need, Captain?"

"We need toilet paper right now, gunny."

"Yes sir. I'm working on it. I only heard about it at breakfast. I have some coming over from wing in a jeep right now."

"Good. Get that all over to the shit houses fast, when it arrives. Why the hell did we run out?"

"I don't know, Captain. I always requisition enough. Some grunts must have gotten into our backyard supply boxes or something."

The landline phone rang on my desk. I picked it up.

"Captain, get some shit paper up to the colonel's outhouse. He can't make it to his briefing until it arrives."

I promised the executive officer of the group that the vital paper was on its way. Then the phone rang again.

"Captain, do you have a Sears Roebuck catalog down in your supply?"

"Excuse me. Who is this?" I asked.

"This is the CO of HMH-463. My enlisted men tell me that the latrines are out of ass-wipe paper. Let's get some out there for the troops."

"Yes sir. It's on its way, Colonel."

Finally, a jeep pulled up. It only had a few boxes of toilet paper. Not enough for the full day. I thought for a fleeting second that I'll bet Lily Ann has plenty of toilet paper in her Da Nang warehouse. I can't imagine what she would charge me for it under this shortage problem of supply and demand. I got into my jeep and drove over to a nearby base, where one of our communication-battalion headquarters was located. I made a fast trade for ten wooden telephone poles that I had lying around the base. There were no tall wooden trees growing in the Da Nang or beach areas. All wood had to come out of the inland jungles. Therefore all electrical and telephone lines in the city of Da Nang and even on our bases were strung over concrete poles. The comm battalion was thrilled with the lighter-weight wooden poles but couldn't fully understand how I could be so enthused about getting several days' worth of toilet paper in return.

I purposely missed lunch and dinner at the mess hall that day because the verbal harassment got to me. The next morning there was enough toilet paper in all of the latrines for the Chinese army. Not another word was said to me about this critical combat shortage.

On a sunny afternoon, while flying a Huey chopper, returning from a routine flight from An Hoi to my base at Marble Mountain AF, I was about three miles south of Marble Mountain, only five miles from my base. At two thousand feet of altitude above the beautiful white China Beach, I glanced down to my right to watch the automobile-sized hammerhead sharks swimming along parallel with me northward along the coast below. I then glanced down to my left, inland, and saw action.

At my lower ten o'clock position, I witnessed a scene from a Hollywood movie. A single Huey from VMO-2 squadron was in about a shallow thirty-degree dive with four forward M-60 machine guns blazing and both side M-60 gunners hanging out, guns swung forward and firing. On the sandy beach below was a person staked out in the sand, spread-eagle and face skyward. There were three black-pajama-clad, conical-hatted Vietnamese with weapons standing at the head of the staked-down victim. A few meters inland toward the dense vegetation were seven apparent VC falling from the impacts of the 7.62-mm bullets of the attacking UH-1E helo. Farther west, along the thickets, were more Viet Cong, now shooting back at the attacking Huey gunship.

I immediately rolled in for attack, throwing my guns and rocket-arming switches to the on position. I was still too far away to render immediate assistance, as I dove at 180 knots. The three VC close to the victim turned and ran toward the treeline, only to be felled by the hail of bullets from the attacking chopper's blazing guns. As I continued down as a backup, I observed the Huey come to hover at the feet of the tied-down victim, blowing sand all over as the six M-60 machine guns continued to rake the fleeing VC. As soon as the chopper landed, the pilot in command jumped from his left seat to the sand, the six M-60 machine guns stopped firing for a few seconds to allow the pilot to run to the victim. The heroic pilot pulled out his survival knife and cut the ropes from the four stakes. Due to the momentary ceasefire of the Huey to prevent hitting the pilot out front and the victim he began picking up, the VC along the treeline again opened fire. The pilot, half-carrying, half-dragging the victim the few feet to the UH-1E, pulled out his .38 survival pistol and began cranking off rounds at the VC. About the time the pilot lifted the victim into the Huey fuselage with a gunner's assistance, I was in a perfect gun-run position and began firing and walking my rudders to spray the area. I didn't fire any rockets for fear shrapnel could hit my squadron mate's chopper. As I pulled off to the east for another roll-in, I saw the Huey lift slightly off the ground with all six guns firing; then a salvo of four 2.75-inch rockets tore from the hovering helo's rocket pods. The chopper then did a 180-degree turn on the spot and climbed toward the South China Sea for safety. I rolled back in with six guns walking 7.62-mm bullets up the sand to the running VC. Then I fired four 2.75-inch high-explosive rockets into the treeline and pulled off to the northeast to join the rescue helo. I escorted them back to nearby Marble Mountain and our flight line. There we all witnessed a very weak but elated marine POW. Capt. Jack Steele, the heroic, gutsy Huey pilot from VMO-2, and his aggressive copilot and crew were rewarded by the knowledge that they had personally saved a POW who was being beaten to death on that sandy beach.

Captain Steele was put in for the Medal of Honor and his crew was recommended for other heroism awards. However, I heard later that headquarters at FMFPAC in Hawaii had downgraded the recommendation of Captain Steele's to a Navy Cross. Much later, Captain Steele was killed and his attaining the medal, whatever kind, was meaningless. The important thing was that a young marine who had been captured by the VC, held one week, and who was apparently going to be beaten to death and left staked out on the open beach for all Americans and South Vietnamese villagers to see, made it back alive.

I received my first Christmas card from Stateside. It was a card from my wife, Eleanor, and the children with Santa Claus in a department store. It brightened my December. Another uplift was when we heard that Bob Hope was coming to Da Nang before Christmas to perform for us. The day of his arrival, the rain was on and off. I arrived at Freedom Hill east of Da Nang in my jeep. The rain had stopped. I was early so I got down around the sixth row of the thousands of multiservice troops. I sat on my helmet, which was submerged in about four inches of water, and waited until the show began.

General Walt, III MAF commander, introduced Bob Hope to a thunderous ovation. Then Bob Hope introduced the USO girls. I don't know how Bob Hope could stand receiving an ovation less than the girls, but he joked about it. The rain started again and Hope and the girls had to perform holding open umbrellas. Ann-Margret left memories for the troops of the American dream girl.

Halfway through the show, the VC tried to attack through an area about a quarter mile southeast of the show. Unfortunately, about one-fourth of the ground units attending the show had to leave to reinforce whoever was involved in fending off the ground attack. Christmas day itself came and went just like any other day. Since Asians celebrate New Year's in a grand manner, our troops decided to make New Year's Eve a spectacle. All over the I Corps tactical zone (ICTZ) our troops spontaneously fired their weapons into the air at midnight. The sky was ablaze with tracer fire in every direction. Where all those descending slugs fell, I'll never know. But I did not hear of anyone getting hit, nor did we have to launch our Huey medevac bird for wounded. The VC did not mortar or attack our base that night. With all that firing into the sky, the VC must have thought the Americans were crazy.

Thus 1965 passed into history. We all knew that 1966, or at least tomorrow, was not going to be too much different for us. Many a marine, if in a position to do so, mixed his drinks that New Year's Eve with much emotion, not knowing if he'd make it to another one.

chapter 3

Vietnam, 1966

At 0800 on New Year's Day 1966, the hired maid for our tent, Missy Bau, came into our tent and gave me a New Year's present. It was the horn of a large caribou (Asian cow). The horn had been cleaned and was very shiny. Three posts had been mounted on the inside curvature of the horn, each having a yellow-brown tortoise shell cut in the shape of a sail. This three masted sail ship looked similar to the Asian fishing junks that were along our coast. I was thrilled to receive a gift from a local. But I was very embarrassed that I had no New Year's gift to give to this poor woman who daily swept the tent of the mounds of sand blown in and washed all of our clothing.

The rains continued and we now had tin huts to live in instead of leaking tents. Support to the marines and ARVNs continued with sorties flown day and night. The area became more familiar to us helicopter pilots than our own hometown areas back in the real world. The Hai Van Pass, Elephant Valley, Charlie Ridge just west of Hill 55, and the Que Son Mountains twenty-two miles south of Da Nang became everyday places to fly to. We knew every hill, every ridge and valley. Often, we teamed up with HMM-163, a UH-34D squadron, stationed aboard the LPH USS *Iwo Jima,* and I flew a couple of missions in their choppers.

Based upon the Southeast Asia Treaty Organization (SEATO), the Koreans sent their own "Tiger" Division aboard U.S. amphibious ships of the Seventh Fleet. This relieved our Battalion Landing Team 2/7 from protecting the Qui Nhon area to our immediate south.

The VC continued to press their attacks. They had overrun the ARVN outpost at Hiep Duc and then attacked an ARVN outpost at Thack Tru. The ARVNs then decided to abandon Hiep Duc, rather than reinforce it. During this battle our helicopters suffered seventeen hits, with three choppers badly damaged and one crew member killed.

The winter and spring months now merged. Some missions were a piece of cake; others too violent to describe except in a movie. On one of these numerous rainy-season missions, I was flying lead aircraft of a four-plane division to resupply the marines at the base of Charlie Ridge. As I came in at about 120 knots and flared nose-high for a fast landing behind some of our assault troops, my crew chief yelled, "Take her off! Punji sticks!" It was too late. I had already touched down in tall elephant grass, pushing the collective down and unwinding some of the engine RPM with my throttle.

"Dash Two, Three, and Four . . . go around. I've landed on big punji sticks in this LZ," I broadcast rapidly. My three wingmen orbited until our ground unit cleared a better landing zone where there were no hidden bamboo punji sticks. The VC had started putting these tall sharpened bamboo sticks in places which they thought might be logical helicopter landing zones. I had accidently landed smack on an area where there were hundreds of five-foot sharpened bamboo sticks sticking straight up. They were a little below the tall elephant grass. Four of these thick sharpened bamboo shoots had punched through the thin fuselage undercarriage skin of my UH-34D helicopter and had punctured my fuel cells. I thought I'd be stuck there and have to get the chopper externally lifted out by an HR-2S helicopter. However, upon lifting into a hover, my crew chief and gunners pulled out the sharp sticks, and I had only minor fuel leakage because of the self-sealing live rubber on the inside of the fuel cells. I flew en route to base, watching my fuel gauge go down slowly.

On a dreary, overcast afternoon, I briefed for a two-plane UH-34D flight to a company-size unit located in a flatland area outside of a village called Chu Buoi. It was about three miles north of Highway 14 and about fifteen miles west of Hoi An.

"Hunter Four, this is Blackbird One; inbound with two supplies, over," I called to the ground unit over the FM radio.

"Blackbird, we see you. You are cleared in to land. No enemy contacts. LZ is marked and smoke is on its way."

"Hunter Four, Blackbird flight will be coming in on the deck from the west, after I see your smoke," I replied.

"Roger. You will be inbound on the deck. Cleared to land."

I had decided that instead of spiraling straight downward as we usually did to minimize getting hits, I would go a few miles west at about five hundred feet, under the overcast, and dive for the deck and level just above the trees. I saw the unit's green smoke and it was rising well upward above the trees, blowing gently from east to west. I lined up with a slightly bending road that ran west to east and I nosed her over, picking up 160 knots. With my wingman closely stepped up on my port side, I continued down below the trees following the road, which lead straight to the marked and smoke-identified LZ about three miles east. It was a hell of a fast-moving trip with the tall trees blurring past our both sides. Gunners were tense, since if we got shot at, they would barely have time to return fire at the enemy now behind them. Abruptly I came upon an open area of tall green grass that the dirt road bisected. As we flashed by at about 150 knots, we all saw about ten caribou, or water buffalo. What really surprised us was that all of the caribou had wide straps around their bodies, and under their bellies were many AK-47 rifles packed in fishing nets. On the back of each caribou sat a single Vietnamese wearing the customary black pajamas, black baggy silk shirt, and the usual conical straw farmer's hat. They each held a long skinny branch for prodding the slow-moving animals along.

"Did you see all those weapons?" shouted one of my gunners over the intercom.

"Dash One, this is Two. Did you see those living trucks of weapons?" transmitted my wingman.

"Roger. We'll report them to the grunts." I answered.

As I closed on the green smoke drifting towards me from the LZ, I reached up and patted my instrument panel for my wingman to see my signal that we were landing. I pulled up on the collective and added a little engine RPM as the nose rose to a climb so that I could see the LZ dead ahead and down behind the trees. I then pushed down hard on the collective, and twisted off the engine RPM to idle while pulling aft on my cyclic. We flared to a slow forward motion at about twenty feet. I then twisted on high RPM and pulled up on the collective to make a smooth, slightly forward-moving landing on the H-shaped panel of the LZ on the grass. As the grunts unloaded the C-rations, water, and ammunition, I described the movement of weapons underneath what appeared to be peaceful grazing caribou and their watchful farmers riding on their backs. The company commander lost no time in calling for artillery support on known enemy weapons transportation, just about three miles away.

As my wingman and I climbed eastward toward Hoi An and the beach leading north to home field, we watched our marine 105-mm howitzers from the 2nd Battalion, 12th Marines, placing impacts all over the open area where we saw the weapons being transported. I don't know if they destroyed those weapons. However, it made it more dangerous for the VC to move their weapons supplies during the daylight hours. If we had not come into our LZ below the treelines, down that dirt road, those caribou would have looked like the usual harmless grazing cattle that are all over the countryside.

During February 1966, our fixed-wing jets, despite terrible winter rains, resumed air strikes against North Vietnam. In early

March, we supported the marine operation Utah, near Quang Ngai, about ninety miles south of Da Nang.

Early in the morning of March 10, the U.S. Army Special Forces camp of Ashau, up north toward Quang Tri, was overrun by a North Vietnamese regiment. The battle raged for three days. The clouds were generally down to five hundred feet above the terrain. Our jets had a hell of a time trying to drop bombs under such weather and TPQs weren't effective, since the enemy was so close into the base. Ashau had an airstrip on its elevated location. As the North Vietnamese captured about one-third of the western part of the camp and runway, HMM-161 from Phu Bai was flying in supplies and taking out wounded from the east end of the field. On Friday morning, the second day of the attack, Capt. Ray Perry, a UH-34D helicopter pilot from HMM-161, was shot down while trying to lift off from the east end of the runway while overloaded with wounded and frantic ARVNs climbing aboard and hanging onto the wheel struts. HMM-161 spent the next two days searching for Ray and his crew in the vicinity of the east end of the Ashau complex. The North Vietnamese over-ran all of the base. I had heard about this at Marble Mountain Airfield. I felt bad about Ray Perry, since I had flown with him in HMM-161 in Hawaii and my wife knew his wife quite well. I figured that there was a possibility that the NVA had captured him and were dragging him through the jungle with a rope around his neck, like they were seen doing to one of our MABS-16 men that they had captured last summer near Da Nang. As Ashau fell to the North Vietnamese, I heard a real heroic story coming out of there at the time. A section of U.S. Air Force A-1 Skyraider (SPAD) piston-engine attack bombers had been bombing and strafing the NVA on the western part of the air-field. The NVA hit one of the A-1 SPADs and the pilot somehow managed to land his burning SPAD downwind, stopping on the Special Forces–held east end of the runway. His wingman, to-tally disregarding his own safety, flew a downwind approach right over the attacking NVA, landed and taxied up to his burn-ing leader's aircraft. The pilot opened his canopy and the downed pilot jumped into his lap and they took off. They climbed back over the enemy-held third of the runway. Somehow they were not shot down.

On Sunday, I was eating brunch in our Marble Mountain mess hall. I was shocked and thrilled to see Capt. Ray Perry walk into the mess hall.

"Ray, welcome back. We heard you were missing for two days. I thought that you had been killed or captured," I excitedly said.

Ray then related the following story:

"Bob, I'm so darn lucky. When they shot me down I crashed off the end of the camp down into the jungles. When I climbed out of the wreckage, the ARVN troops up the hill on the airstrip had already begun retreating from the attacking NVA. As they ran from the camp down the hill, they saw me. I assumed that they figured that more helicopters would come to rescue me. So they all ran toward me, as I ran deeper into the jungle to the east. The NVA had overrun the entire field by then, and some of them were chasing the ARVN down the hillside. I kept on running and the ARVN stayed right behind me until dark. Then they simply joined me and acted like I should be their leader. During the first night, I traveled to an area that we had designated as a safe pickup area for downed pilots. The next day we held very still under the dense jungle canopy awaiting helicopters to come near this slightly open area. No helicopters came. I heard them all over the area, but more toward the west and Ashau. That night, while slowly moving toward a second safe area for possible pickup, the band of ARVN followed me. I heard a noise up front. I stopped. The ARVN stopped. Then I heard the crackling of branches and bushes. I figured that the NVA somehow had outflanked us and were directly in front of us. I laid down with my .38 drawn and pointing straight ahead of me. The crashing noise continued toward me. I thought I may as well go out shooting. I cocked my pistol, got up on my one knee and as the noise was now immediately to my front, I moved some branches aside with my left hand. I figured to shoot an NVA face-to-face. Instead, an enormous head came out of the thick mangrove area. It was the orange and black head of Bengal tiger that reflected under the shaft of moonlight that pierced the jungle canopy. Its large eyes, set much wider than mine, glared at me from about two feet away. It had not expected me, though it must have been smelling all of us sweating, dirty creatures for some time. It leaped up in the air, but backwards, landed, and turned and ran into the jungle. I don't know who was more frightened, the tiger or me."

"What a hell of a scare. Did you get hit or badly scratched up from the crash or thickets up there?" I asked Ray.

"No. But my body is badly torn up from the blood-sucking leeches. Somehow they got under my armor vest and under my flight suit and all over my body. I couldn't burn them off because I was afraid that the NVA might see my lighted matches. When I was finally picked up by our squadron helicopter, it took our corpsman hours to burn every leech off me."

I saw Ray Perry several more times in Nam during this first combat tour of mine. Every time that I saw him, I thought of his coming eyeball-to-eyeball with that tiger.

The VC and NVA had by this time broadened the war. We increased troop strengths to match their aggressive invasion forces. To me it seemed like ten years ago, but it had only been nine months, during last summer, that we wore Australian bush hats and any kind of shoulder holster and pistol that met our fancy. Those days as "jungle fighters" were long gone, when in August 1965 General Walt banned those colorful costumes and made all marines look like marines.

However, there were holdouts that still sported the long, curled handle bar moustaches. One such proud moustache-wearer was our MABS-16 senior staff noncommissioned officer in charge of the crash crew. One day our group commander called the SNCO into his office to reprimand him for not meeting Marine Corps moustache regulations. I happened to run into this SNCO immediately after he came out of the group commander's office.

"Top, what did the group commander say?" I quizzed.

"Well, I first explained to the colonel that I had worn a handle-bar moustache during WWII. Then when the war ended, I shaved it off and mounted it in a butterfly case. I then told him that I did the same during the Korean War and that I saved that beauty the same way, in a butterfly case. And so, I would like to do the same during this war."

"What did the colonel say, Top?"

"He said, 'If you don't shave that handlebar moustache off right now, I'll put you in a butterfly case and send you home!'"

That was the last handlebar moustache on an American marine that I saw in Nam. The Australians, of course, had real championship handlebar moustaches approved by their command.

As I flew along in a Dog—UH-34 transport helo—I scanned the beautiful countryside. The winter rains had really turned everything green. The rivers were swollen and brown from the increased water gushing through tributaries coming from the mountains near Laos and the Ho Chi Minh Trail areas. I was leading a flight of four birds, carrying rations, ammo, and water to a battalion to the west of Tam Ky.

We landed in the center of a small no-name village and I came to a full stop next to the village water well. As our four rotor blades churned the loose red mud and rain water, I looked about the village. The ground unit was unloading the supplies and placing them on a motorized "mule." There was about a company of marine infantry in the vil.

All of a sudden, off to my left, the ground rose up in a long line about twenty meters long. Straw mats with mud and sand rose into the air as at least twenty Viet Cong rose from a covered trenchline, firing AK-47 automatic rifles. Three marines on my left side of my chopper fell bleeding. My portside gunner returned the fire, blasting the four closest VC back into the opened tunnel. The remaining VC jumped from the trenchline, charging and shooting at our four choppers. To the left rear of the VC, four marines came out of a grass shack firing into the VC. One marine had a Browning automatic rifle, a BAR, and he must have cut down at least seven VC himself. When the noise and smoke settled, all the VC were dead or wounded. Four marines were KIA and five wounded. We quickly, but carefully, checked our helicopters over for battle damage. Unbelievably, none of our chopper crewmen were hit despite numerous holes all over the four helos. Our grunts tied up the VC wounded and I carefully checked them over for grenades as they were thrown into my helo. The five marines wounded were placed in my wingman's aircraft, and the four dead marines were placed in my section leader's aircraft.

As we rapidly climbed out to take all wounded, VC included, to Charlie Med, I tried to figure out exactly what the hell happened. Best I could guess, our grunts had been searching through what had been a VC-controlled village. The VC might have escaped detection in the mat-and-dirt-covered trenchline. Possibly when our four choppers landed so very close to them with all that noise, they thought a larger force was coming in to attack and they now didn't have a chance. So, they may have decided to fight and came up out of their hiding place.

When I returned to base to check for battle damage, I counted thirty-seven AK-47 bullet holes in my UH-34 helo. One hydraulic line was shot out, but no other critical damage was found. A good metal patch job was all that was needed.

I was so pissed that I had once again been stuck sitting up high, fully exposed, in a transport assault helicopter with nothing but my .38 pistol and .45-caliber grease gun. I walked directly from the UH-34 flight line over to the VMO-2 Huey line to get on the next day's Huey gunship flight schedule. I was going to go into tomorrow's hot LZ with guns and rockets firing like hell to get back at these bastardly gooners. This sitting-duck business in the transport helos was getting old.

The next morning was dark with a thick gray overcast. I cranked on the throttle and pulled up on the collective, pushing forward on the cyclic stick as my Huey gunship climbed from our base in China Beach. I was joined by three other UH-1E gunships as we rapidly caught up with the slower-moving UH-34 assault transport helos. This was a planned regimental assault on a known North Vietnamese unit operating on Charlie Ridge, a small mountain range just eighteen miles southwest of Da Nang.

The LZ was prepped by four marine A-4 Skyhawk attack bombers dropping pairs of 250-pound bombs and controlled by a VMO-2 FACA in a UH-1E Slick ship. As the A-4s departed, my wingman and I rolled in to the north of the LZ and my other section of two Huey gunships rolled in to the south side, laying salvos of rockets into the treelines. If NVA were there, they were dead, wounded or dug deeply into the ground. No heavy antiaircraft gunfire was received on our four runs. I told my division wingmen to follow me to start hitting the edges of the LZ to the hilly terrain to the west. The UH-34s were now closing fast toward the LZ with their troops ready to jump out in the LZ and attack upon landing. As I rolled in from the north for an attack on the west treeline, all hell broke loose. The dark jungle below came alive with flashes like summer fireflies at night. I fired rockets, then my trigger finger squeezed the gun trigger on the cyclic, firing my four forward-fixed guns. The upcoming fire was intense as we continued in the attack. It was all small arms, no triple-A guns, but a hell of a lot of AK-47 stuff. Before I pulled off target I saw at least four holes in my windscreen. As I turned downwind, I heard number three UH-1E pilot, my second section leader, shout, "Dash Three is hit in the transmission, going down!"

I looked back and saw his Huey smoking at first, then flames erupted above and behind the crew compartment as he swung toward the LZ to avoid a jungle crash. As I continued around and began my roll in again, the first four UH-34 choppers touched down westward in the LZ, and our burning UH-1E gunship landed next to them.

As I dove firing rockets and guns, the trees were flashing back at us as the determined NVA returned our fire. As I rolled up in a left turn, my copilot, 1st Lt. Dan Wallace, shouted over the intercom, "I'm hit. Fuck, I'm hit . . . god, it hurts like hell."

I looked over at him and he was holding his lower stomach, which now turned black with liquid on his green flight suit. He was bleeding like a stuck pig. I told my wingman to join Dash Four, my section leader's wingman, and continue working the western vegetated area as briefed, and until our FACA gets another section of attack bombers to work over that heavy NVA area. I then headed straight for Da Nang and asked the FACA in his UH-1E when the next bombers were inbound. He stated that four marine F-4s just checked in with him. They had five-hundred-pound bombs and had just been given the western target briefing by the FACA.

At full throttle and at two thousand feet heading for Charlie Med, my two side gunners had pulled the bleeding copilot back into the rear compartment and had unzipped his bloody flight suit.

"Jesus, he's really bleeding badly, Captain," said one gunner to me.

"See if you can stop the bleeding. I have Charlie Med standing by at the hospital LZ waiting for him," I responded.

The copilot, who appeared to have almost passed out now, spoke in a quivering voice, "I think those fuckers shot me in my dick. It hurts so much, I'm not sure . . . but I think that's where I'm hit."

He was now ash white and I think going into shock. Charlie Med was coming up fast on my nose. I started a rapid descent to the large red cross painted on the pierced-steel-planking LZ.

Very worried about my copilot, but wanting to keep him going, I tried making a joke to him and saying, "Hang in there, Dan. Charlie Med will put a big bandage on that prick of yours and you'll be out in Da Nang city tomorrow night chasing those Vietnamese gals and sporting the biggest throbber in town."

I don't think Dan heard me. I glanced back and he was passed out, probably from loss of blood.

I went to see him that night at Charlie Med. He was still very white, receiving transfusions. He told me that the bullet had shot off a small part of the tip of his penis. However, other than the excessive bleeding, he said he'd be normal again. I responded, "Normal! Hell, you won't need a French tickler condom anymore to thrill the girls. You'll have your own built-in tickler."

He thought that was funny and said, "It could have been worse." (Six years later, Dan was a reserve pilot in one of my several squadrons of the air reserve group in Detroit, Michigan, that I commanded. He was constantly teased there by his fellow pilots, mostly now commercial pilots, who called him the Tickler or Bent Twig, etc. He always took the ribbing very well. I suppose he kept thinking, It could have been worse.)

We were now allowed to have an American flag on a flagpole on our bases. When I first arrived in Vietnam in 1965, I brought my own small flag. I had placed it on a stick outside of my tent. I promptly had to take it down because the group commander informed me that we had not been given permission from the Vietnamese to fly our colors. For the rest of my combat tour, I had the flag hanging next to my cot inside of my tent.

A big operation called Operation Orange came up. It was a big sweep up a valley that Highway 14 entered from the lowlands as it came west from Hoi An about twenty miles away. The valley ran along the Song Vu Gia River. Very steep cliffs were on both sides of the narrow entry into the valley. Beyond the entrance, the valley broadened to about two miles wide. The whole area near the many villages had piles of orange peppers. The peppers had been harvested and the numerous piles of orange made the countryside strangely altered, especially as it appeared from the air. Therefore the operation was called Operation Orange. Many pitched battles took place here, as the marines pushed the VC and NVA regulars back up the valley. This valley had been one of the major inbound routes from the Ho Chi Minh Trail, so the resistance was fierce when the marines entered the valley. I don't think that I ever made a flight there without getting some hits. On one resupply flight I counted twenty-two bullet holes in my UH-34D, upon return to home base.

Padre Roland saw me at lunch one rainy day and said, "Bob, looks like I can't visit the leper colony anymore at Nha Tho. The North Vietnamese captured it last night and killed the European missionary and his wife who ran it. They chased the lepers out of the building and off of the grounds. They are now using it as a headquarters."

I responded, "Well, I'm glad that you're not running down there anymore. I don't know why you'd hang your ass out like that—going so far south of Marble Mountain into bad-man's country alone in a jeep. Additionally, you better quit going down to Ap Nuoc Man village. They have many plague cases down there just south of the Marble Mountain."

"It's my job, Bob. Besides, we all have the plague shot," responded the chaplain.

The next afternoon our grunts retook the leper colony. The building had a few Huey gunship rocket holes in it. But otherwise, it was usable. However, with the missionary and his wife killed by the NVA, there was nobody to care for the lepers. Our marines stayed there a few days to make sure that the North Vietnamese did not return, and then they pushed southward. All of us at Marble Mountain AF felt very sorry about that missionary and his wife. Why the NVA killed them we didn't know. I flew past the former leper colony many times over the next few weeks, looking down at its desolation. And then, like everything else, it was lost in the memory due to more terrible atrocities by the invading North Vietnamese.

Late one afternoon, while sitting out in front of my SEA (Southeast Asia) hut, a full squadron of strange-looking new helicopters came roaring in from the sea. It was my first sight of the new CH-46 helicopters. The squadron of about eighteen troop transports came in at about five hundred feet over our runway and made a standard aircraft-carrier breakaway from each other for taking spacing intervals between each other for landing. I walked down to the flight line to see this new type of helicopter. It was large, with tandem rotor blades (blades in front and rear) and no tail rotor. It carried about twenty-four troops, in contrast to the maximum of eight troops that we carried in the UH-34D (we could lift only five on a hot day). It was armed with a .50-caliber machine gun on both sides of the fuselage. Our UH-34D had two lighter M-60 machine guns (7.62-mm shells). Additionally, the pilots told me that their CH-46 could cruise at about 140 knots. Our cruise was at about 100 knots. Overall, I was highly impressed with this flying machine that would eventually replace our time-tested aircraft.

The very next morning I was flying a routine ARVN resupply mission from an airstrip at Tam Ky, about seventy miles south of Da Nang. Our UH-34 squadron was helo-lifting troops and tons of bags of rice inland to Hoi Lam, not too far away from fallen Hiep Duc. There were several hundred ARVN troops with piles and hills of rice along the Tam Ky runway. We had flown two sorties already and it didn't put a dent in the quantity to be airlifted. I figured that today would be another eight-hour day of flying, but then I looked in my rearview mirror, while parked at the south end of the strip loading up. To my rear, twelve CH-46 helicopters had landed and were also loading up. We were thrilled to have them join us. We flew two more sorties in our UH-34 choppers and returned to Tam Ky. As we approached for a landing, the CH-46 flight commander came up on our common operating frequency and told us that they could finish the job and that we could go home. Right then and there I knew that this was going to be easier for us, with the CH-46s capable of carrying more than twice our load. That evening the CH-46s returned home after a long hard day. They had not encountered any enemy fire on their first day on the job. However, the very next day, four CH-46s were flying support missions for marines to the west of An Hoa and they ran into intensive NVA ground fire. All four CH-46 crews returned fire, but everyone of the eight .50-caliber machine guns jammed, and the CH-46s had to get the hell out of their fight fast. Back at base, it was discovered that only three bullets fired on each gun because the linkage on the ammo where it feeds into the gun had jammed. So for the following three days, each of the CH-46s sat, taking turns, on our beach firing their .50-cal machine guns to make sure that they had solved their link-jamming problems. In the meantime, we resumed our heavy workload of flying supplies until the CH-46s would join us again.

Then more assistance came. The free world's largest helicopters arrived. It was a squadron of CH-53s. Each CH-53 could carry thirty-eight troops, and a hell of a lot more smaller Vietnamese troops. Its speed was up around 150 knots. Now we really had a huge helicopter-airlift capability for our hard-working ground pounders in the bush. The CH-53 squadron also had to solve the .50-cal-machine-gun link problem, so there was much gunfire out on our beach for a few more days.

A one-week rest-and-relaxation period was now offered to anyone in the country over six months. This R&R included a free round-trip flight to Hong Kong, Bangkok, Japan or Australia. Costs once you were there were your own. I selected Bangkok, Thailand, and got scheduled for a Da Nang flight out on an air force C-130. I arrived at Da Nang Airfield two hours early. As the driver took several of us lucky ones over in a small truck, I felt naked. It was the first time that I had left my base without my .38 pistol hung over my shoulder. Even when we got onto the security of the Da Nang Airfield, it felt very strange not to have the reassurance of that personal weapon.

It was unusually active at the field. There were all sorts of Vietnamese air force (VNAF) aircraft flying in. I checked into a tent on the U.S. Air Force side of the field—the tent had a sign saying "R&R BANGKOK" posted on it. The airman there told me that since the airfield is closed to air traffic, the C-130 had to land at Tan Son Nhut Airfield near Saigon. It would fly up here to get us only after the airfield was open to normal traffic.

"What is the field closed for?" I asked.

"There's some kind of local revolution going on," responded the airman.

I stepped back out of the tent. It was true. The area was active. A large number of South Vietnamese troops had arrived by transport from Saigon's Tan Son Nhut Airfield. They quickly moved in assault waves off the airfield and east toward the ARVN I Corps headquarters. I had heard that there was a Buddhist revolution going on in Da Nang and Hue. But there had been demonstrations before, so I didn't think that this was different. However, as I stood outside the air force tent watching ARVN airborne troops and Vietnamese marines heading for the northeastern area of the field toward Da Nang city, I figured that this was serious. Shortly, another group of VNAF transports and A-1 fighter-bombers arrived to back up Prime Minister Nguyen Cao Ky, the hard-charging former air marshal and pilot. It looked to me like a large-scale battle between the Buddhist-backed I Corps ARVN troops of Da Nang and Premier Ky was about to take place. All of us along the U.S. Air Force flight line stood confused; we were concerned for our safety and wondering who the hell's side we were on.

Since I didn't even have my .38 pistol along for personal safety and knew that our R&R bird would not land at Da Nang until this confrontation was over, I thought that there was no sense in standing out in the open flight line. I felt that the safest and most comfortable place to wait this confusion out was in the famous Red Dog Saloon on the Marine Corps side of the field. I made sure that my bag was secure in the Bangkok R&R check-in tent, and told the airmen there that I'd be back in a couple of hours—"I'm going to the Red Dog and relax."

I walked the two miles around the southern end of the field because Ky's tanks were now rolling off of VNAF transports at the northeastern end of the field. Walking along the west side of the field, behind our F-4s and A-6s, I saw a VNAF O-1 Bird Dog single-engine, prop-driven observation airplane (same as a marine OE-1) flying north from Marble Mountain Airfield and passing to the north of the Da Nang bridge, along the Da Nang

River. The O-1 was flying at about a thousand feet, and as it came adjacent to downtown Da Nang on the east side of the river, I saw tracers from a .50-cal machine gun going up at it. The O-1 turned away to the east, but got hit and went down smoking, somewhere to the northeast of the Da Nang bridge and south of Monkey Mountain—in the vicinity of where Chaplain Roland and I had gone for a visit to a village to get church kneelers constructed. I thought, Who needs this on the way to R&R? I quickly went into the Red Dog, lit a good long cigar, and ordered a scotch and water. The drink came with ice in it these days. I drank for hours and listened only half heartedly to the rumors from those coming in the western-style swinging bar doors. I thought, Who cares? I'm on a week's vacation. The only problem is that I'm still not in Bangkok. I didn't even bother to leave the bar for lunch at the MAG-11 air wing mess hall. After many dart games and drinks, I decided to go back across the airfield to see if my transportation to Bangkok was able to land here. There still was much VNAF air activity, along with the normal marine F-4 and A-6 departures and landings. As I approached the air force side, I saw a U.S. Air Force C-130 parked near the R&R tents. By gosh, we were loading up for Bangkok! Before dark, it was wheels in the wheel wells and climbing up north over Hai Van Pass. A turn west caught the setting sun over Laos and behind that was my destination—Thailand. In a very short time I saw the gleaming Mekong River, which divided Laos from Thailand. I sat back wondering what that was all about back there at Da Nang. It was May 14, 1966, and I was heading for a week of R&R.

The next morning, while eating a late breakfast in a plush Bangkok hotel, I read the English-version newspaper. It covered the rebellion of the Buddhists of Hue and Da Nang. It described how back in March 1966, Premier Ky had flown up to Da Nang and fired the I Corps commander, Gen. Nguyen Chan Thi, and replaced him with General Chuan. General Chuan, it turned out, supported the local Da Nang Buddhists, who wanted Ky kicked out of office along with the rest of the government hierarchy. The period from March to May had seen numerous Buddhist-led labor strikes in Hue and Da Nang. There were marches by the demonstrators across the Perfume River in Hue, where the Buddhist leader Tri Quang had hoped to start a full-scale South Vietnamese revolution. He was supported by the Hue-located ARVN 1st Division commander, General Nhuan. The Buddhists in Da Nang had captured the Da Nang radio station and the municipal buildings. The Vietnamese I Corps fully supported them, as did units in Quang Nam and Quang Da provinces. Therefore, on the morning that I, unfortunately, was to leave for R&R, Premier Ky had moved his forces into Da Nang to stop the rebellion. The news article did not divulge just what the hell our III MAF commander, Gen. Lewis Walt, was doing, caught in the middle of this web with his troops and aviators. By the end of the third day it was over. Ky had won and had taken Tri Quang from Hue to Saigon.

During my wonderful vacation in Bangkok, I walked into a store that had a very large Bengal tiger rug with the immense tiger head intact. That exquisite rug was for sale for only six hundred dollars. I thought I should buy it for such an unbelievable deal. Then I thought how angry my wife would get, since she is a staunch conservationist for all wildlife. The thought also occurred to me what Ray Perry might think of it lying in my SEA hut. He might have some mixed emotions seeing it after that close encounter with a live tiger while he was evading the NVA after being shot down.

I kept my money in my wallet.

chapter 4

Return from R&R

Soon, Bangkok and its tremendous purchases of quality precious gems and jewelry passed too quickly. I was back at Marble Mountain Airfield, as if Bangkok had never happened. There, my fellow pilots brought me up to speed on the three-day revolution I had missed. This impacting activity among the Vietnamese at Da Nang and Hue simply added to our fighting men's disenchantment and confusion with the war effort on our part.

I was no sooner back from R&R when Padre Roland wanted help finding out where in the Da Nang area he could get a bell cast for his forthcoming wooden chapel. I asked all around the city. Even Lily Ann didn't know of an iron-casting place in Da Nang. Somehow the chaplain found one himself. In three weeks' time he had a very large chapel bell created at a foundry. This helped expedite construction of his now overdue wooden chapel, with a little bell tower. However, when the tower was completed, it turned out that the bell was too heavy and large to hang in it. So Father Roland had a stand built just in front of the chapel for the bell.

The spring and summer heat was now again with us. On one standard resupply mission to a unit back in the Que Son Mountains (the Hon Nui Tau area), I was number three plane in a four-plane division. We had already made three sorties carrying rations, water, and ammo from nearby An Hoa to an 886-meter-high mountaintop. On taking off to the east for a final sortie, all four of us were receiving fire from the opposite mountain peak across a deep valley. We all turned north, following the leader. I then noticed that my transmission fluid temperature was pegged in the red-line danger area. I must have gotten a round or two in the transmission, causing loss of transmission fluid. If the transmission were to freeze from lack of fluid, my rotors would stop and I wouldn't even be able to autorotate to a landing. I declared an emergency and my wingman followed me down to the flatlands near a village called Phu Loc. The other two planes of the first section returned to An Hoa, and two Huey gunships quickly came out from An Hoa to cover us while we were on the ground. No enemy appeared to be in our immediate area. In about an hour, a mighty CH-53 helicopter arrived and externally carried our sick UH-34D back to Marble Mountain AF. I rode back in my wingman's chopper. Previously, I had not known that the Que Son Mountains were so high and rugged until I now had to sit an hour at the very base of them near Phu Loc, with my downed bird.

A few days later I landed to drop off some deep reconnaissance troops out in the jungle to the west of Da Nang, south of Dong Den. While we sat in a small clearing as the troops disembarked, an air force herbicide-drop aircraft came low and almost directly over us spraying the defoliant vapor. It fell all over us, as well as on the dense vegetation. My rotating helicopter blades churned it up into a misty dust storm. It reminded me of the strong smell of chemicals that are spread upon the Southern California crops. Its odor was very repugnant and caused us to start drinking water from our canteens to kill the taste. The defoliant was being used to deny the enemy cover and concealment, thereby allowing us to push them farther back toward the Ho Chi Minh Trail and away from the population centers of the flatlands. It worked, causing the NVA to relocate many times.

A base was under construction to our immediate north, near our living-area tents and perimeter wire. It was built for the mountain people called Hmongs. They are tribesmen who do not look like the Vietnamese. They look like Indonesians and had lived in the mountains along the Ho Chi Minh Trail. They had been driven from the flatlands years ago by the Vietnamese. Now the North Vietnamese were forcing them to do coolie labor carrying ammunition and food south along the trail. The Hmongs hated the North Vietnamese, and our CIA and Special Forces had given them weapons to protect themselves from the NVA. They were paid for each set of NVA ears that they brought in. However, with the ever-increasing numbers of NVA flowing down the trail from North Vietnam, the Hmongs had to get out of the mountains if they were to survive and avoid slavery. They poured into the camp next to where I lived, bringing their families. They sure were a noisy group. Anytime, day or night, they would fire a rifle or machine gun—at what, I never knew.

Directly to our south, army Special Forces built a camp right off the end of our runway 18 departure. Below their camp and at the very base of Marble Mountain a POW camp was constructed.

On our own base, next to the parked helicopters on the west side, the U.S. Army began building wooden, two-story barracks for an L-19 (O-1) Bird Dog observation squadron. While the barracks were under construction, the army personnel lived in downtown Da Nang at the White Elephant Hotel. As we lived in leaking tents and then rusting sheds, we naturally were jealous watching the army ground and flight crews commute to our field from a hotel to fly their combat observation missions. Finally, several months later their barracks were completed and they moved onto our base as tenants. Shortly after, a small group of

U.S. Air Force personnel arrived to join the L-19 (O-1) squadron and to fly O-2 Super Skymaster, Cessna twin-engine observation (push-me, pull-you) aircraft that they brought with them. They also located on the west side of our now busy airfield and directly across from where the Seabees were progressing with construction of the navy hospital.

June 1966 arrived and I was scheduled to leave Vietnam on July 1, 1966. I had already received orders to report to Amphibious Warfare School in Quantico, Virginia. I had written to Eleanor to get ready to move to Quantico with the children. I flew normal day and night missions until one week before my scheduled departure date. I needed a full week to conduct a joint inventory of my hundreds of supply-line items with my relieving officer. We flew to Phu Bai and Tam Ky inventorying everything from individual rifles to tents and trucks. At the end of June, the inventory was complete. And, remarkably, there were only two things that I could not account for: an M-16 rifle and a tarpaulin. For three days I searched for both. I conducted another personal inspection of 620 rifles held by our MABS-16 personnel located all over from Tam Ky to Phu Bai. I went over the serial numbers until my vision was blurred. However, we had just gotten a new lieutenant colonel as commanding officer of MABS-16. He had just arrived in Nam several days before. He still felt like he was Stateside and didn't know what terrible events had happened and were continuing to happen. He not only insisted on my finding the missing rifle, but also the inexpensive missing tarpaulin. I offered to have the costs deducted from my pay. He refused that approach. He canceled my July 1 scheduled flight out of Da Nang on the Air America (Freedom Bird) jet airliner. I was furious. Here I had hundreds of line items from trucks, jeeps, Bay City cranes, generators, tents, walk-in refrigerators, and 620 rifles in combat and he is worried to death about a single rifle and a tarp. After my having been here well over a year, this asshole lieutenant colonel now cancels my flight home! I couldn't believe it was happening to me. Word spread and a lot of people tried to help me out.

While having a drink at our beach bar one night and wondering just when I would get out of this hellhole, another lieutenant colonel approached me.

"Bob, I've been reviewing the entire wing's pilot log books and I found out that you had twelve hundred flight hours in the old OE-1 Bird Dog back in Okinawa and North Carolina as a forward air controller airborne."

"Yes sir. That's a fact. What about it?" I asked.

"Well, we need an OE-1 instructor pilot here at Marble Mountain to get some new pilots trained to fly six OE-1 observation planes that we got out of mothballs from the States. It would only be about a three-month period and they would be fully ready for daily missions alone."

"Sir, what does that have to do with me? I was scheduled to leave tomorrow and hope to be out of here within a few days," I said.

"Well, I was hoping that you would like to volunteer to stay an extra three months," was his response.

"Colonel, I wouldn't want to tell you the words that I really have in mind for you. But I will say no thanks for the fine offer. I'm getting the hell out of here as fast as I can. Besides, you wouldn't want me to miss the fun of attending amphibious warfare school, would you?" At that time, I couldn't conceive of staying there another three months. In fact, I didn't know how I could last the next few extra days I was given to solve the missing rifle case.

As I sat in my hot supply tent on the second of July, my supply SNCO and three troopers came in. They had a cardboard box and the SNCO handed it to me.

"Sir, here's a going-home present for you."

I quickly took the top off the box. I almost fell over. It was a shiny M-16 rifle stock mounted on a shiny wooden base. A plaque on the wooden rifle stock read, "To Captain Stoffey—From the NCOs and Men of MABS-16."

"Top, I don't know how to thank you for such a fine going-away gift. Believe me, it will be a memorable sayonara gift. Particularly in view of the fact that I am still stuck here in hell, two extra days already because of that missing rifle in inventory."

"Well sir, we had planned to give you this before the missing rifle issue came up. So here it is."

"Top, this isn't the missing rifle, is it?"

"No sir," the SNCO replied and ran out to the MABS-16 utilities tent to produce the rifle part. He handed me a bent, rusty rifle. I looked closely at the serial number. It was not from our serial numbers lot.

"Where did you get this piece of junk?" I asked.

"Somebody brought it back from the field in a chopper. It was badly damaged in combat. But the stock was good enough to make a gift for you."

"Thanks. Thanks very much," I answered and then walked over to Major Bates's utilities section to thank them for doing such a nice job on making the rifle stock look so good.

The next morning, Maj. Joe Mix, the MAG-16 group supply officer, came into my tent. He handed me an almost new-looking M-16 rifle and his sergeant carried in a tarpaulin.

"Here you are, Captain. Your ticket to the real world via the Freedom Bird," said Major Mix.

I didn't know how to thank the major and simply asked, "Where did you get the rifle?"

"Don't ask me. But I have cleared this with your CO. The records are straight, although this serial number is different."

It took me just thirty minutes to check out and get to Da Nang. To my dismay, the next several days of commercial airline jets were booked by departing GIs. The marines had a C-130 MARLOG flight departing the next morning. I got scheduled on that.

The next morning, July 4, 1966, I was airborne en route to Okinawa. As the plane climbed out over the South China Sea, I looked back at Marble Mountain Airfield and Vietnam fading away. It only then occurred to me as to what happened to the missing rifle. It was the rifle that the MABS-16 water truck driver had with him when he drove the truck over the mine, just minutes before the October 27, 1965, attack upon our airfield. That was eight months ago. We all had forgotten that when the mine blew up the truck and killed the driver, the rifle was destroyed. My armory personnel simply had not properly recorded the loss of that weapon. Then my mind swept over the entire night of October 27 and morning of October 28. I personally had directed some of my reaction-force personnel to throw a tarpaulin into a dump truck. I didn't want to get a lot of VC blood all over the truck and I wanted to make it easier for pulling out the seventeen dead VC near the Da Nang bridge. The missing tarp was left under the dead VC at the Da Nang bridge that morning.

As we flew along, I saw land to our left. I thought, What the hell is that? We're not crossing to Okinawa; that's the coastline of China. I crawled up into the C-130 pilots' compartment and asked the pilot, "Where are we going?"

"We're making a short stop in Hong Kong. I dropped off my crew chief there yesterday to buy me a few items. He'll be at Kai Tak Airfield in Kowloon when we land. It'll only take a few minutes."

We landed at about 1130 on the Fourth of July. The crew chief was not there waiting for his C-130. It must have been 115 degrees in the C-130 fuselage.

"Gentlemen, you are free to get out of the aircraft and stretch a little. But do not leave the area of the aircraft. None of you have R&R orders to Hong Kong, nor a passport. So you can't even go into the air terminal," shouted the pilot in command, while inside the belly of the cargo aircraft.

The crew chief then arrived carrying several large boxes of purchases. Then the pilot in command shouted to all of us, "Sorry. Bad news. We can't take off until 1300. Kai Tak Airfield closes daily from 1200 to 1300."

So we all sat under the wings of the C-130. It was a hot Fourth of July. But not as hot as Vietnam. It wasn't Vietnam, so it couldn't be all that bad. We sat there on the hot parking apron looking across the bay to Hong Kong at the many white skyscrapers of bustling Hong Kong and at the beat-up old, large Chinese junks all over the bay. We weren't in Okinawa on our way home. But we weren't in Vietnam.

Finally, after 1300, we were airborne and en route to Okinawa. While looking down below at the puffy white clouds, I reviewed my good and bad memories of my first combat tour in Vietnam. To go along with those memories, I had a bagful of 8-mm personal movies that I had taken flying and on the ground. The movies included scenes of the smoldering ruins of our helicopters. I took that scene as the sun was coming up on the morning of October 28, 1965, after the ground attack against us at Marble Mountain Airfield.

After landing in Okinawa, I purchased a new khaki uniform to replace the mildewed and rotted uniform that had lain unused in my SEA hut over a year in Nam. I then soaked a year's dirt from my body in a "hotsy" bath for hours.

Soon, I was flying back across our great country to Newark Airport for an extremely happy reunion with Eleanor, Monica, and Bobby.

Within days, Nam was truly seven thousand miles away. Unable to sell our home during my thirty-day leave period, we left it empty in the hands of a realtor and headed for Quantico, Virginia, and attendance at a five-month amphibious warfare school.

At Quantico, I was soon to learn that my thirteen months of combat experience did not match the school's curriculum. The Marine Corps Principles of Warfare presented at the school were sound, basic, historically proven ways to militarily run a war; not at all the way our stupid government was forcing our military leaders to defend South Vietnam. The other Vietnam vets and I were completely disillusioned by the classroom work that was not relevant to "our war."

After graduation, I received orders to Marine Corps Air Facility, Santa Ana, California. Another mid-school-year move for the family located us in San Juan Capistrano. Here, I flew helicopters from Santa Ana and fixed-wing aircraft from Marine Corps Air Station (MCAS) El Toro for two years.

I was then very lucky. I received orders to transition to the new North American Rockwell OV-10A Bronco at Camp Pendleton, California. In January 1969, I was assigned to be officer in charge of an eight-plane OV-10A detachment to take ten pilots, eight aerial observers, and forty enlisted men to Vietnam for my second combat tour.

PART II

Captain Stoffey outside of pilot's ready room tent of HMM-365, Marine Medium Helicopter Squadron, at Da Nang Airfield in early 1965.

Flight crew of a gunned-down H-34 Dog running toward a rescue helicopter, and carrying an M-60 machine gun from their downed bird, south of Da Nang in 1965. (*USMC photo*)

Army of the Republic of Vietnam (ARVN) troops being dropped off in Landing Zone (LZ) Charlie Ridge from U.S. Marine Corps H-34 helo. (*USMC photo*)

Colonel "Pappy" Boyington, left, of World War II "Ba Ba Black Sheep" squadron fame, visiting Marine F-4 Phantom fighter lines at Da Nang in summer of 1965. (*USMC photo*)

Marine Air Group 16 (MAG-16) chaplain serving local Vietnamese civilians to the east of Da Nang in early fall 1965. (*USMC photo*)

Marine H-34 Dog lifting off near Da Nang during summer of 1965. (*Courtesy of Roger Herman, President of USMC Vietnam Helicopter Pilots Association*)

M-60 machine gun emplacement overlooking VMO-2 Huey gunship flight line at Marble Mountain Airfield three miles east of Da Nang. This particular gun position stopped a fair amount of attacking North Vietnamese on their raid of the airfield in October 1965. This same sand dune was later the site of the South Korean observation commander's living quarters bunker that the author removed in 1969.

VMO-2 Huey destroyed by enemy sapper attack on Marble Mountain Airfield. On the last night of the October 1965 battle, the enemy ground forces destroyed nineteen helicopters and damaged thirty-five others so badly that they were evacuated to Taiwan for repair. (USMC photo)

VIET-NAM — 1965

Marine Air Group 16 chaplain conducting services on China Beach in 1965. (*USMC photo*)

Here come the CH-46 helos and they have .50-caliber machine guns. The older, more tired H-34 choppers only had M-60 7.62mm machine guns. (*USMC photo*)

Marines charge from a CH-46 rear ramp in Nam in 1966. *(USMC photo)*

OV-10 on rocket attack against North Vietnamese. Note that top of wing is painted white to enable attack jet bombers to see forward air controller (FAC) against the green countryside of Vietnam. *(USMC photo)*

A Marine OV-10 with full ordnance load of four rocket pods, center line Gatling gun, and four M-60 machine guns. *(Courtesy of North American Rockwell)*

LZ Grant at BT 069638—a large rice paddy sixteen miles south of Da Nang in 1969.

Sunset in Vietnam as two VMO-2 single-engine Cobras return from a mission to Marble Mountain Airfield in 1969.
(Courtesy of Bell Helicopter Textron)

Marine F-4 B Phantom dropping a 500-pound retarded "snakeye" bomb on Viet Cong trenches concealed in a tree line south of Da Nang. *(National Archives)*

VMO-2 achieves 30,000 accident-free flight hours. CO, Lieutenant Colonel Stoffey to left of sign; maintenance officer, Major Wickersham to left of CO; maintenance chief, Master Sergeant Suarez, second row between CO and maintenance officer; XO, Major Ellis to right of sign; and Sergeant Major Yodler on extreme far left. *(USMC photo)*

VMO-2 squadron ready to launch all eighteen aircraft, led by Skipper, Lieutenant Colonel Stoffey in "00" aircraft. (*USMC photo*)

Lieutenant Colonel Stoffey receiving Vietnamese Air Cross of Gallantry from Vice Admiral James L. Holloway III, Commander, Seventh Fleet, November 9, 1972, on board USS *Oklahoma City*. (*USN photo*)

chapter 5

Vietnam, 1969–1970

It was a dark, overcast morning at 0200 when our Flying Tiger Airline jet transport touched down at Cam Ranh Bay, Republic of Vietnam. Cam Ranh Bay had a U.S. Air Force air group of F-4 Phantoms and a U.S. Navy patrol squadron of P-3 Orions. All fifty-four of us were tired and sleepy from the long trip from California. I checked into the navy air traffic coordinating office and woke up a sailor who had the night duty.

"I have a detachment of fifty-four people and we'll be staying here at Cam Ranh Bay for about a week. Did the 1st Marine

Aircraft Wing at Da Nang make reservations for us here in your barracks?" I asked the sleepy sailor.

"No sir. We never heard of any marines scheduled to come through here."

"Well, start looking for sleeping quarters for fourteen officers and forty enlisted personnel."

"I'll have to wake up the officer of the day," the sailor said.

"Wake him up. I have some very tired people here from a trip from CONUS."

After an hour of trying to find sleeping quarters for my detachment, the OD returned saying that he could come up with only forty beds. I told him that the officers will sleep here on the floor of the terminal and give the beds to the enlisted men. We'll get some officers' sleeping areas in the morning when everybody around here is awake. I then asked the OD how I could call Da Nang and the 1st Marine Aircraft Wing. He showed me the phone and left to resume his sleep.

I got in touch with the wing duty officer and told him that the OV-10A detachment had arrived in Cam Ranh Bay. I asked him if he had any instructions for me.

"OV-10A detachment? Nobody told me about a detachment coming into Cam Ranh Bay. I'll have to check with the operations officer when he comes into work at 0700," he responded.

I told the enlisted men that we would have a muster here at the terminal at 1400. They shoved off for the barracks and much-needed sleep. The officers and I fell asleep on the floor of the terminal.

At 0730, I was awakened by the phone ringing. The navy ATCO told me that it was the wing operations officer up in Da Nang.

The operations officer told me, "None of us at Da Nang expected an OV-10 detachment until next week. Why are you a week early?"

"Colonel, your general sent a message to our 3rd Wing commander and asked for us to get out here a week early."

"Major, I never saw such a message. However, I'll ask the general about it at breakfast shortly. I'll call you back later this morning to discuss it."

"Okay, Colonel. Be aware that I have fifty-four people here

with eight OV-10A Broncos. We will have to get the aircraft off of the aircraft carrier and tear off the cocoon skins. Then we'll have to test-fly each aircraft here and repair any deficiencies. Therefore, I figure it'll take us five working days from tomorrow to be ready to fly 'em north."

"I'll tell the general and we'll pass that on to your group commander at MAG-16, over at Marble Mountain Airfield."

"Colonel, that brings up another question. Are all eight aircraft and all of the people going to Marble Mountain?"

"Hell, Major, I don't know. Nobody here even expected you. I'll have to staff that up here and get back with you on that too."

At 1100 I received a call from the wing operations officer. "I talked to the general. He was surprised that you are a week early. He said that he did not request your general in California to send you a week early. Additionally, he said that he doesn't know where to send you. I'll staff it and talk to the two air groups and get back with you later."

"Yes sir, Colonel. But don't tell any of my officers and men here, just not yet, that nobody wanted them out here a week early. I had one man cut short a honeymoon, another man left a partially painted house, and the rest aren't happy about leaving their families, for thirteen months, a week earlier than necessary."

"I'm sorry, Major. Sounds like some overeager decision makers back at your old command screwed you all up. I'll talk with you later."

By noon, I was down at the bay dockside getting the large cranes to offload the OV-10s from the carrier that had arrived just a day before.

At 1400 I held muster of my detachment and simply told them that I didn't know where we'd be going after we test-flew the aircraft. We all went down and tore the cocoons of rubber skin off of the aircraft. A few days went by and we had test-flown half of them.

A marine R-4D transport landed one afternoon and a warrant officer and SNCO came out of it looking for me. He was a personnel officer from the 1st MAW headquarters.

"Major, the chief of staff sent me down to help you decide where you should take your detachment," he smartly told me.

"I thought that you knew where we were going."

"Well, nobody made any plans to absorb eight aircraft and crews."

"Gunner, there's only two places that OV-10s can go: VMO-6 at Quang Tri, or VMO-2 at Marble Mountain. Now where do you want to send us?"

"Major, I don't care where you want to go. Just let me know, and I'll handle the administrative papers of assignments at wing."

"I'll tell you what, Gunner. I'm going to hold a muster and ask the troops where *they* want to go. I've decided to split it down the middle; half the unit to Quang Tri and the other half to Marble Mountain. That goes for the aircraft too."

I did just that, and surprisingly it worked out that everybody got exactly what they wanted. I didn't have to tell anybody to go to either of the bases. The gunner was happy and took all the names and to what base they were going. He then departed for Da Nang on the R-4D.

Several days later, all eight aircraft were ready and the wing sent the same R-4D down to take the forty maintenance men to both Quang Tri and Marble Mountain Airfield.

I was to take four planes to Marble Mountain and the other four were going to Quang Tri, located above Hue city near the DMZ. Therefore, we broke down into two four-plane divisions. However, we briefed the weather and flight-planned separately. Captains Bart Nole, Ron Macky, Bob Bracket, and Paul Brown decided to go with me to Marble Mountain.

We all took off with the eight aircraft together and climbed out, heading north from Cam Ranh Bay. The January winter rains precluded us from seeing much of the countryside as we flew up the coast, skirting the large thunderbumpers. I really didn't see any of the once familiar landscape of Vietnam as we continued past Nha Trang and Qui Nhon toward Da Nang.

At ten miles on the 170 radial of the Da Nang TACAN, I kissed off the second division of four OV-10s and descended through and around puffy clouds to enter a thousand-foot downwind leg of Marble Mountain Airfield's runway 18. Coming down through the weather, I had fleeting thoughts of my friend Bill Miller, in his F-4, crashing into Monkey Mountain one night during my last tour. Now I was below the weather, and saw Marble Mountain first, then Monkey Mountain and Da Nang Bay. The familiar city of Da Nang loomed on my nose as I passed through the 180-degree turn to final landing. The other four OV-10s continued north toward Quang Tri.

After landing our four OV-10 aircraft on the runway, we taxied onto the VMO-2 parking apron. It now was on the east side of the runway, along with the helicopter parking areas. All those squadrons had been on the west side of the runway two and a half years ago. Now I saw U.S. Army choppers and OV-1B Mohawk Grumman twin-turboprop sensor aircraft, U.S. Air Force O-2 Skymaster, push-me–pull-you Cessna twin-engine FAC spotter aircraft, and Korean OE-1 FAC spotter aircraft all parked on our old west side of the runway. The airfield no longer was just marines, but all services and a mix of aircraft.

After parking the aircraft, we walked into the pilots' ready room. I checked in with the executive officer, Maj. Mark Hall, who said, "Nobody at group or wing said that more pilots and OV-10s were coming. The CO isn't here now. But you can meet him in the morning."

The XO got a truck for us to get to our new homes. I moved into a Quonset hut that had a plyboard wall divider allowing for two field-grade officers to live in each half. Four of us to a Quonset hut was pretty good living for a major, in contrast to a large group of us crowded into a tent during my first tour of duty here. I walked over to the old tent area that we had changed into SEA huts two and a half years before. I stood in front of my old tent and had several flashbacks. The SEA hut was now old and rusty and occupied by senior enlisted flight crews. Never in my wildest dreams did I ever think that I'd ever be back here at the same place in the same stinking war.

There now was an officers' mess hall in the beachside officers' club. I had dinner, then went into the club bar. I asked around for the commanding officer of VMO-2. Someone pointed him out to me. He was sitting at the bar with a major. I walked up and introduced myself to him. I explained that we'd brought eight aircraft into the country and that I'd brought four here along with half the number of crews and maintenance personnel.

"Major, nobody told me that I had four more aircraft and

crews coming now. I'll see you in the squadron in the morning."

That was it. No welcome aboard; no handshake. He abruptly turned away from me to resume his conversation with the other major. I thought, Shit, this guy could care less that he has new planes and people. I walked away to the other end of the bar. To my surprise, Maj. Frank Adams was there. I hadn't seen him in years. He was the angel chopper pilot that had pulled my friend George Gross out of the Atlantic when his OE-1 crashed upon one of our returns from the Caribbean, with my two cases of rum aboard. Frank also flew with me in the HRS-3 helicopters in Japan. We small-talked and he told me that he had gotten out of the Corps but had now returned to fly CH-46 helicopters in this war. I then ran into some VMO-2 pilots. They were captains. I told them about the CO not being too friendly on the welcome aboard. They said that he talked only to a handful of his pilots— only the ones that he came over to Vietnam with, and soon that group would all be going home with him. I thought that was odd, but believable, after his cool reception of me at the bar.

After a few drinks, I returned to my new home in the Quonset hut. To my surprise two of my closest friends were there waiting to greet me, Maj. Len Bland and Maj. George Gross. Each had a drink in his hand when I walked into my hootch. George was fast to give me a rum and Coke, and we discussed where each of us had been the previous two and a half years. None of us could believe we were back here in Nam. Len didn't have to be here. He already had his twenty years of service in and could have retired right after his last combat tour here. However, he wanted to try for lieutenant colonel, so he decided to stay and they shipped him back here like George and me. We drank late into the night, talking about our earlier days of flying in Okinawa and the Caribbean. George and I laughed at ourselves when discussing our rum-and-Coke drinking in our foxhole at our old tent here in Nam back in '65. The very tent area located just about thirty yards from where we were living now. Then Len hit us both with a hard one.

"You know guys, I just don't feel right about this tour here. I don't feel like I felt during my last combat tour. I just don't see beyond this trip. I hate to say it, but I have a very strong feeling that I'm not going to make it out of here this time."

"Damn it, Len. Your drinks are cut off now. Go to your hootch. Don't be talking so damn silly," said George.

I didn't comment. This was my first night back in town. So we broke up for the night feeling very uneasy about Len's comment.

As soon as George and Len left, Maj. Benny Bart came in and introduced himself to me as my roommate in this half of the Quonset hut, and also as a VMO-2 pilot. He had just returned from a night OV-10A mission. This was my first meeting with Benny. Somehow, over the years, we had never served together. Benny was too tired to give me much of a briefing on the squadron, its flying activities, and the war situation in general. He hit the rack from exhaustion.

The next morning I checked in with the executive officer. He assigned me to be the personnel and administrative officer of the squadron. I then drew my survival pistol from the squadron armory. I just then realized that in the OV-10A you did not wear body armor like we did flying the helicopters during my last combat tour. I hadn't thought about that until the moment that I drew my weapon from the armory. In the OV-10 you wore a G suit and a torso harness plus a chest-pack survival kit with a .38 pistol. Your torso harness attached you to the ejection seat, which had a parachute attached to it. There simply was no room for body armor to be worn.

I walked into the pilots' ready room. It reminded me of a football player's locker room. Here all the players were suited up with their flight suits on; helmets next to them. They were getting briefed on their next mission, like football players getting their last-minute instructions. In the next room, intelligence (S-2) was conducting debriefings of the pilots who had just returned from a mission. What did they see, what did they do, what went wrong, how many NVA did they kill, what changed out on the battlefield? Yep, I thought, just like a football game; except that the stakes are higher and the pay is much lower.

At this time, VMO-2 still had three UH-1E Hueys left and were transferring these within a few weeks to another squadron that had formed an HML, or light helicopter squadron. Since receipt of the OV-10A Bronco aircraft during June 1968, the UH-1Es began phasing out as more OV-10s came into the inventory. One of the Huey pilots who had been in-country a year and a half already, Capt. Frank Wick, had decided to volunteer to stay longer and to fly the OV-10A. So Frank didn't transfer to the new HML squadron with the Hueys, nor did he go home as he could have. We would soon be strictly an OV-10 squadron. There are two crew members in the OV-10. The pilot flew the armed reconnaissance aircraft from the front seat. The aerial observer (AO) sat in the rear seat to assist in seeking out the enemy. The OV-10 pilot had to be a designated forward air controller (FAC). He also had to be trained in naval gunfire support control and artillery control. The rear-seated AO had to have had a minimum of six months of ground combat experience as a ground officer. He had to have been an artillery or infantry officer. The AO was a volunteer who wanted to fly. He was then sent to the States for an AO training period and returned to fly in Vietnam in the OV-10A. The pilot and AO team both were capable of controlling and coordinating all supporting arms of close air support (FAC), naval gunfire (NGFS), and artillery. The missions normally were single-plane FAC missions, and generally we had three OV-10s airborne in different areas of the Da Nang TAOR (tactical area of responsibility) at any given time. VMO-6, with its OV-10s at Quang Tri, covered the DMZ and Hue city areas.

On my second day in VMO-2, I had my first familiarization flight with Capt. Herman A. Graves, "Hostage Victor," on January 29, 1969. It was flight-coded 1V3, meaning daylight, reconnaissance, visual gunfire spotting.

Captain Graves took me up over the TAOR, and we flew a FAM hop all over that area in about a thirty-mile arc. I was completely shocked. The South Vietnamese countryside was like the moon. I wasn't mentally ready to observe the destruction that had been wrought over this once beautiful green countryside since I left here just two and a half years ago. Village after village had been burned down. The villagers were now probably living as refugees in the Da Nang city area—those who were still alive. Bomb craters were all over the rice paddies; many were filled with water from the winter's rain. The Vietnamese bury their dead in burial sites that are covered with round mounds of dirt next to their villages. These thousands of burial mounds used to stand out from the rice paddies and hills when I flew over them in my helicopter during my previous tour of duty. Now there were so many bomb, naval gunfire, and artillery craters dotting the countryside that it was hard to distinguish grave-site mounds from bomb craters as I flew rapidly overhead. If our Congress had backed any of the presidents who were controlling the war here, and if we had been directed to expend that amount of ordnance on Hanoi and Haiphong in North Vietnam, the war would have been over in several days.

Captain Graves then said, "Major, that's just about the entire area that we daily work in. So now I'll show you how easily you can spot an NVA gooner from this OV-10A. We'll fly over to the Arizona free-kill zone."

We headed for a large, flat area located two miles to the west of our An Hoa airstrip and artillery base. Just west, across the Song Thi Bon River and about three miles north of the Coal Mines, was an area that our marines had fought hard over. It had many villages throughout, including Quang Dai, Phu Xuan, An Phu. Each time our marines withdrew, the North Vietnamese troops moved back into the villages. All we pilots had to do was check with our grunts on the ground at An Hoa to determine if we had reconnaissance patrols or assault companies in that flat, contested area named after an operation called Arizona. If there were no friendlies in the area, we could shoot at any NVA without any ground coordination.

Captain Graves and I were over this approximately ten-mile-square area. We were there only about five minutes when we saw two NVA regulars dashing from a water well in the village of Tap Phuc. They had heard our noisy OV-10 and then seen it approaching. They ran north from Tap Phuc and into a dense treeline. Captain Graves turned the OV-10 away and back toward An Hoa and climbed into the sun. Sure enough, as I looked back, the NVA troops came back out of the treeline and were walking toward the village, thinking that we were gone. Captain Graves had us passing through four thousand feet and then he rolled the aircraft into a wingover maneuver turning 180 degrees and lowering the nose for airspeed and dive-angle attack. I looked around his left shoulder and through the nose windscreen and saw the two NVA each carrying a rifle and still heading back to the village. Captain Graves now had them in his sight picture in the front cockpit. Coming out of the sun and at that altitude, the two enemy soldiers never saw the attack. *Woom!*—one rocket fired and Captain Graves executed a positive six-G pullup. The six Gs sunk me into the back seat and I couldn't look back to see what the hit result was. I then, for the first time, realized how much more the guy in the rear seat felt the six-G pullups in the OV-10. I always tried to remember this for my rear-seat AOs during my numerous later missions. The guy actually flying the aircraft doesn't mind the G-force pulls as much as a passenger, because he's busy flying the aircraft with the controls.

When Captain Graves passed through 3,500 feet, he rolled the aircraft over so we could look for our single rocket impact. Beside a large black smudge on the green ground, I saw only a single rifle and some piles of dirt. That was two less gooners that would be trying to kill South Vietnamese or U.S. Marines. While heading back from the FAM hop, Captain Graves said, "If you look for them, you can get two to ten per day without even being involved in a battle."

From now on it would be me and an aerial observer flying our assigned missions. The FAM hop was over.

My assigned personal call sign was "Hostage Uniform." Unlike all the jet attack fixed-wing squadrons or helicopter squadrons, we in VMO squadrons had personal call signs. The other pilots used the squadron call sign only. In our case, the squadron call sign was "Hostage." Added to that was a call sign for each FAC pilot. My call sign, "Uniform," was simply added to the "Hostage." Additionally, the aerial observer in the rear seat had the AO call sign of "Cowpoke" and then a number assigned to each AO. For example, the senior aerial observer at the time was Capt. T. J. Hart, "Cowpoke Six," and Capt. J. W. Spruce was designated "Cowpoke Fifteen." The obvious reason for this personalizing of call signs was that since we controlled most of the close-air-support bombing and much of the artillery and naval gunfire, we could very easily accidentally kill or injure our own friendly troops. Therefore, there never was a question as to who it was in the OV-10A that ran the airstrike or other supporting arms.

The next day, as I climbed out from runway 18 at Marble Mountain Airfield, I rapidly passed over new installations next to our base. Immediately after takeoff to the south of the airfield there was now a marine reconnaissance base. Next to that, toward the mountain called Marble Mountain, was a prisoner of war camp. As my landing gear retracted up into my fuselage, I glanced down at these POWs. They were mostly North Vietnamese. Personally, by now I believed most of the Viet Cong guerrillas were killed, except for a few holding out in the jungles waiting for the North Vietnamese to take South Vietnam. The POWs looked like they had a pretty good deal down there walking around their wired-in cantonment, rather than living in the bush and getting shot at. As I continued to climb south directly over Marble Mountain, I instinctively scanned toward the southwest. I was looking for the old abandoned leper colony that the North Vietnamese briefly captured during my last tour. The damaged buildings were still there. No sign of life or activity was seen. I had flown over this part of the country so much that I felt that I knew every inch, every hill, every village. It all came back to me now, as I leveled at five thousand feet and flew toward Hill 55. The old names came back rapidly—"Charlie Ridge," "Elephant Valley," "Hoa Van Pass." Everything was the same except for the battle-scarred land. I checked in, on my assigned frequency, with the major air-controlling agency in the area—"Da Nang DASC."

"Da Nang DASC, this is Hostage Uniform checking in on flight three-zero with a single OV-10. Over."

"Roger, Hostage Uniform. This is Da Nang DASC. We have you relieving Hostage Sierra"—Maj. R. L. Peters—"who was working with Hanover Sue. Report to Hanover Sue on button Orange now."*

"Roger DASC, Hanover Sue on Orange. Hostage Uniform out."

I switched my FM radio to 60.45 and headed for the artillery unit located at An Hoa Airfield, about twenty-five miles south of Da Nang.

"Hanover Sue, this is Hostage Uniform with Cowpoke Four reporting in." Cowpoke Four was 1st Lt. William Berry.

---

*This refers to switching FM radio to frequency numbers identified by code of colors as orange, purple, green, and so on.

"Roger, Hostage Uniform. We have you in sight. We are firing two batteries, and the other Hostage aircraft has just left the area. We are ready to resume firing as soon as you are set up for spotting and adjustments. You are cleared into the area. Over."

"Roger, Hostage. Break. Cowpoke Four, are you ready for fire adjustments?"

"This is Cowpoke Four. Go ahead and give me your gun-target line, targets that you have been shooting at, and number of guns you are going to fire."

We received the gun-target line, or line of fire from the known artillery positions to the target. We would stay well clear of that imaginary line so as not to cross it and accidentally get shot down by our own artillery shells. The target area was a complex of caves three-quarters of the way up the western cliff of the Que Son Mountains to the southeast of An Hoa. The area was called Hon Nui Tau. The mountains rose to 886 meters high. My AO picked up the artillery mission and adjusted the hits in the hills until we started getting hits right on the caves. I simply flew the aircraft around so that when the arty unit said, "On the way," we would be in a good visual position to see the shells impact on the targets. The AO would then say, "Splash . . . wait one." He then would call in the corrections to adjust the artillery to improve the hits. When enough shells were impacting on the targets, he then would call the artillery and direct them to "Fire for effect." This would then have four, eight, or twelve guns firing at the same time and really impacting the target area. After two hours of artillery spotting it was time to head for home. The artillery had pretty much destroyed the caves. If there were gooners in there, they were now buried under rocks and rubble. It was a boring first mission for me. But while some of the combat missions were boring, others were too exciting.

Like the other pilots in the VMO, I generally flew two missions a day, each a two-and-a-half-hour mission. Again, as in the previous combat tour, war knew no Saturdays or Sundays. Every day and night is work time.

I quickly fell into the routine of flying and doing my squadron's administrative paperwork. Our squadron operating area was vastly improved over my previous tour. We occupied a large metal prefabricated building hangar. All offices easily fit into this large hangar, except the aircraft maintenance office. Maintenance offices were located on the aircraft flight line, which had six SEA huts for the various service divisions, called work centers, such as hydraulics, avionics, ordnance, engines, and so forth. Next to our large hangar, we had four other similar hangars for a CH-53 squadron of heavy-hauler helicopters and for three CH-46 squadrons. Their aircraft, like ours, were parked out in front of the hangars and flight-line shacks. Each squadron had its aircraft protected from mortar and rocket attacks by lines of fifty-five gallon drums filled with sand and stacked three tiers high. Only the CH-53 rotors and the OV-10 tails stood higher than the protective barrels of sand forming parking revetments.

A typical mission occurred on February 2, 1969, when I flew aircraft serial number 155451. My AO, Cowpoke Eighteen, was 1st Lt. R. Towne. We briefed in S-2 on what the latest friendly and enemy situation was, particularly in the area of the 3rd Battalion, 26th Marine Regiment, in the vicinity of AT 868527. This unit was undergoing intensive automatic-weapons-fire attack during a sweep of this area in the Arizona zone near the village of Phu Xuan. The 3rd Battalion had been conducting a large-scale sweep when the resistance increased, and they were expecting an NVA counterattack.

As Lieutenant Towne checked the three fuel refiller caps in the top of the wing to make sure that they were secured and then checked the array of circuit breakers behind his rear ejection seat, I preflighted all around the outside of the OV-10. I particularly checked the guns and their 7.62-mm bullets and linkage and feed in the sponsons. I checked the wiring and security of the rockets in the pods attached below the sponsons. The aircraft ordnance normal combat load consisted of four rocket pods of nineteen 2.75-inch FFARs (folding-fin aircraft rockets); thirty-eight of these long rockets had high-explosive heads for destruction of targets and thirty-eight had white phosphorus warheads for marking the targets for our jet close-air-support bombers. The four rocket pods were attached at stations located on the two sponsons. Within these two sponsons were located a total of four M-60 machine guns, each loaded with a thousand rounds of 7.62-mm NATO bullets. Additionally, on the centerline station, where an external fuel tank is carried in peacetime, was located an SUU-11 A/A "Gatling" machine gun with 7.62-mm bullets. This external store of the SUU-11 Gatling gun placed an airspeed carriage limitation of 350 knots and a maximum speed of 325 knots when firing this gun. It also placed a maximum acceleration limit of plus six Gs and negative one G to the aircraft's capabilities. The maximum speed of the OV-10 was not the problem. For good, low-altitude FAC work, the problem was to fly slowly enough to see the enemy. With all of that ordnance aboard, it was difficult to slow down below 110 knots and do much maneuvering to see the enemy on the ground clearly, avoid getting hit by ground fire, and avoid stalling out a wing. Once you burned down on fuel and expended many of your rockets, you could slow down to 100 knots, but not too comfortably.

After preflighting the outside of the bird, the AO and I climb into our cockpits. The lengthy checklist is then gone over in a routine to avoid missing something. The ejection seats are first checked: ejection seat D-ring pin removed and stowed, emergency radio beacon lanyard lines secured, speed/altitude sensor checked, seat-man separator secured, thruster safety pin removed, thruster line slug secured, chute thruster static line secured, catapult retention bolt secured.

After the ejection-seat inspection, it is time to make the cockpit check: fasten survival kit, fasten lap belt and riser straps, remove landing gear pins and stow in map case, then close canopy and secure canopy brace; HF radio off, flap-handle set for thirty degrees for takeoff, yaw damper off, external lights as desired, power levers in flight idle, condition levers on fuel shutoff, battery off, generator switches automatic, UHF radio switch off, master armaments switch off, set clock, radar altimeter off, alternate TACAN power switch off, TACAN off, fuel gauge select to internal tanks, fuel emergency shutoff switches normal, pitot heat off, windscreen wiper off, anticollision light on, oxygen regulators checked for quantity, oxygen diluter set at 100 percent, IFF (identification friend or foe) master transponder switch off, bleed air normal, interior lights as desired, circuit breakers all in.

Now for the prestart checklist: set parking brakes locked, close access steps, have ground crew remove wheel chocks, clear propellers, throw battery switch on and check voltage, test-fire detection warning lights, and have ground crew turn on plugged-in external power unit.

For starting one engine at a time: clear that prop, turn on start switch, and as engine comes up to 10 percent RPM, move condition lever to normal flight position; inverter number one switch on, monitor EGT (exhaust-gas temperature), engine RPM and oil pressure, generator light out, test-fire detection lights, turn on FM, UHF, and HF radios, check gunsight, have ground crew disconnect external power. Repeat the engine-start sequence for the second turbine engine.

Before taxiing the aircraft: check instrument power inverter number two and reset to number one, turn on radar altimeter and set desired altitude for warning light to come on, slave compass, ammeter check on both generators, set compass, trim aircraft for neutral rudder and aileron and one unit down for elevator trim, cage attitude gyro indicator, set TACAN channel, test fuel gauge and quantity, set IFF to standby, check full travel of flight control stick and rudder pedals, check operation of flaps and reset to thirty degrees, make sure that ejection-seat D-ring pin is removed, hold brakes with toe pressure, reverse one power lever momentarily and note 71 percent RPM after propeller unlocks, repeat reverse power lever to unlock other prop and check 71 percent RPM at flight idle, set altimeter, check brakes to ascertain working order, roll forward and check nose wheel steering, and test yaw damper. Taxi out to the ordnance arming area. The arming crew connects the electrical circuitry to the weapons and checks for stray electrical voltage in armament systems, and aircraft is armed. Taxi to runway.

Prior to taking the active-duty runway, go over the before-takeoff checklist: seats armed, check fuel quantity, check 260 pounds of fuel in center feed fuel tank, external fuel transfer off, pitot heat as desired, cockpit heat as desired, flap handle set for thirty degrees, set takeoff trim, compute temperature and torque limits based on outside air temperature, canopy locked, shoulder harness locked. Switch from ground control to tower frequency for departure.

"Tower, this is Hostage Uniform, ready for takeoff."

"Hostage Uniform is cleared to take the duty runway and

cleared for immediate takeoff. Please expedite. Army CV-2 Caribou inbound on final. Switch frequencies passing three miles."

"Roger Tower. Hostage Uniform cleared for takeoff."

I took the duty runway and gave a quick glance around the cockpit and pushed both condition levers to takeoff position of 95 percent, lined up with the centerline and held the brakes, switched on the IFF to normal, checked full movement of the stick and rudder controls . . . pushed both power levers to military power of 101 percent and began rolling, using a little rudder pedal action to ensure a perfect roll down the runway and transmitted, "Tower, Hostage Uniform on the roll."

Rolling until I reached 106 knots of airspeed because of my twelve thousand pounds of gross weight due to my heavy ordnance load, I then pulled back on the stick and lifted the OV-10 off the runway. When well clear of the runway and after checking engine RPM, EGT, and oil pressure, I raised the landing-gear handle. Passing through 115 knots, I raised the flap handle from the thirty-degree position to zero degrees flaps. In a 160-knot climb and departing the field at three miles on my TACAN, I switched from control tower frequency to Da Nang DASC.

"Da Nang DASC, Hostage Uniform on flight five-dash-zero checking in with a single aircraft."

"Roger, Hostage Uniform. You are cleared to report to Pony Boy, who is in heavy contact with NVA. I'm sending you a Hellborne Two-Seven flight of two. They'll report to you on button Orange. Report BDA on return to home plate."

"Wilco, DASC. Going button Rose now. Out."

I leveled at seven thousand feet. Despite the February rainy weather today, there were many clear spots, including the Arizona area to my southwest. I was over the area twelve minutes after takeoff. I switched my FM to the Pony Boy frequency of 49.85, and stayed on Rose on my UHF at 361.1.

"Pony Boy, this is Hostage Uniform with Cowpoke One-Eight, ready for some work. Understand you have heavy contact."

"Hostage Uniform, that's affirmative. We have large quantity of Charlie in the vicinity of Alpha Tango eight-six-seven, five-three-zero. They are dispersed along a treeline to the south of a village."

"Pony Boy, do you have any artillery firing into your area at present?"

"Negative artillery. We were waiting for you to arrive to adjust, since we can't see past the dense treeline. Be advised that we are firing mortars into the treeline."

"Roger, negative arty. I see your mortar impacts now. They are impacting in the treeline that is running north and south. What is the distance of your closest troops to that treeline?"

"Roger. Understand that you have the treeline where the NVA are. Our closest friendlies are four-zero-zero meters in paddies."

"Roger. Four-zero-zero meters. Am I clear to fire into that treeline right now?"

"Affirmative, Hostage. Cleared to fire into that treeline."

"Roger. Understand cleared to fire. I'm going to bring in some fixed-wing aircraft to fix those badasses down there. Stand by."

"Roger, Hostage. Fixed-wing. They are also cleared into the area and cleared to fire on that target area."

I quickly called DASC on my UHF radio after switching from button Rose. "Da Nang DASC. This is Hostage Uniform with Pony Boy. They are still in hot contact. Has Hellborne flight checked in yet?"

"Roger, Hostage Uniform. Hellborne out of Chu Lai about fifteen minutes. Should be there soon."

"Roger, DASC. Uniform waiting."

I switched back to button Rose on my UHF and came up on my FM radio, "Pony Boy, Hostage Uniform waiting for a flight of A-4s. Request clearance to fire my on-board ordnance right now, until the A-4s arrive. Over."

"Roger, A-4s inbound. Hostage Uniform, you are cleared on that treeline now. Clear to fire."

"Roger, Pony Boy, I'm cleared to fire. I'll put just one Willie Peter"—white phosphorus—"rocket in there. You then confirm that I have the right treeline."

"Roger Hostage. One Willie Pete. Be advised that we are now getting mortars from that vicinity and the automatic weapons incoming is very intense."

"Understand you have heavy incoming. I'm rolling in for attack."

I leveled at 5,000 feet AGL and set up for a 2.75-inch-rocket attack run. I decided on a thirty-degree dive angle, so the chart called for a 4,500-foot roll-in, sight setting of thirty-four mils at 250 knots of airspeed with firing at exactly 2,000 feet AGL with a six-G pulloff. The maximum fragmentation pattern for a high-explosive (HE) rocket warhead was 1,000 feet high six seconds after firing. So a minimum pullout altitude of 1,500 feet had to be executed, even though I was shooting WP. I might be going to HE warheads on the second run. I lit the reticle light on the gunsight shield and cranked in thirty-four mils on the gunsight in front of me, and located above my instrument panel. I then turned the master arm switch on. As I came downwind of the treeline, I could see numerous muzzle flashes in the dense vegetation. As I approached the 180 turn-in to target line-up, I turned the number one rocket-pod station to ARM and made sure that I was set for single shot, not ripple of all nineteen rockets in that pod. I picked a point midway in the treeline as an impact point and began a roll so as to be totally inverted and lined up with the target line. Rolling inverted prevented my losing sight of the target. I always preferred this to a simple roll-in to target. When inverted and lined up with the target and nose down, simple, smooth rudder pressure and aileron rolling with the stick to an upright position and establishing a thirty-degree dive places the aircraft in a smooth track to the target, avoiding a skid or excessive rudder control, which is sometimes encountered when using a simple, noninverted roll-in. At thirty degrees dive, the aircraft airspeed increased to 250 knots from the 200 knots of level flight, as the altimeter unwound rapidly. Exactly at 2,000 feet AGL (in this case it was 2,075 feet indicated on the altimeter), I kept the target in the center of my gunsight and pressed the red thumb-button on the control stick. *Woomp!* One rocket away . . . and I pulled straight up, wings level at six Gs on the G meter. Passing through 3,000 feet, I looked back as I rolled left. My white phosphorus rocket smoke began to rise from the treeline.

"Hostage Uniform, you put it smack in the middle of the correct treeline. Be advised that you took small-arms fire on your pull-up."

"Roger, Pony Boy. I'm in for a standard high-explosive rocket run; two rockets."

I selected single shot on number two and number three stations, giving me HE rockets. I rolled in and fired two rockets at the closest end of the treeline. As I pulled off target, I heard:

"Hostage Uniform, this is Hellborne Two-Seven flight. Over."

"Hellborne Two-Seven, this is Hostage Uniform. Give me your posit and ripple."

"Hellborne Two-Seven is flight of two A-4 at angels two-zero on the Da Nang TACAN at one-five-zero degrees, four-zero miles."

"Hellborne, come to the Da Nang TACAN at two-zero-zero, two-five miles and descend to five thousand feet."

"Roger, Hostage. We each have six Delta Ones"—MK-81, 250-pound general-purpose bombs—"aboard and 20 Mike-Mike"—20-mm guns.

"Hellborne, roger ordnance. Are you ready to copy mission?"

"Roger. Send mission, Hostage."

"Target is troops in heavy treeline, conducting heavy fire at friendlies. Treeline is at Alpha Tango eight-six-seven, five-three -zero. I want two Delta One per bird. I want a one-eight-zero run-in and a right pull. Be advised you'll probably get small-arms fire at you. Friendlies at nine o'clock to target on run-in heading. Give me three-second roll-in intervals. Call in hot and off target. Read back. Over."

"Hostage. Hellborne has a solid copy. Readback is . . ." and the A-4 lead attack pilot read back the mission. His readback was precise.

"Okay, Hellborne. I'm going to stay over the friendlies at two thousand. I see your smoke trail now. I have a good tallyho on both of you. You're all set up. I'm at your two o'clock low."

"Tallyho, Hostage. I see the white top of your wings."

"Roger, Hellborne. I'm rolling in for Willie Peter target mark now."

I rolled inverted, lined up with the target, rolled around the line-up to the upright position and fired a single WP 2.75-inch marking rocket. As I pulled off, I heard:

"I have your smoke, Hostage. Dash Two, do you see the smoke?"

"Affirmative, Dash One."

"Hostage. We're in hot."

"Hellborne Dash One, cleared hot."

"I see two bombs away, Dash One."

"Roger, two away. Dash One off target."

I looked at the two explosions from the 250-pound bombs. They had a 268-meter kill or damage radius. Both fell near my smoke mark, right on the northern end of the treeline.

"Dash Two. Go six o'clock at two-zero meters from One's hits."

"Roger, six o'clock at two-zero. Dash Two in hot."

"You're cleared hot, Dash Two."

I had them reverse to a 360-degree heading run-in and we repeated two more attacks, expending their twelve bombs on the enemy-held treeline.

As soon as the surviving NVA saw the two jets departing, those not seriously wounded began running out of the treeline for the village. I called my AO in my rear seat on my intercom. "Lieutenant Towne, would you work up an arty fire mission on this village?"

"Major, I've had one made up since the jets first arrived. I'm ready to go."

"Good. You start calling it into the artillery unit near An Hoa and I'm going to kill some gooners in the meantime.

"Pony Boy, this is Hostage Uniform rolling in with rockets. We have gooners running all over from that treeline toward a village. Cowpoke One-Eight is setting up an artillery mission into that village located behind the treeline. Can you get clearance from your battalion for us to fire artillery in there?"

"Roger. I'll get the clearance for you."

I rolled in with two rocket pods armed and fired. The NVA were now shooting back at me as they ran for their lives into the numerous grass shacks. There were about fifty NVA that made it out of the trees, and except for about five that I shot in the open, they made the village. I came around again and circled west of the village. It looked like the whole damn village of people were outside of the village running westward. They must have cleared out of their homes when our bombs started hitting the treeline. I rolled back in from the rear of the village and this time switched my four M-60 machine guns to ARM and fired all four while coming down in a twenty-degree angle of attack. I walked my rudders, pushing left and right causing the aircraft to yaw left and right. This gave me the capability to spray the whole area with 7.62-mm bullets. Still in my attack dive and with my tracers arcing into the huts, some of the huts caught fire. Some of the NVA ran out of the burning shacks into a hail of bullets. As I got back up to 3,500 feet, Lieutenant Towne, in the rear seat, already had an established gun-target line from the arty and was giving the arty a "fire." The ground unit below, Pony Boy, was up on the same FM frequency now and listening to the artillery coordination.

Within five minutes, Lieutenant Towne had one gun fire a single shot into the village to start his adjusting fire. Within twenty minutes, he had a fire-for-effect on those fifty or sixty NVA in the grass huts.

Hostage Quebec—Maj. Mike Cole—arrived in his OV-10 to relieve us, since we only had thirty minutes of fuel left. I briefed Mike and my AO briefed Mike's AO on the arty shoot and I departed the area. I assume that Mike continued to wipe out that now disorganized NVA unit with arty or close air support. Pony Boy stated that they had not received any more incoming small arms or mortars, and they would soon be moving through that village after the next artillery shoot was over.

Walking back from my squadron area, I briefly stopped at the now old-looking chapel that Chaplain Roland had MABS-16 build three years ago. The large steel bell that the chaplain had cast in Da Nang was still out in front of the wooden chapel. The white paint of the chapel was badly faded. Someone should get some paint brushes to it, I thought, and then walked back to my Quonset hut.

That night, Len Bland, George Gross, and I went over to the nearby officers' club for a few beers. The clubhouse was made of large stones with a wooden roof. It had a back porch that overlooked the beach and South China Sea. George got into a serious card game, and Len and I sat on the stone wall, or banister of the porch. We had a big spotlight on the beach to enable us to see any assaults from the water. The spotlight lit up the beach and sand and surf. It was tranquil and beautiful, as I gazed out over the water toward the east and wondered, Where the hell are the reserves? This war has been going on seriously for four years and still Congress hasn't activated the reserves of any of our armed forces. What the hell have they been getting paid for in the reserves all these years? Without them coming over here, the same guys are back again. That's why I was back again; so were George and Len and hundreds of infantry officers and other pilots.

My quiet thoughts were rudely interrupted by the wailing of the siren mounted on the control tower. The night tower crew apparently saw rockets streaking toward our base and set off the attack-warning siren. We generally had five to six seconds to find our sandbagged hole to dive into before the six-foot-long Russian-made 122-mm rockets began impacting from their seven-miles-distant launch area. We didn't have any sandbagged bunkers built near the officers' club, just outside of our own living hootches. So the only thing all the pilots could do was hit the deck. Len and I jumped off the porch railing and hit the stone floor. Almost immediately there was a very loud *WAAAMMM!* and chunks of rocket steel and sand pounded right against the very banister where Len and I had been seated. The damn rocket hit just outside of the club on the north side. Within a second, another rocket impacted about twenty yards from us on the beach. I prayed that the next one didn't hit our club. It had a wooden roof. So many of us would die. A third rocket came screaming in over the club and hit just on the water breakers of the beach. A fourth and fifth fell on the beach at about thirty and forty yards away, near the staff NCO club. The siren wailed . . . all clear. The music in the club resumed playing. Len and I picked up our beers that somehow still stood on the banister. We wiped off the sand that had been thrown against them and then we drank the cool, pacifying liquid. George and Lt. Col. Gene Borden, CO of the "Purple Foxes" CH-46 squadron, were picking up their playing cards from the stone floor of the porch. It was like nothing had happened—except we on the porch were thankful that the banister railing had also been built of stone, like the club walls.

Soon the national Tet holiday would be upon South Vietnam. The III MAF command had decided to attack on several fronts to knock the North Vietnamese off balance and prevent them from massing for large-scale attacks. Our ground units began aggressive probes north, west, and south. Intelligence reported that a full NVA regiment and headquarters was located about forty miles southwest of Da Nang in dense jungles and mountains. The general area was at AT 600420 on the map, or about ten miles west of our An Hoa fire-support base. This meant that a large-scale attack into that dense jungle area would require a hell of a lot of work on everybody's part. The CH-46 helicopters began airlifting large numbers of assault troops. The CH-53 choppers began hauling 105-mm howitzers to hilltop artillery firebases, well into the jungle. Our UH-1E gunship choppers and OV-10 aircraft gave the troop helicopters close-in fire cover, as OV-10 FAC pilots ran marine F-4J Phantoms and A-4 Skyhawks in for close-air-support bombing. The marines landed by helicopters to the west of the NVA positions and cut them off from their Ho Chi Minh Trail supply routes. As our ground units moved eastward through the dense forests, the enemy realized that they were in for a real battle, so they stood and fought. It may have been one of our toughest jungle fights. It went on for days, as the marines kept heavy contact on the NVA units. The NVA was subject to artillery fire from their other side on the east mountains. The daily battles were intense. We in VMO-2 received permission to load our OV-10s with 5-inch Zuni rockets, instead of our normal load of thirty-six 2.75-inch rockets. Firing the 5-inch Zuni HE rockets changed our attack data only slightly. We still used a thirty-degree dive angle and 250 knots of attack airspeed, but we changed the gunsight setting to thirty mils from thirty-four mils. Roll-in altitude now was 5,000 feet instead of 4,500 feet, because of the altitude of the Zuni fragments after impact. We also loaded the centerline station with a GPU-2 (20-mm) Gatling gun, and for that usage we set up our 250-knot dives at twenty degrees, mil setting at fifty-three mils and fired at 1,000 feet AGL with a pull-off at 800 feet AGL.

During this period of keeping the NVA from forming up for a Tet offensive, I flew twice daily, and some of the situations were interesting because of the rough terrain and the daily movements of both marines and NVA. One afternoon I checked in with a battalion that was moving east and was about to cross a river at AT 801420. I had just started talking on the FM radio with their ground FAC when I spotted the marine lead element coming out of dense jungle and begin wading, chest deep, across the winding river. As I talked to the ground FAC, Capt. Clint Ennis, who ironically was temporarily assigned to this battalion from our VMO-2 squadron, I watched four of the lead marines cross to the east side of the river and head across open sandy ground for a dense ridgeline. As I passed over the open area, neither my rear-seat AO nor I saw any signs of Charlie. I turned westward across the river to come back and see if the area was clear. I then saw all four marines fall down on the sand. They either got shot, or shot at.

"Impressive Five, this is Hostage Uniform overhead. It looks like your lead men just got hit. I'm calling for air cover," I called to Clint Ennis on the ground over my FM radio.

"That's affirmative, this is Hostage Juliet"—Clint Ennis—"here on the ground with Impressive. Our guys up front got hit by a machine gun somewhere at the base of that ridgeline, just east of the river crossing. It was a trap. The NVA were sitting waiting for the lead marines to cross the river and then they opened fire on them. We're pulling back from the open side of the river. We could use some air on that other side of the river. You're cleared to run anything that you have in there. We can't see much from the thick jungle on this side of the river."

"Roger that, Clint."

I called Da Nang DASC. "Da Nang DASC, this is Hostage Uniform in contact. Request two sections of marine attack air. I'm at four-zero miles on the Da Nang two-seven-zero TACAN."

"Roger Hostage Uniform. We have two sections of A-4 airborne in your area at this time with wall-to-wall nape. Call sign is Hellborne One-Two-Zero. I'll have them report to you on button Blue."

I told my backseat AO, Cowpoke Three (First Lieutenant Grady) to get in contact with the Hellborne One-Two-Zero flight of A-4s as I made rocket and gun runs on the east side of the river in front of our four marines that were still lying out on the sand. Just as I was about to roll in, I saw muzzle flashes from the edge of the treeline, just behind a large dead, leafless tree trunk. It was a concrete-bunker machine-gun nest—here, right in the middle of the jungle. These NVA must have been in this area a long time to pour concrete for a gun emplacement, I thought. I rolled in from west to east and figured that I'd fire high, or beyond the machine-gun nest on the first run. This way I'll make sure that I don't hit our four dead or wounded marines lying just out in front of the NVA machine-gun bunker. As I came wings level in the dive, I could hardly see the concrete bunker because of the tree stump in front of it. But what I saw scared the hell out of me. The whole dense hillside behind the bunker was flashing like the Fourth of July fireworks—all of it at me. As tracers poured up at us, I told the AO that we had better make ourselves small in this aircraft because that's a lot of shit coming up at us. I fired two rockets and pulled up, not daring to look out of the Plexiglas side canopy, because of the wall of tracers coming up at us. At four thousand feet, I saw my smoke from my rocket impacts. They hit about twenty meters uphill, behind the bunker. My AO was already talking to Hellborne flight inbound as I rolled in for another rocket run. This time I let four rockets go, one from each rocket pod. I aimed directly at the bunker, hoping no rocket would fall short on our marines lying out in front of the bunker. Again, the muzzle flashes deep down inside of the dark canopied jungle sparkled at us as I fired and pulled hard at six Gs.

"Hostage Uniform, this is Hostage Juliet down here on the ground. You got the concrete bunker. It has stopped firing. We're crossing the river now. We're going after that ridgeline. From what we saw shooting at you, that ridgeline is crawling with Charlie. How are you doing on getting attack air?"

"Clint, I must have got a lucky rocket into that bunker; a rocket against a concrete bunker would just dust it off. I see you now crossing the river. I hope those four marines out in front of the bunker aren't dead. I now have A-4s with nape and I'm going to work that ridgeline over good."

I quickly got the A-4s on the radio and gave them a simple but very dangerously low mission of dropping napalm on a very heavy concentration of enemy troops. The NVA will be firing at them very heavily as they come in slow and low for nape release. Each of the four A-4s had four Delta Eight (MK-77) five-hundred-pound napalm tanks. We worked that ridgeline over with the sixteen napalm bombs. When my relief, Hostage King (Capt. Don Kapon) arrived, the whole hill was burning, and our marines, Clint Ennis included, were charging up that burning ridge-line to engage the NVA force.

I felt a lot of satisfaction knocking out that machine-gun bunker. However, I wondered if we lost those four marines out in front of the bunker. (A year and a half later, while I was serving as the operations officer of VMO-1 in New River, North Carolina, Capt. Clint Ennis told me, "Major, one of your rockets had gone right through a small machine-gun window of that concrete bunker. It exploded into the concrete wall behind the two gunners and blew the backs of their heads off. As far as the four marines lying out in front of the bunker, two had been killed by the machine-gun nest and two were wounded and helicopter medevacked out of the battle area later.")

This major thrust at the NVA before Tet apparently paid off. There were no major large-scale NVA attacks against the Da Nang area during Tet 1969. There were attacks by large numbers of NVA, but not anywhere near the scale of the previous year of 1968.

The war continued at a fast pace. Congress, never allowing any of our presidents to let us destroy North Vietnam, win the war, and go home, caused the battlefield to remain in devastated South Vietnam. The North Vietnamese kept coming. I kept seeing more and more NVA in the fields, on the rivers in boats and coming out of the mountains. They were fresh troops in new uniforms and helmets. Sometimes they were so new to the tactical situation that they didn't know what to do when I dove at them shooting my guns or rockets. They paid the price for their hesitancy or lack of field leadership.

Our pilots flew fearlessly and daily attacked the NVA troops firing automatic weapons or .50-cal machine guns, with both the UH-1E gunships and the OV-10As. I never saw any of the pilots hesitate to attack no matter what volume of fire was directed at them.

A typical night situation occurred when we had a CH-46 helicopter shot down, and the crew of Yankee Kilo Five was stranded on the ground under enemy fire. Hostage Charlie (Maj. C. Kurz) arrived immediately over the downed chopper crew in an OV-10A to coordinate an extract of the YK-5 crew. He

brought with him two of VMO-2's remaining Huey gunships. In
the lead UH-1E, 3-0, Lieutenant Brent was the pilot, and his
copilot was Captain Crib. Their M-60 side gunners were Lance
Corporal Roberts and Corporal Anderson. The wingman, 3-2,
gunship crew consisted of Lieutenant Morgan as the pilot and
Lieutenant Carwell as the copilot. Their two gunners were Corporal Frank and Corporal Himes.

As the rescue CH-46 from the Purple Foxes came in for the
extract, it came under intense enemy automatic-weapons fire
from a treeline. Hostage Charlie coordinated the UH-1Es to
attack on one side of the rescue pickup point as he rolled in with
rocket and machine-gun runs suppressing the heavy enemy fire.
The enemy, to survive the air attacks, shifted their attention to
the OV-10 and the Hueys as the CH-46 landed and brought out
the downed flyers. The enemy was within fifty meters of the
downed crew members and aggressively attempted to annihilate
them until driven off by the air attack. The UH-1E and CH-46
gun crews really liked a gun fight. They constantly volunteered
for the jobs as crew gunners and would be upset when some other
duty precluded them from going on a good mission.

Another typical night situation that comes to mind was on a
night in February. M Company, 3rd Battalion, 26th Marines,
was involved in an operation called Taylor Common. That night
the NVA launched an attack against M Company. The company
soon required more ammunition. A CH-46 was dispatched carrying an external load of ammunition in a cargo net. As the
CH-46 came into the Mike Company area in the darkness, heavy
automatic-weapons fire began hitting the chopper. To survive,
the chopper crew dropped the cargo net full of ammunition and
the chopper limped out of the hail of bullets. The load of ammunition fell beyond the marine lines and the marines were concerned, as Charlie began picking up the ammunition and
grenades. Hostage King—Capt. Don Kapon—came by in his
trusty OV-10 and immediately began attacking the gooners near
the ammo pile despite the dark night. He knew that the marines
couldn't get out near the ammo to salvage it. He proceeded to try
to blow it all up with his on-board rockets. After blowing some
of it up, he ran low on fuel and had to fly to nearby An Hoa
Airfield to refuel. He returned and had his rear-seat AO, Cow-

poke Fifteen (Capt. J. W. Spruce), run a flight of marine F-4 Phantoms on the ammunition. The F-4s, using two five-hundred-pound bombs on each of their first runs, blew all the remaining ammunition away, along with some overly aggressive NVA. This prevented Charlie from using the ammo on Mike Company.

The winds and rains of the winter continued into March and so did the low flying, day and night. One afternoon, Lieutenant Brent as pilot and Lieutenant Good as copilot, with gunners Private First Class McRae and Lance Corporal Lovell, flew the lead Huey gunship of a two-ship formation. Lieutenant Pask was the pilot of the second bird with his copilot, Lieutenant Baker. They had Staff Sergeant Thompson as crew chief and gunner and Corporal Moss as gunner. The two UH-1Es were escorting a CH-46 medevac helicopter to M Company, 3rd Battalion, 5th Marines. M Company had been under heavy attack by the NVA near LZ Maxwell. Five marines in M Company had been killed and several marines were badly wounded during an intensive skirmish with Charlie, so the CH-46 medevac helo had been requested for the wounded. The firefight was so intense that the Hueys had asked for two OV-10 smoke birds instead of the usual one smoke bird. The OV-10 smoke birds were loaded with four nineteen-rocket pods of white phosphorus smoke rockets instead of a mix of high explosives. This wall-to-wall smoke made an excellent smoke screen. VMO-2 normally had two OV-10s always standing by loaded for smoke attack to assist any medevac CH-46s if the enemy fire was too intense. In this case, two OV-10s came in and fired all smoke rockets, giving an excellent smoke screen for the CH-46 to come in and land behind the smoke cover. Because of the two UH-1Es' relentless attacks upon the large number of NVA, the CH-46 medevac helicopter was able to get in and get the seriously wounded marines as well as the five KIA. Despite all the gunfire, the CH-46 did not get a single hit. This was unusual not to get hits under such heavy enemy fire.

One early morning during March, I was flying over the TAOR in my OV-10 simply checking in with various units to see if they needed any close air support, artillery spotting, or naval-gunfire control. It was a quiet morning with nothing going on. All of a sudden I got a call on my FM radio from Red Bird, an eight-man deep reconnaissance unit from our reconnaissance battalion.

"Hostage Uniform, this is Red Bird. We are completely surrounded and got to get the hell out of here now. Over."

"Red Bird. This is Hostage Uniform. I read you loud and clear. Give me your posit. I'm on my way now."

"Hostage Uniform. We are Alpha Tango eight-zero-one, eight-eight-niner on top of a five-hundred-meter hill."

I glanced at my map. They were located about twelve miles northwest of Da Nang in dense jungle mountains and west of Elephant Valley. I was about ten miles south of Da Nang. I jammed both power condition levers forward to military power and headed for the surrounded marines. On my UHF radio, I called Da Nang DASC. "Da Nang DASC, this Hostage Uniform. I have troops in contact. I have Red Bird, an eight-man recon team, surrounded at Alpha Tango eight-zero-one, eight-eight-niner. Get me some fixed-wing attack aircraft to rendezvous with me at those coordinates or at the Da Nang two-niner-zero at one-one miles. I'll be there in five minutes."

"Roger, Hostage Uniform. We copied that. We'll have a flight of Gunslingers from the Da Nang hot pad meet you there in a few minutes. I'll have them come up on button Purple."

"Roger, Gunslingers to report to me on button Purple. Will you call Babe Ruth for me and tell them that I have a shit sandwich going on out here and that I need a CH-46 extract bird and two Huey gunships for escort to execute an immediate extract of this eight-man team?"

"Roger, Hostage Uniform. I'll have that extract package report to you on UHF, button Purple."

As I flew slightly northwest at seven thousand feet, I looked to my lower right, while passing Da Nang Airfield. I could see the two Air Force F-4 Phantoms, Gunslinger aircraft, leaving the hot pad and blazing away down runway 36 on a fast climb-out to meet with me to the northwest.

I soon arrived over the dense-canopied jungle hills.

"Red Bird, this is Hostage Uniform overhead. Give me your sitrep and help me find you in that dense jungle."

"Hostage Uniform. We are an eight-man team. We've been here a week now. Somehow Charlie has found us and now has us surrounded. They are shooting all kinds of weapons at us, including mortars. We're sitting on top of a hill with the gooners all around below us. They've been working their way up the hill. If we keep shooting at them like this much longer, we'll be out of ammo. I hear your OV-10 flying over us right now. Now I can see you. You just went over us and you're going west."

"Roger, Red Bird. Understand that I just passed over you. I think I have the right hill, but I don't see anything but jungle trees. Shoot me a pencil flare straight up through the trees. Make sure that it's fired straight up. The gooners know exactly where you are now so no sweat if they see the flare. I need to know exactly where you are. I have Air Force F-4s inbound right now. Hang on. I also have choppers coming out to get you."

"Roger that, Hostage. We don't know how long we can keep these guys from getting up this hill at us."

"Hostage Uniform, this is Gunslinger Three-Zero. Over."

"Roger, Gunslinger Three-Zero. This is Hostage Uniform in an OV-10. What's your position?"

"Hostage, we're at niner-thousand on the Da Nang two-niner-zero at one-three miles with two Fox-fours."

"Okay, Gunslinger. I see you both above me now, heading west. Come back east. What's your ordnance line-up?"

"Hostage, we have six Delta Three and 20-Mike-Mike each."

"Roger. Understand six Delta Three and 20-Mike-Mike. What's your roll-in altitude?"

"Roll-in is at eight thousand."

"Roger, Gunslinger, you are cleared to descend to eight thousand. Are you ready to copy the mission?"

"Roger. Go Hostage."

"Mission is . . . eight recon troops on a mountaintop, surrounded by unknown-sized NVA force. Since you have one thousand pounders, I can't get you in too close to the friendlies. So I'll have you drop around the bottom of the hill. I want two bombs per run. I want four-second roll-in intervals. Call in hot and call off target. Give me a run-in heading of two-seven-zero with a pull left on the first runs. I'll be inside of your turns at about five hundred feet above the ground. My wings are painted white, the rest of the plane is green. You should see my white wing tops against the green jungle below, when you enter downwind. How do you copy?"

"Roger. Solid copy," and he read all of it back to me correctly.

"Gunslinger. I see you arcing for the downwind now. I'm leaving this frequency for one minute to Da Nang DASC. I'll be back up shortly.

"Da Nang DASC. This is Hostage Uniform working Red Bird with Gunslinger aboard now. This is a serious problem here and I'll need another couple of flights out here. Send me marine air. I can't use the Air Force one-thousand-pound bombs after this flight. I'll need five-hundred pounders or napalm. Also, what is the status of the extract choppers?"

"Hostage Uniform, winter winds are now at four-five knots with gusts to five-five at zero-niner-zero. No choppers can take off at Marble Mountain due to these extreme winds. Nor are any more jets taking off at Da Nang due to dangerous crosswinds on the runway. I have a section of A-4s from Chu Lai that I can divert up to you. I'll get them to you right away."

"Roger, DASC . . . keep in touch with me on Purple, especially if those choppers get airborne. I'm returning to Purple now."

"Gunslinger, this is Hostage Uniform back up. I have you entering downwind now. I'm in with a Willie Pete marking rocket now."

"Roger, Hostage. I see you rolling in for your mark. . . . I now have the smoke in sight."

I rolled in, fired, and pulled back up to a low orbit inside the jets' attack orbit.

"Gunslinger, put your first two bombs at four o'clock at twenty meters from my smoke. You're cleared hot."

"Roger, Hostage. Gunslinger One in hot with two Delta Three."

The Air Force F-4 hits were exactly where I wanted them. The pilots were sharp. I only wished that they had five-hundred-pound bombs instead of these thousand pounders, so that I could press their attack up the hill, closer to our surrounded marines. But at least the NVA knew that we were there and that we'll keep bombing them until we get our guys out of there.

Then I heard over my earphones, "All aircraft in the Da Nang Airfield area, be advised that Da Nang Airfield is now closed due to excessive crosswinds and gusts. . . . Repeat, Da Nang Airfield is now closed to traffic. Diverts to Chu Lai, Cam Ranh Bay, Udorn are directed, based upon your fuel state. We will announce when the field is again open for normal traffic. Da Nang Airfield out." What all airborne aircraft crews heard over the guard UHF emergency channel was that nobody could now land at Da Nang.

"Gunslinger Three-Zero Dash Two, did you hear Da Nang Tower's transmission?"

"Roger, Dash One. This is Dash Two. I read that loud and clear. I don't have too much fuel for a distant divert. I can't make it to Cam Ranh. I can make it to Udorn, Ubon, or Chu Lai with what I have now."

"Roger that, Dash Two. We'll divert to Udorn after this last drop."

The F-4s ran their last run with pinpoint accuracy at the base of the hill. We had run strikes in a complete circle of the base of the mountain. The jungle below was burning intensely. I'm sure no reinforcements of NVA were going to try to get through that to attack up that hill.

"Hostage, Gunslinger flight winchester . . . going high and dry and switching to Da Nang DASC. Thanks for the action today. It sure was dull sitting there on the hot pad waiting for something to do."

"Roger, Gunslinger. Give Da Nang DASC a BDA of direct hits on unknown number of enemy troops in contact with friendlies. Thanks for the fast service."

I switched to my FM radio. "Red Bird. How were those hits? Did they help keep the gooners back a little?"

"Hostage, thanks. They were loud bastards impacting all around the base of the hill. That will hold back reinforcements for a while. But we have gooners about halfway up the hill at all quadrants."

"Roger, Red Bird. I have another section of air coming in. It's marines, so we'll be able to work them in much closer to you with five-hundred-pound bombs and napalm."

"Hostage Uniform, any inbound on the choppers to get us the hell out of here?"

"That's a negative, Red Bird. As soon as they check in, I'll let you know. I'm leaving your frequency a minute to call my home base to see what's happening with the choppers."

I didn't have the guts to tell these poor bastards that both Da Nang and Marble Mountain airfields were closed due to excessive crosswinds and winter gusts. I called my VMO-2 squadron ready room on my FM radio on our squadron common frequency of 35.6. "Hostage Base, this is Hostage Uniform. Over."

"Uniform, this is base. Go."

"Base, I have a real shit sandwich out here and I'm getting very low on fuel and ordnance. Plus my extract birds and escorts haven't arrived yet."

"Uniform, the field is closed for both choppers and fixed-wing. You are the only guy airborne. After you took off, the wind picked up off the China Sea. It's bad; something like forty-five knots crosswind. We can't launch an OV-10 to relieve you. Plus you won't see your extract helos until this wind dies down."

"Holy shit! Man, I have an eight-man recon team surrounded. I need those choppers now. Call the group ops officer and let him know my situation out here. I'll push down on them from Da Nang DASC. Something's got to get out here soon or these guys will die."

"Roger. Understand. I'll talk to the old man and we'll get everybody involved. I'll have two OV-10s sitting at the end of the runway ready to roll . . . when the winds die down and tower can clear them for takeoff."

"Roger, base. Check with me periodically on Red Bird FM frequency. Let me know when aircraft are coming out."

I checked back in with Red Bird. The lieutenant and his seven-man recon team were now concerned. They knew it was taking too long a time for the choppers to arrive.

"Hostage, we have gooners in so close now that we can see them coming up the hill all around us."

"Roger. Just hang in there. I'm rolling in with rockets. Keep your heads down. I'm going to put some very close into your area." I rolled in and shot four high-explosive rockets. I climbed back up and ran in lower with my four M-60 guns blazing on the other side of the hill.

"Hostage Uniform, this is Mad Dog Four, with two Alpha

Fours checking in for a mission. I understand that you have a hot one."

"Roger, Mad Dog. It's hot all right. I have a real problem. I need your bombs, but I need helicopters and can't get 'em. What's your posit and load?"

"We're a section of Alpha Fours at the Da Nang two-seven-zero at ten and at angels one-eight. We each have eight Delta One Alphas aboard. We don't have much fuel time on station for a return to Chu Lai. Go ahead. We're ready to copy mission."

"Roger. Understand eight five-hundred-pound-snakeye bombs aboard each. I could kiss you for bringing snakeyes." Snakeye bombs are retarded finned bombs—bombs that have fins that open like an umbrella to slow the descent of the bomb, allowing for very low, accurate delivery. "I have no fancy brief for you. Simply put your first bombs on my smoke-rocket marks and I'll talk you through the rest. You'll be aiming for an area about halfway up a hill from where all that burning jungle is. Join me at the Da Nang two-niner-zero at eleven miles. You're cleared to descend to three thousand. I'm at one thousand in an OV-10."

We married up and I rolled in with a WP rocket for marking to get them started on their drops. The marine A-4s came in slow and low, and their open-finned snakeye bombs were extremely accurate. However, they received automatic-weapons fire on each run due to their slow and low bomb-run patterns. They must have been really killing gooners because those hits were exactly where the recon leader had told me he had seen the assaulting NVA.

"Hostage, What a hell of a job: those bombs were right on those mothers!"

"Roger, Red Bird. I have another flight ready to go. Just stay down."

I ran three more flights of bombers and then briefed two more who were stacked up in holding patterns. Da Nang DASC had alerted Chu Lai's MAG-12, since Da Nang was closed. So all of the aircraft coming up to me were A-4s with five-hundred-pound bombs or napalm—just what I needed. I was now very low on fuel and almost out of rockets. I quickly briefed the last two flights that were stacked in orbit overhead. I gave them detailed bombing instructions to lay their bombs halfway up the hill in a circle around the mountain and then strafe with their 20-mm guns closer to the top, and then brief any other flights coming up to do the same until I returned from refueling. I then contacted Red Bird on FM and told them that I had to leave to refuel and that the A-4s would continue bombing downslope to keep the gooners from massing. Red Bird didn't like my leaving, but my thirty-minute low-fuel warning light had been on at least ten minutes. I had to leave—or join Red Bird on the ground. I headed for Da Nang Airfield and called the tower. "Da Nang Tower. This is Hostage Uniform, a single OV-10 inbound from the north at four miles."

"Hostage Uniform, be advised that Da Nang Airfield is closed due to crosswinds in excess of forty-five knots."

"Tower, this is Hostage Uniform inbound on an emergency. I'm almost out of fuel. I have to land. Am I cleared?"

"Roger, Hostage Uniform. Understand low fuel state and declaring an emergency. You are cleared to land runway one-eight. Winds four-six knots at zero-niner; gusting to five-five. Crash trucks alerted."

I was worried. The OV-10A is a high-wing aircraft, which is affected much more by crosswinds than a low- or mid-wing aircraft. I knew that I was exceeding the crosswind-landing maximum winds of forty-five knots by at least ten knots plus gusts as far as the OV-10 flight manual was concerned. I also was well aware that the Da Nang runway was 150 feet wide, while the Marble Mountain airfield runway was only 50 feet wide. So I set up for my straight-in approach well to the left or east of the runway line-up. I lowered my left wing considerably, while pushing in top right rudder causing me to be in a big skid, but a good crab to stay aligned with the runway's east side to fight the easterly winds. The winds were strong. I fought to keep to the extreme left side of the runway as I approached with landing gear down and no flaps extended. On touchdown, the winds from my left side lifted my left wing high and I thought that my right wing would strike the runway, despite it being a high-wing aircraft. Having approached with full left stick and full right rudder in a crabbing skid, I now kept the stick full left and forward and on the runway I had to reverse pedals, pushing full left rudder on the rollout. But the wind was too strong. It pushed me across the runway as my 110 knots decelerated down through 50 knots and I pulled both power condition levers into full reverse, giving reverse thrust to the turbine engine props. By now, slowing to 30 knots, the wind swept me diagonally across the 150-foot-wide runway. I soon ran out of runway width. I was almost standing on the left brake and rudder and yet the winds and gusts striking both below the left high wing and against the twin massive vertical stabilizers forced me off the runway, as I rolled out on the gravel along the runway to finally stop the aircraft. I tried taxiing the aircraft but could not control it. I asked the tower to send out a tow truck to tow me to the marine MAG-11 flight line at the northwest corner of the field. I was towed into the MAG-11 F-4 flight line and parked.

I quickly exited the aircraft and told the nearest ground crewman to fill my aircraft with JP-5 fuel. I asked where the flight-line officer was and soon found a busy warrant officer.

"Gunner, I need that OV-10 loaded with thirty-eight 2.75-inch WP rockets and thirty-eight 2.75-inch HE rockets. Also reload my four 7.62-mm machine guns. I have an emergency extract in process right now."

"Major, I don't have authority to give you rockets or machine-gun bullets. You're not from our squadron or air group. I can give you fuel, if you sign a fuel chit. Besides, I don't even have Willie Pete marking rockets; we only have high-explosive 2.75-inch rockets."

"Okay, Gunner. Have them refuel the bird and have your ordnance crew load the seventy-six 2.75-inch HE rockets and the 7.62-mm guns. I'll find your CO or group commander and explain the situation. I'll be back as soon as possible."

"Yes sir. We'll load it for you. But we may have to download if our CO doesn't give approval."

I ran all over their squadron tented operating area and couldn't find the commanding officer. So I ran a little way up the road to the MAG-11 headquarters.

"Where is the group commander?" I asked.

"He's in the briefing area near the flight line," said a captain.

I ran back to find the briefing room and entered it. To my surprise, it was air conditioned. So here is where our jet jocks briefed: in an air-conditioned briefing room . . . and then they went to fly their air-conditioned jets, as we suffer in 120-degree heat in our glaring canopied non-air-conditioned OV-10s and helicopters at low, hot altitudes. Interesting how some people operate under different working conditions. But then there were those recon guys out there, surrounded, under *extreme* working conditions!

I found the group commander briefing with three other flight-crew members.

"Colonel, I hate to disturb your briefing. However, I have a bad shit sandwich to the northwest of here and need your help."

"Major, what the hell is a shit sandwich?"

"Sir, in the OV-10 and helicopter community it is when we have a recon team totally surrounded and we have to extract them. It's fairly common to find ourselves in this situation. But today I can't get helicopters and I had to refuel here instead of at Marble Mountain Airfield due to the high winds."

"Well major, I'm not going anywhere right now with the air-field closed due to those winds. By the way, how the hell did you land in those winds? Go ahead, brief me on your exact situation."

I briefed the very interested colonel. It happened that he was briefing with his crew to respond to DASC's request for more bombers to come out to me at the recon site. He would be joining me as soon as the winds subsided and the field opened. He quickly picked up the phone and called the F-4 squadron flight line to tell them to load my aircraft with anything that I requested. He then called that squadron executive officer to make sure that it was done rapidly and to pass that on to the commanding officer, who was not in the area at this moment.

I thanked the colonel and ran back to my aircraft. In minutes, I had them tow me back onto the closed runway. I declared another emergency with Da Nang tower and somehow got airborne in those terrible winds. It was a very hairy takeoff, fully loaded with fuel and ordnance. I ran out of full left rudder on initial roll and knew that I had burned my left brake, thoroughly damaging it, trying to stay on the runway. I again was blown diagonally across the runway from the far left side as I rolled down runway 18 and staggered into the air.

As I approached the beleaguered recon team and the smoking hill, I saw two A-4s making a napalm delivery. I came up on the UHF radio and transmitted, "This is Hostage Uniform, the tactical air controller airborne here. I'm returning from refueling. What is the call sign of the A-4s on the attack run?"

"Hostage, this is Hellborne Six-Zero. We are winchester and departing. Our relief above us is Hellborne Seven-Zero. He's ready to work with you. Sayonara."

"Thanks, Hellborne Six-Zero. Break. Hellborne Seven-Zero, what's your ordnance load?"

"Hostage Uniform, this is Hellborne Seven-Zero with a flight of two Alpha Fours and six Delta Niners each and with 20-Mike-Mike. We've been over the target area, saw the impacts of the previous birds and know the situation. We only have one-zero minutes of station time left due to fuel state."

"Roger, Hellborne Seven-Zero. You are cleared down to attack orbit. Set up for a three-six-zero run and right pull. Drop two napalm tanks per run. Keep the pattern tight so we can get three fast runs in due to your low fuel. I'm switching to the recon unit on FM for a minute."

"I'll be back to you in a minute."

"Red Bird, this is Hostage Uniform back on station with rockets and plenty of fuel. How you doing down there?"

"Thank God you're back. Did you bring the choppers?"

"The choppers are on their way. How's it going?"

"Not too good. I have three men wounded and the gooners are now so close in that we're throwing hand grenades at each other."

"Roger. Get down again. Here comes some more napalm below you."

I switched back to the UHF radio. "Hellborne, drop that nape on the western slope, midway up the hill; then set up the next run for the north-side slope with a heading of zero-niner-zero and a left pull."

"Roger, Hostage. Dash One in hot."

"You're cleared hot, Dash One."

As the A-4s were dropping their nape tanks on their second run, Da Nang DASC came up on the radio. "Hostage Uniform, this is Da Nang DASC. Your choppers are now on their way.

They are about five minutes out. It'll be Hostage Able"—Maj. Steve Cross— "with a flight of two Huey gunships and two CH-46 extract choppers, Lady Ace Four-Zero flight. Also, I have another flight of F-4s for you. They are Fast Cat One-Zero out of Da Nang. The winds have subsided and the airfield is now open."

"Roger, DASC. Hostage looking for 'em."

"Hostage Uniform, this is Hostage Able inbound to your area for an extract with two gunships and two extract birds."

"Roger Able. You can easily see the smoke out here. Head straight for it. I'll run some more attack air in there, and then you and I can lay some close-in stuff on those gooners for the CH-46 to get in there for his extract."

I ran the F-4s in. They had five-hundred-pound bombs. It was the group commander that I had just talked to at MAG-11 when I refueled. He led his flight in and they dropped superbly as Hostage Able joined me with his two Hueys.

"Red Bird, this is the last bombing run. Stay down. Right after it, two Hueys and me will be shooting very close into your area to pin down Charlie so the single CH-46 can get in to get your team. The CH-46 will drop a rope ladder. Get your wounded strapped to it as the chopper hovers. There is no landing spot that I can see on that hill."

"We're ready. These gooners are almost face-to-face with us now."

Hostage Able had one CH-46 orbit back about a mile as an emergency backup extract bird for all of us. The other CH-46 began a rapid approach to the hilltop.

"Hostage Able, you Hueys take the area near the top of the hill and work the north and west side. I'll take the enemy half way down the slope on the south and east side. I can't fire as close in as you. I have MAG-11 rockets aboard. They are not chamfered rockets for slow-aircraft delivery. They're for the fast movers, so they'll spiral more and are less accurate at slow-speed delivery."

The MAG-11 group commander dropped his last bombs and he and his wingman departed for Da Nang. As I rolled in firing four rockets per run, the Hueys did the same. It was very close-in fire support within twenty meters of friendlies and closer. The NVA could only bury themselves to survive our rockets and the

Huey gunners' M-60 machine guns as they swept by the hill. The CH-46 dashed in and hovered as a long aerial rope ladder dropped from the side door. The recon team, wearing chest-attached quick-snap hooks, placed their wounded near the bottom rungs of the ladder and snapped them to the rope ladder. Then the lieutenant had the rest of the troops climb the ladder attaching themselves to it with their metal clips. The lieutenant then hooked onto the bottom of the ladder, below the three wounded, and the chopper lifted off the hill area from its hovering position. During the hover and critical lift off, Maj. Steve Cross and his wingman were closer in, shooting their M-60s, and I was doing the same with my four M-60s. I wished I had my centerline Gatling gun aboard, but I just didn't have one loaded aboard the aircraft that day. It would have been nice to have along. There is nothing more accurate than machine-gun fire from an aircraft. The NVA couldn't raise up to fire at the fully exposed recon team or the CH-46 when it hovered and then lifted off the mountaintop area, due to our fire. I then slowed to 110 knots of airspeed, dropping my flaps to thirty degrees to fly alongside this unusual sight. As the CH-46 left the five-hundred-meter hilltop, it flew out over Elephant Valley, where it was at three thousand feet above the valley. At three thousand feet, this ladder was dangling there with eight reconnaissance marines hanging and hooked on, flying through the air at about sixty-five knots. It was a real aerial circus act—better than Circus-Circus at Las Vegas. I passed them by and headed for Marble Mountain Airfield. The Hueys escorted the CH-46 and his wingman to a secure hill that marines controlled. Here the recon team unhooked from the ladder and climbed in with their wounded and headed for Charlie Med and then to the recon pad, located at the recon base just south of Marble Mountain Airfield.

Two days later, while I was in our squadron ready room drinking coffee, a grunt lieutenant walked in and asked for me.

"What can I do for you, Lieutenant?" I asked.

"It's for what you've already done for us that I'm here. I want to personally thank you for saving my ass and my team's lives. I really didn't think that we'd get out of that trap on that hill the other day."

I was thrilled to meet this young gung ho lieutenant who

frequently had his ass hanging out miles into enemy territory counting gooners on infiltration routes. He asked me to come outside to see something. I went out and there was a six-by truck full of all kinds of Russian and Chinese weapons plus three old American .50-caliber machine guns. All of these weapons had been captured by these recon guys over a period of time. I met and talked with three more members of that team that we had just extracted two days before. Then the lieutenant said, "Here's a gift of souvenir weapons for you. Take them all, Major."

"Thanks, Lieutenant. I'd just like a Russian AK-47 assault rifle. The rest I'll pass out to our troops and then pilots."

"We don't happen to have any Russian-built AK-47s, but there are plenty of Chinese-made AK-47s; they're identical except that they have Chinese characters stamped on their metal."

He dug through the pile of weapons and found a wooden box. He opened it and he showed me a brand-new, never-used Chinese AK-47 automatic rifle. It was beautiful, with its bright, yellowish tan stock. It was still covered with packing oil and wrapped with cloth. I took it, thanked him, and then went into our building to tell our CO that we had a truck full of weapons for our troops and pilots for their tent souvenirs. (It was against federal law to mail or ship weapons back to CONUS. So they could keep them in their tents during their combat tour and then pass them on to their tentmates when they left for the real world.) I made a wooden plaque and mounted my AK-47 on it and hung it behind my homemade bar that I had in my Quonset-hut living area.

On February 13, 1969, I took off on a naval-gunfire mission with my AO, 1st Lt. Bill Berry, Cowpoke Four. The battleship USS *New Jersey* had entered the Vietnam War from mothballs, and this would be my first time to control its big sixteen-inch guns. I flew south to an area about seven miles southwest of the coastal city of Hoi An. We had an intelligence report that there was a large NVA underground ammunition storage area in the vicinity of BT 110440, near the intersection of Highway 22 and the abandoned north-south railroad that paralleled Highway 1. On the way down to check in with the USS *New Jersey,* which was now on station and available for naval-gunfire support, I flew along the coast to see if I could see this majestic World War II battleship. Then my AO spotted it out in the misty waters and said, "Look at that big sucker." It was large. She was sitting just south of the island of Cu Lao Cham, about twelve miles off the coast of Hoi An. Her call sign was "Thunder," so I looked up her frequency on my classified freq list and cranked in the HF radio.

"Thunder, this is Hostage Uniform with Cowpoke Four checking in for NGFS fire mission. Over."

"We have you loud and clear, Hostage Uniform. We are standing by for a fire mission. Over."

"Thunder, this is Hostage Uniform. I am en route to a suspected large NVA ammunition dump. How many guns will you be firing?"

"This is Thunder. We'll fire a single sixteen-inch gun for registration and then three sixteen-inch guns for fire for effect."

"Roger Thunder. I'll give you a mission shortly."

I flew past Hoi An and toward the eastern base of the Que Son Mountains until I saw the intersection of Highway 22 and the damaged railroad. I got down to about eight hundred feet and started a slow, jinking flight over the suspected area with both me and the AO looking carefully for anything that might tip us off to an ammo dump being in this area. Then Bill Berry said, "Look, near the village of Nhan Xu. There's about ten NVA running into what looks like a mine opening." I poured the coal to the OV-10 but by the time that I got over to the mine opening, the gooners were inside and had closed massive wooden doors that had trees and brush tied to them. You now couldn't tell, even at a low eight-hundred-foot pass that I made, that there was a large doorway or entry into a small rising hill to the west.

"Well, Major, that could very well be the ammo storage area that intelligence gave us as a target today."

"Yeah. Work up an NGFS fire mission. You go ahead and control this one today. I'll keep my eyes peeled for more gooner activity. See if the *New Jersey* is good enough to hurl a sixteen-inch shell through that front door of whatever that is down there."

In seconds, Lieutenant Berry was calling in a fire mission to the *New Jersey*. It took just a little longer to get set up than with an artillery unit, due to the ship moving about and having to feed data into its gun radar system. Then I heard the ship's gunnery crew say, "Thunder . . . shot."

I had flown well south of the target so as not to be in the way of the hurtling shell, the weight of an automobile, traveling through the air about fifteen miles to our target.

"Splash. Thunder standing by."

"Roger, splash. Wait one."

I maneuvered about the area and neither Lieutenant Berry nor I could see an explosion.

"How the hell could we not see the explosion of a sixteen-inch shell? Hell, even if it was a dud, it would have kicked up dust and sand," I said.

"It must have been a dud and hit down in some trees. It certainly wasn't near our targeted underground entry."

Lieutenant Berry came up on the air, "Thunder, no hit. First shot must have been a dud. Give me a second shot, same target grids."

"Roger Cowpoke Four. Wait one."

"Cowpoke Four . . . shot."

"Roger, shot."

"Cowpoke Four, Thunder . . . splash."

"Roger, Thunder. Splash; wait one."

Then there was one hell of an explosion. It was a single big red-and-orange impact with white smoke at about four hundred meters to the west and upslope of the target.

"Thunder, we got a good impact that time. But we have to adjust. Make adjustments . . . right two hundred, drop six hundred. Over."

"Roger, Cowpoke. Right two hundred, drop six hundred. Ready."

"Cowpoke, Thunder . . . shot."

"Roger, shot."

"Cowpoke, splash."

"Roger. Splash. Wait."

This third shot landed about fifty feet from the cave entrance, and the impact and shrapnel knocked down the camouflage of trees and bushes from the doorway.

A fourth shot was a little long, but off to the left. One more adjustment and the fifth shell fell near the entry, caving it in under tons of dirt and sand. Not knowing where that entry led to, we simply assumed that it went straight west into the higher terrain. So Lieutenant Berry adjusted a little more west and then said, "Thunder. Fire for effect. Over."

"Roger Cowpoke. Fire for effect with three."

"Cowpoke, Thunder, shot with three."

"Roger, shot three."

"Cowpoke, splash three."

"Roger Thunder. Splash three."

We saw the first explosion. This sure was the biggest explosion from a shell or bomb that we had seen so far in this war. Then a second impact exploded. All of a sudden the earth erupted where the third shell apparently fell. There was an immense explosion, throwing up dirt at least five hundred feet into the air. Then we saw the ground caving in over several areas. The strangest pink smoke began to rise as I circled the suspected ammo storage area. Then more of that strange pink smoke came out of what used to be the entryway that had caved in. Neither Lieutenant Berry nor I had ever seen that color of smoke from secondary explosions before.

"Major, look to the west about two hundred meters from that big secondary. There's gooners coming out of another exit. There's about ten of them."

"I see 'em now. I'm in with guns."

I switched on my four M-60 machine-gun switches and dove for the fleeing NVA.

"Thunder, This is Cowpoke Four. You just got one hell of a secondary on a suspected ammo storage area. We now have a few NVA trying to get out of the underground fire that you started. We'll get that small number with our on-board weapons. I'm giving you end of mission now. We'll call in another fire mission, if we find a worthy target for such expenditure."

"Roger. End of mission. Understand Thunder got large secondary. I'll pass that on to our ship's captain. We'll be standing by in the event that you can use our guns again this afternoon."

I was now on my gun run at 350 knots and twenty-degree dive. The approximately ten NVA split into two groups as my 7.62-mm bullets walked up behind them, so I picked one group and walked my rudders while I held my finger down on the machine-gun trigger located on my control stick. Five NVA hit the dust. I climbed back up for another run, but the other five gooners ran into a thick treeline. I strafed the treeline then climbed for altitude and fired a dozen HE rockets into the treeline. As I passed over the original five that I had shot at, the AO counted four still there probably dead. The other one had gotten back up and ditty-bopped into the dense vegetation. The AO then spotted about twenty NVA digging their way out of the caved-in entrance located to the east. He quickly called in Thunder again with another fire mission. The ship's crew was happy to oblige and sent three two-thousand-pound sixteen-inch shells crashing back into the damaged entrance and immediate surrounding area. At least half of the NVA were killed and the rest were just punched back into the holes of the cave that was crumbling.

We left the area feeling that for once intelligence was right. There really was some sort of ammunition storage area right at the grid coordinates that they had given us. We also felt that the *New Jersey* had destroyed or damaged most of the storage area and the ammunition in it. We still couldn't figure out what that pink smoke was that rose out from all of those cracks in the earth where the storage areas had caved in. It certainly wasn't from the *New Jersey*'s shells. Maybe it was very old gunpowder. It wasn't from various smoke grenades. I saw a lot of different colors from explosions and secondary explosions, but never saw this pink color before or after that incident.

As the North Vietnamese continued to pour down the Ho Chi Minh Trail, we observation pilots in our OV-10s daily continued to see more and more of them out in the open flatlands. It was common everyday practice for all of our OV-10 pilots to see groups of five to twenty fresh NVA troops moving from village to village, or forming up for a ground assault. Therefore, every day, each OV-10 pilot would kill anywhere from two to six NVA out on the flatlands, or on open trails back in the jungles with their OV-10 on-board ordnance. These kills were generally confirmed by body count by our deep force recon or our division recon teams out in the bush, or by a company passing through the area. It became obvious to our local division and marine amphibious force intelligence that the OV-10s were getting many, many more kills with their guns and rockets than the sophisticated marine jet attack fighters with their bombs. It was really the nature of the battlefield that resulted in this situation. Cost-effectively, the bombers should have been allowed to bomb the hell out of North Vietnam as the South Vietnamese invaded North Vietnam to carry the war there and end it rapidly. But our congressmen didn't want to win the war, only our succeeding presidents did.

However, as these kills were reported through the system back to Headquarters Marine Corps and then on to the Defense Department, some eyebrows were raised. The civilian bean counters—accountants and statisticians in the Department of Defense—began to question the Marine Corps. How can a very inexpensive twin-turboprop armed reconnaissance aircraft be accounting for so many NVA kills against the expensive operating costs of the A-4s and F-4s? It even went so far that some bean counter in the DOD recommended, in writing, that the Corps do away with several A-4 squadrons and add replacement OV-10 squadrons, based upon kills per operating costs of aircraft. Here was a statistician who hadn't the foggiest idea of how the Marine Corps air-ground team operated and what was needed for the projection of naval sea power ashore. The simple fact, for example, that the OV-10s don't have landing hooks for aircraft-carrier operations was one of hundreds of simple items overlooked on such a stupid report.

The big picture of world operations was lost in the Vietnam numbers game. As a result, definitive directives came down through the chain of command explicitly stating: "Marine Corps OV-10A aircraft must not be used as attack aircraft, but must be relegated to performing their assigned missions as observation, target marking for forward air control, naval-gunfire spotting and artillery adjusting." We in VMO-2, on the receiving end of this, changed our intelligence reporting. When we killed four or five NVA with our OV-10A ordnance, we simply told the debriefing intelligence officer, upon our return from a mission, that we'd marked four targets with our marking rockets. The intelligence officer knew better, but he reported "five targets marked." Nothing on the battlefield changed. If we saw ten NVA, we didn't quickly call in an A-4 or F-4 section, which was always airborne above us at about twenty thousand feet. We'd simply roll in and shoot the NVA. On the other hand, if we had hard targets, like concrete bunkers or large numbers of NVA, a hundred or more, then we'd call in our brothers in their air-conditioned jets to drop their bombs on that more lucrative target. If we ran into two or three .50-caliber anti-air machine guns, the specific situation dictated if we in an OV-10 would duke it out to knock 'em out, or whether we'd put a fast-mover jet load on their heads.

I saw remarkable heroism daily as a way of life in this squadron. One of the many examples was the case of First Lieutenant Pask from Hazleton, Pennsylvania, and his flight crew in a UH-1E gunship. On March 17, 1969, Lieutenant Pask was the pilot in command of a Huey from VMO-2. His copilot was First Lieutenant Blanc. The crew chief was Corporal Lefler and the volunteer gunner was Master Sergeant Robert L. Cover. They were assigned for the day as the standby medevac crew at An Hoa Airfield. While sitting around their Huey, Lieutenant Pask noticed one of the squadron's OV-10A Bronco aircraft making strafing and rocket runs just about three miles northwest of An Hoa. He saw that there were no other aircraft in the area, so he decided to join the OV-10 to see if he could assist in whatever was going on. So they took off, notifying the An Hoa tower that they would only be flying about three miles away, in the event that an emergency medevac call came in for them. Lieutenant Pask joined the OV-10 and reported to its pilot, Capt. L. Gold, Hostage Oscar. Captain Gold briefed Lieutenant Pask that L Company, 3rd Battalion, 26th Marines, was in a critical situation below. L Company had been moving across open ground toward an objective on high ground. Just as their lead element reached that high ground, the NVA opened up with a heavy volume of fire from fortified positions, killing and wounding numerous lead-element members. The intense fire pinned down the lead element as well as the other marines caught in the open field. Captain Gold with his AO, 1st Lt. D. D. Perks, in their OV-10 had called in attack fixed-wing aircraft. However, because of the enemy's heavy fire, the lead element could not move to retrieve their wounded lying close to the enemy's fortified positions. Captain Gold knew that he couldn't fire any of his HE rockets: the shrapnel from the high explosives would hit the wounded and other surviving lead-element members. So he rolled in with his OV-10 and fired a 2.75-inch WP marking rocket at the concrete machine-gun emplacement. He described the situation to Lieutenant Pask, who began making numerous rocket and gun runs from the slower, lower-flying Huey gunship. He had hoped that his own intensive firing would allow L Company to withdraw. The enemy was persistent despite Lieutenant Pask's forward-firing ordnance and the intensive M-60 firing by crew members Master Sergeant Cover and Corporal Lefler.

Captain Gold brought a flight of jets down below the clouds to attack the target. However, the weather was so bad that a 1,200-foot ceiling required the jets to be at an unsafe altitude. This resulted in three NVA .50-caliber machine guns lacing the sky at the jets, which couldn't drop their bombs from such a low altitude. So the jets had to climb back up through the low overcast. The marines were still pinned down. Lieutenant Pask was out of WP rockets. So he left for nearby An Hoa and rearmed. Capt. Herman A. Graves, Hostage Victor, and his AO, 1st Lt. D. J. Scrop, arrived in another OV-10 to relieve Captain Gold, who was dangerously low on fuel.

Lieutenant Pask returned with his Huey well armed and began to fire WP smoke rockets at the enemy positions to lay down a smoke screen. Captain Graves rolled in with his OV-10 and fired HE rockets at a safe distance from our wounded. Ten NVA ran from the smoking treeline into a structure. Lieutenant Pask in his UH-1E and Captain Graves in his OV-10 immediately attacked the structure, blowing it up. L Company was able to move farther back because of the smoke screen, but was still not capable of tactically maneuvering, because they were carrying wounded with them. As Lieutenant Pask began an approach to land to pick up wounded, another OV-10, piloted by Capt. Paul Hughes, Hostage India, and his aerial observer, Capt. John Bright, arrived overhead to assist. Both OV-10s continued a series of rocket and gun runs upon the large enemy force dug in along the treelines and in concrete bunkers. Even with the heavy air attack, the NVA, in well-camouflaged, fortified positions, continued to rake the friendlies with heavy fire. Despite the heavy enemy fire, Lieutenant Pask landed his Huey in the open area near the wounded marines. The incoming enemy fire was so intense that none of L Company's marines were able to get up to carry any of the wounded to Pask's chopper. So the gunship's crew chief, Corporal Lefler, and the volunteer gunner, Master Sergeant Cover, jumped from the helicopter carrying their M-60 machine guns, which they had taken from their mounts in the helicopter. They both shot their way more than fifty meters to the first wounded marine lying out in the open. Lieutenant Blanc, the Huey copilot, had his own M-16 rifle out and was also laying down a base of fire as the chopper was parked out in the open under heavy incoming fire. As Corporal Lefler and Master Sergeant Cover arrived by the wounded, one wounded marine died. They left him and then picked up a seriously wounded platoon leader who had a deep skull wound and was unconscious. Despite the crisscrossing deadly fire, they carried the wounded marine to the helicopter, as Lieutenant Blanc fired his M-16 to protect them. Master Sergeant Cover was hit by a .50-caliber bullet that struck at an angle to the body armor on his chest. The shredding steel tore into his left arm, giving him a deep three-inch-long wound on his forearm, but he continued with Lefler and they placed the wounded marine in the helicopter. Lieutenant Pask then lifted up the helicopter and they flew to An Hoa where a CH-46 landed and took the wounded platoon leader to Da Nang. Lieutenant Pask refueled and rearmed at An Hoa and returned to the battle scene. He joined the two OV-10s in making a series of gun and rocket runs on the enemy positions. Running out of ordnance again, he flew back to An Hoa as the OV-10s continued air strikes under the low, 1,200-foot overcast skies.

Upon his return to the battle area, Lieutenant Pask was told by L Company that they had two emergency medevacs ready for pickup. At this time the CH-46 returned from Da Nang. Lieutenant Pask told the CH-46 pilot to wait for medevacs at An Hoa, since the enemy fire was still too intense. Lieutenant Pask rolled in, expending his rockets at the enemy, who was well dug in in a thick treeline. As the two OV-10s continued gun runs, Lieutenant Pask landed again and his wounded Master Sergeant Cover and Corporal Lefler, for the second time, ran from the gunship firing their hand-held M-60 machine guns and set up a base of fire for the L Company marines to carry one of the wounded to the helicopter. The L Company grunts were unable to make it to the helicopter with another wounded marine. Lieutenant Pask quickly lifted off and flew the one wounded to the waiting CH-46 helicopter at An Hoa. He again refueled, rearmed rapidly, and flew back to the L Company area. He made several more attack runs on the enemy as Captain Graves ran low on fuel and had to leave in his OV-10. Captain Hughes was now running A-4s on low-altitude bomb drops, despite the 1,200-foot overcast. L Company called to Lieutenant Pask to come in to pick up three dead marines and two wounded so that the company could get some mobility tactically. While on his approach to land, an enemy .50-caliber machine gun bracketed his aircraft. Then two more .50-cal guns opened fire, and Captain Hughes attacked them. However, Lieutenant Pask's UH-1E's tail pylon got hit by a .50-caliber bullet as he landed in the zone. Captain Hughes destroyed one of the .50s. Lieutenant Pask climbed back up and quickly returned to An Hoa. Ironically, as he and his crew were loading rockets and refueling, An Hoa came under rocket attack. It was not uncommon for daytime rocket attacks to be launched upon An Hoa, particularly at noon. This contrasted to the at-least-once-a-week rocket attacks upon Marble Mountain Airfield that usually occurred between 2300 and midnight.

Again, Lieutenant Pask flew out to L Company, where he found Captain Hughes fighting it out with two .50-cal guns. Captain Hughes knocked one .50-cal gun out, and Lieutenant Pask, in his UH-1E, destroyed the other. I Company, located nearby this battle scene, called for an emergency medevac, and Lieutenant Pask flew over there and picked up a wounded marine and flew him to Da Nang because the CH-46 had not yet returned from Da Nang. He landed his battle-damaged Huey, and Master Sergeant Cover was taken to our dispensary in the meatwagon to have his wound attended to.

The next morning, the ground units counted 240 dead enemy in this exact vicinity. It had been a day-long raging fight that the remaining participants will long remember.

There were continual incidents similar to the foregoing. Some people lived through them. Some did not.

* * *

One morning our CO held a pilots' meeting to raise hell about our flying too low. This was the CO who didn't talk to anyone. The captains in the squadron particularly disliked this lack of communication. They avoided him in the officers' club bar, since he wouldn't communicate with them. In fact, the captains quit going to the club and set up a small bar in their own Quonset living area as a mild form of protest of these circumstances. As a major and a department head, I didn't fall into this group and actively avoided this rather unusual conflict. However, they were partly right. In the five months that this individual had command of the squadron, I worked for him three months. It's hard to believe that during three full months he never uttered a word to me. He spoke very little to his executive officer, who then passed the word to me and other officers. This was unusual, but even more it was annoying, since this was combat and we were seeking cohesiveness, not individuality, or aloofness from the other pilots. I not only observed this obvious relational problem, but I remembered it well so that I would never approach duplicating it when I would rise to command. Later, when I had command of this same squadron, VMO-2, for eighteen months, I often thought of that unconventional commander and his way of running a squadron in combat.

But here he was. It was a very rare occasion. He was standing up front in the ready room lecturing to all of the pilots.

"There are five pilots in this squadron who are consistently getting all of the hits in our aircraft. I've been checking in maintenance for the names of who has been flying the aircraft requiring most of the patches. This indicates to me that those five pilots are flying too low."

I was going to say something to the effect that these are the pilots getting all the kills. Then I thought, Why bother? He's leaving in a matter of weeks for the States anyway. But it was true, the gooner killers *were* the guys that received the largest number of hits on their OV-10s. If you don't take risks, you're not going to kill NVA.

The CO continued, "If I'm flying around the TAOR and see one of my OV-10s below a thousand feet, I'm sending you right back and grounding you. Do you all understand that?"

We then broke up. I won't repeat what some of the hard-charging captains said.

The next day I was in my S-1 personnel office doing some administrative paperwork when I heard the crash-crew siren and the sickbay meatwagon siren heading for the runway. I walked out to see what the emergency situation was. An OV-10 was on final approach with one of its two props feathered. I thought there must be more to this than just a single engine out. Most of us had had several of those. A flare was shot up at the end of the runway as the tower closed the runway to fixed-wing traffic because of the emergency. The OV-10 landed safely. But due to only one engine operating, it could not taxi. It was towed up to our squadron flight-line area, as we all gathered outside to see what had happened. To our surprise it was our CO with the damaged OV-10. We walked over to look the aircraft over. The whole underside of the fuselage and gun sponsons were torn up. There were dirt marks all over the rippled skin of the underbelly. There were thick bamboo shoots sticking up into the undercarriage and into the wheel wells. It was amazing that the wheel-well doors opened to allow for the landing gear to come down.

The OV-10 has its two turbine engines mounted high on the high wing. Despite that high location, both of the oil coolers located above the engines had bamboo shoots sticking in them. The one oil cooler apparently had been pierced by several bamboo shoots, causing loss of oil and engine damage and failure of that engine. Everybody just shook their heads in wonderment. This was the CO who had just the day before told us not to be flying below a thousand feet. Hell, he must have been on a gun run and ran into a hill full of bamboo. He must have been at three feet on the bottom of that gun run. He was sure lucky to be alive.

One thing was certain at Marble Mountain Airfield. Or that's what we thought. When the German nurses visited our air group officers' club, we knew that the NVA would not rocket us that night. The West Germans had a hospital ship tied up to a pier in downtown Da Nang. They took care of the seriously injured Vietnamese troops, since we had our own hospital ship, the USS *Repose,* in Da Nang Harbor for backup to perform serious surgery cases and other cases that couldn't be performed in the land-based navy hospital. After undergoing many NVA rocket attacks, we began to notice that the German ship occasionally would leave the pier and go out into the middle of the Da Nang Harbor where the *Repose* was. When it did that, we at Marble Mountain and Da Nang airfields would get rocketed. So we always asked the last daylight pilots who had just landed whether the ship was in at the pier or out in the harbor.

There's an exception to everything. One night we were all partying at the O club. Another Australian band was up entertaining us with mostly World War I and II songs sung in England during those periods. We heard that a group of German nurses was visiting our living-area Quonset huts. Naturally many of us took drinks over for them to the Quonset-hut area and began grilling food on the beach and talking with the nurses. At about 2330, the siren went off in our tower. Everybody was reluctant to run for our underground bunkers. After all, the German nurses were here. How could rockets come in tonight? But when the first rocket exploded into one of the nearby Quonset huts, blowing half of it away with a hell of a *bwwaang!* everybody ran and dove into the nearest bunkers—German nurses included. Six more Russian rockets rained in upon our living area. Some were too close to my secure hole in the ground. Major Bob Wagner asked one of the German nurses, while we all sat in the darkness of the sandbagged bunker, what had gone wrong tonight? The German nurses were as amazed at being rocketed as we were. It was the first time in the year that they had been there that they almost got killed by NVA rockets.

About midnight, one of our medevac pilots landed and joined us. He said that the German ship is out in the harbor. Apparently, the German ship's crew got the word that there would be a rocket attack somewhere near Da Nang tonight. But they got the word very late, after the nurses left the ship to come out and visit us. The German nurses didn't come around for a long time after that rocket-attack night. We never did find out how the Germans knew what night there would be a rocket attack in the Da Nang area.

Chapter 6

The NVA Continue South

A few days later, I was assigned as the Tactical Air Coordinator Airborne (TACA) for a regimental-sized assault against known NVA units. It was an encirclement plan that would be executed with helicopters landing into two landing zones from the south and north; assault from the west by tanks and by infantry marines from the northwest and east. The two LZs were Grant at BT 069638 and Sherman at BT 086648. The first wave of helicopters was to land into LZ Grant. LZ Grant was a large rice-growing area consisting of many rice paddies. I arrived on station in the vicinity of LZ Grant at one thousand feet with two flights of F-4s. I ran both sections, having them drop their five-hundred-pound bombs into the area. I then saw the approaching first wave of twelve CH-46 helicopters with their two UH-1E escort gunships. I quickly ran an A-4 smoke-screen aircraft into the LZ so that the choppers could approach the LZ from behind the smoke. As I circled about, I saw several NVA running from the bombed treelines, so I alerted the approaching CH-46s and Hueys to expect resistance despite our bombings. The two VMO-2 UH-1Es covering the HMM-364 squadron of CH-46s were led by my roomie, Maj. Benny Bart, Hostage Bear. Major Bart placed one of his Hueys on the one side of the LZ, and he took the other side. They proceeded to fire rockets and their forward M-60s into the treelines to keep the NVA down as the CH-46s landed with only a few shots being fired at them. Upon landing, the marines jumped out of the helicopters and fanned out northward. Major Bart then had his two gunships join four CH-53 heavy-hauler choppers from HMH-463 that were bringing in jeeps and 105-mm howitzers. I then flew northward to LZ Sherman and ran two A-4 sections in that area for their five-hundred-pound-bomb drops, followed again by an A-4 smoke aircraft to lay another smoke screen. After both LZs were secured and HML-167 UH-1Es began arriving for close-in fire support, I began checking in on my FM radio with each of the advancing ground units, including that of the tank commander. I had several flights of attack jets holding at eighteen thousand and twenty thousand feet above me, if I needed them. I climbed to three thousand feet and from there I could easily see all five major elements closing in on the area where NVA units were last reported. There was much ground action between the NVA and our ground companies, but none that required close air attack by either me, HML-167's Hueys, or the jets. Small-scale fighting took place, and then my roommate, Benny Bart, with his wingman, departed because of low fuel states.

I then spotted about twenty NVA running northwest in an open, sandy area. I called down to the nearest company commander and requested that I have clearance to fire on this small band of NVA. He gave me permission and cleared me hot. I climbed to 3,500 feet to get set up for a rocket run when another voice came up on my radio. It was the call sign of the regimental commander.

"Hostage Uniform, This is Fairfax Six. Permission to fire on those NVA is denied. Let them go. We'll get them on the ground."

"Fairfax, this is Hostage Uniform. On just one rocket run I might get most of them. Request your clearance."

"That's negative, Hostage Uniform. Just keep me and the nearest company commander informed exactly where those NVA are heading. I have it all here on the map. I have a complete circle of marines and tanks around them. We'll kill them on the ground."

"Fairfax Six, this is Hostage Uniform. This would sure simplify it, if you let me get them now while they're in the open. How far away from this scene are you, sir?"

"Hostage Uniform, I'm seven miles away. But I know how to read a map. I really appreciate your air attacks up until now and your continued availability. But I know that I have these bastards trapped and I want my men on the ground to kill them. Do you understand?"

"Roger, Colonel. But if they make the treelines, I may lose them."

"We won't lose them. I have a complete circle around them. Just keep me informed on their whereabouts."

"Yes sir, Colonel."

About that time the twenty NVA ran into an advancing marine company and took fire. So they then ran toward the west and a small river. I so informed the regimental commander.

Just as the NVA got close to the river, our tanks came out of the woods from the west and saw them and began firing at them. The NVA again turned around and headed southeast. I could see that about three miles from them were the lead elements of another company of marines from the battalion that had landed in LZ Grant. I called their lieutenant on the FM radio, and of course the regimental commander listened in on it.

"Flu Shot Six, this is Hostage Uniform. You have about two-zero NVA heading your way. They are all wearing tree branches and bushes on their backs and helmets."

"Roger, Hostage. We see them and we're now firing at them. Thanks."

The NVA again reversed their running direction and headed north across a wide-open sand dune.

"Fairfax Six, Hostage Uniform again requesting permission to fire on those same NVA."

"Negative Hostage. I'm closing in on them now."

"Fairfax, this is Hostage Uniform. Those NVA are now heading for a thick treeline. If I let them make it, they may make a stand in there. It'll be hard to get them without taking any casualties ourselves."

"Hostage, I have the firepower. Let them go."

I did. The NVA all ran into the trees and I expected them to stay there and make a stand for it. They really surprised me. Instead of twenty coming out, thirty came out. So ten more NVA in the trees joined them in their run for life.

"Fairfax, they came out of the trees and now there are three-zero NVA. Can I at least mark them with a smoke rocket for your closest company?"

"Negative. I know how you OV-10s mark a target. You'll kill 'em. I'll get 'em on the ground."

"Fairfax, would you clear Hostage Uniform to make dry diving runs on them? It'll slow them down."

"Roger Hostage Uniform. You are clear for dry runs, but no shooting. Is that clear?"

"Roger. Understand. Hostage Uniform is cleared for dry runs on NVA. I'm rolling in cold."

I dove down on those thirty NVA, and they were still running. I have never seen anyone run so fast so far, especially the original twenty NVA. They must have run at least ten miles in circles. As they saw me diving down from three thousand feet, they knew that now they were going to die. They all fell flat to the ground. I zoomed by them. They were still frozen in fear. They must have thought that my guns jammed or something. They still laid there as I climbed up on a downwind leg. I glanced about the area and then back at them. They really looked like bushes and small trees lying out there. If I hadn't seen them running, I would never have spotted them from three thousand feet. I rolled in again and told the colonel that I was in on another dry run. This time as I pulled up and hadn't fired a second time, they figured that I had nothing on board to shoot with. So they all got up and ran into another treeline. I reported it to the regimental commander. I slowly circled at one thousand feet, and in about three minutes they were all out running again. They picked up another five NVA in those trees. I reported to the colonel that they now were thirty-five. Just then an HML-367 helicopter flown by Capt. Archie Blowers was passing by the area. I asked him to hang around the area a minute as I called the regimental commander.

"Fairfax, this is Hostage Uniform. I have a UH-1E standing by to mark the thirty NVA. He can have a crew member throw out a red smoke grenade on top of those bastards."

"Good idea, Hostage Uniform. But tell them no shooting from that Huey. You understand, no shooting from that Huey. I want those NVA captured or killed from the ground."

"Understand, Colonel. No shooting from the Huey."

I called the Huey and briefed him on the whole no-shoot situation and emphasized that neither he nor his side gunners were to shoot those NVA. He acknowledged that he would have a crewman only throw out a smoke grenade at the NVA. I told the Huey pilot that I'd climb back up to 3,500 feet and cover him, and if he took any fire from those NVA, fire back and I'd roll in and finish them.

I climbed to 3,500 and watched Archie fly down directly over the NVA, who were all lying out flat on the ground. I couldn't believe it. Archie was hovering over them at about twenty feet. The sand was blowing around. The NVA froze and didn't even look up. Both side machine gunners swept their guns over the NVA below, but did not fire. Then I saw the hand of one of the Huey crew members stick out of the left side of the helicopter and throw a smoke grenade out. It was red smoke. The smoke canister fell next to an NVA who had his right arm stretched way out on the ground holding his AK-47 rifle. The burning smoke grenade was too close to his arm and was probably burning it. He quickly withdrew his arm toward his body and away from the burning, red-smoking canister, leaving his weapon lying out on the sand. What a sight—if only I had brought my movie camera along on this flight. Those two Huey crew gunners were looking right down their machine guns at these frightened gooners. They could have easily killed them all in seconds.

"Fairfax, this is Hostage Uniform. The Huey just marked the gooners. He is still hovering over them. Should I have him kill them?"

"Negative. I repeat, negative. My one company commander has seen the smoke and the NVA. He's heading right for them now. Get the Huey out of there."

"Roger, Fairfax. Huey will be told to depart. Understand that your closest company has the enemy in sight."

I called the Huey pilot and thanked him and he continued on for wherever he was going in the first place. But he did say to me over the UHF radio that he thought that the regimental commander must be nuts.

My relief, Capt. Joe Rock, Hostage Bull, arrived above me in his OV-10. I briefed him and his AO, First Lieutenant Marks, Cowpoke Thirteen. They both couldn't believe the situation. Then I told Joe Rock to come down to three thousand feet and join me in circling the NVA. My AO in the rear seat, First Lieutenant Martin, Cowpoke Seven, then added, "Major, you're wrong. There's thirty-six gooners now. I counted them better when they were lying out there under the chopper."

"Fairfax, this is Hostage Uniform. I have to bingo to home plate. My relief, Hostage Bull, is now up on your frequency. You now have three-six NVA out there in the open. I wish you luck. Out."

As I headed for Marble Mountain Airfield, I kept my FM on the same frequency to listen to this ridiculous situation as long as I could. I heard Capt. Joe Rock repeatedly requesting permission to blow the shitbirds away. He was no more successful than me. In fact, the regimental commander threatened to put him on report if he didn't cool it. I finally got close into my base and entered downwind for a landing. Passing through the ninety-degree position, at about five hundred feet, I lost the FM radio transmissions behind Marble Mountain. I would have to ask Capt. Joe Rock what was the outcome of that dumb situation.

I landed, debriefed, and got in my jeep and drove around the runway, out the front gate and down the road about one mile to the navy hospital. I was going to have a few drinks in the doctors' bar. As I drove by the hospital Quonset huts, one of our CH-46 medevac choppers was landing, so I had to stop on the road near the emergency operating room to let the several litters of wounded get carried in front of me from the landing pad. It was routine, so I didn't think much of it, except for the usual sorrow I felt for those poor youngsters all ripped up and bleeding in those litters.

I went into the hospital bar and hung up my .38 shoulder holster on one of the wooden pegs for hanging weapons. I sat down, still sweating from two missions, or five hours of flight time, for the day, and I ordered a rum and Coke. I downed a few cool, refreshing drinks when one of the surgeons came in and sat next to me. He was from Brazil but had joined the U.S. Navy as a doctor. He had just come from the operating room. We small-talked a little, observing that these youngsters that came in here all blown up, missing limbs, and so forth, would not survive except that they had their age going for them. He said that if a forty-year-old person back in the States had suffered in an auto-mobile accident what some of these young marines had suffered, the forty-year-old would have died. He was amazed what a young body can take and still make it. He told me that he had just had two CH-46 helicopters bring in eleven WIA and five KIA. I said that I had seen one of the choppers bringing in some of the WIA just minutes ago when I drove in here. I asked him if he knew the unit that they were from. He told me and I got the chills. They were from one of the companies in this operation that I had been the TACA for today. I thought, I wonder if they are casualties from those NVA that I could have so easily killed with one or two attack runs? They could have been. But then with all the NVA out there, it could have been in some other part of that battle that they were wounded and killed. I sat back, relaxed and continued talking with the Brazilian doctor.

Then someone came to the door and called the bartender. Without telling any of us at the bar anything, the bartender just left and went out the door. The Brazilian doctor said, "I wonder what the hell is going on out there?"

"I can't guess, doc. Let's go see."

We both walked out and I grabbed my .38 pistol on the way. When we got outside, we looked across the street where the navy nurses quarters were. There were at least thirty nurses and the bartender standing outside of the front Quonset hut of the nurses living quarters. Some of the nurses had on only panties and bras; others were only half-dressed. The doc and I ran across the street and asked, "What's going on?"

One nurse responded, "Someone threw a tear-gas grenade into our living quarters. It's a mess. The whole Quonset complex is filled with gas. At first we thought it was a VC or NVA attack. Then we didn't hear any siren or gunfire. Most of the nurses are out here except those working at the hospital. What we're concerned about is that usually when there is a siren or rocket attack, we all dive under our beds. We're worried that maybe one of the girls dove under the bed and knocked herself unconscious. Or possibly passed out from the tear gas while under her bed."

I asked, "Are there any gas masks around?"

"There are, but they are all inside by our beds."

"We have gas masks at the doctors' quarters," said the doctor.

"Okay, doc, you and the bartender go get *three* masks—one for me. In the meantime, I'll try to get in there and find that tear-gas canister."

I ran up to the front door and opened it, and the gas came pouring out at me, closing my eyelids automatically. I ran back out onto the street and wiped my tearing eyes as I coughed. I took a deep gulp of fresh air, then I ran and opened the door, keeping my eyes and mouth tightly closed. The Quonset-hut complex consisted of several interconnecting Quonset huts with a long main passageway. I was now moving in the central passageway, holding my breath and moving my feet out front from wall to wall to feel for the smoking canister. Ah, after only five steps, my foot hit something heavy. By now I was completely out of oxygen. I was ready to pass out. I wanted to take a step or two beyond the canister and then kick it back toward the door that I had come in. I couldn't do it. I simply could not stay in there any longer. All I had oxygen for was to give the smoking canister a hell of a kick and hope that it would sail all the way down to the other exit door. Then I could run around to the other side, open the door and kick it out. So I gave it a big kick and heard it sliding down the passageway. I turned and ran and opened the nearby exit door. Then I heard, loud, but coughingly, "You bastard, *cough, cough.*"

Hell, someone else had been kicking that canister my way with the same idea. It sounded like he must have been halfway down the passageway in all of that gas.

I ran around the outside of the building and quickly opened the door at the other end of the passageway. To my shock, it was my new executive officer. He stumbled out, crying from the stinging tear gas. He was bitching about someone trapping him in the middle of the passageway and kicking the gas canister back past him, after he had almost kicked it out the other side. I took a quick step inside, felt for the canister and kicked it out into the sand. I looked again at my XO. He was still blinded by the gas and couldn't see me. Without saying a word, I got the hell out of there before he would recognize me. I didn't want him even to think I might have been the one who kicked the can back past him. I got into my jeep and drove back to my base and stopped at our O club. I found Joe Rock at the bar.

I asked him, "Captain, what happened with Fairfax and the trapped gooners? When you relieved me, I heard you still arguing with the colonel for permission to kill those thirty-six NVA."

"Well sir, I just did not receive permission to kill 'em, just like you. And just as you said they would, those bastards got into a defensive position. They found several concrete bunkers. The one company had five marines killed and eleven wounded before the tanks arrived and blew the NVA to hell. Shit. We could have killed those gooners on one or two gun runs. I almost got sick over it."

I believed what Joe said. But then I almost couldn't believe it. Just what I feared would happen. It really disturbed me. I left the bar and went back to my Quonset hut. I had had enough of this crazy war for today. I told my roommate, Benny Bart, the whole story.

(I was to find out seven months later from a new AO that he had been one of the company commanders in that battle that day. He informed me that several weeks after that ill-fated day, that colonel or regimental commander was relieved when word of his decisions got back up the chain of command to the generals.)

Benny and I were lying in our racks feeling terrible about those unnecessary KIAs and WIAs when the base siren sounded. I grabbed my steel helmet and flak vest and ran out of the Quonset hut. I barely made it into our bunker when the first rocket hit. It struck up on our flight line. Then eight more came in exploding. I waited five minutes in the dark, damp, sandy bunker, and then the siren wailed the all-clear signal. I went back into my hootch to find Benny Bart still in his rack.

"Benny, one of these nights a goddamn rocket is going to fall on this hut and you'll meet your maker. Why don't you get into the bunker like the rest of us?"

"Shit, if you're gonna get hit, you're gonna get hit. Hell, if a rocket hits directly on that bunker you're dead anyway."

"Yeah. But if you're in the rack and one explodes just outside of the wall, you'll get all that Quonset-hut steel as well as the rocket frags up your ass."

"Oh, it's still a numbers game. Those gooners aren't good enough to hit this Quonset hut."

"I sure as hell hope that you're right, Benny."

The next morning I had the early launch at 0600 and was back in the ready room by late morning. As I enjoyed a cigar and cup of coffee, I heard my new executive officer telling his story to a couple of pilots. He was detailing the incident of last night with the tear-gas canister in the nurses' quarters and about some sonuvabitch who kicked the can back and trapped him in the middle of the passageway with more gas, just when he was almost out of breath. I sipped my coffee, looked at his angry expressions, and decided not to fill him in on all of the facts. (Two years later, in New River, North Carolina, I told him about my heroic efforts of kicking a tear gas can down a passageway of the navy nurses' quarters in Vietnam and about some sonuvabitch kicking it my way. He didn't really appreciate my story.)

Two days later, Capt. Joe Rock and his AO, 1st Lt. Tom Walker, were making rocket and gun runs on an NVA unit only about eighteen miles south of Da Nang and three miles east of Hill 55. On one of his gun runs, Joe got some NVA rounds in the OV-10, and as he climbed for another attack run, the left engine stopped. He quickly feathered the prop and added full power to the right engine, climbing for altitude. All of a sudden, the right engine quit. It also had been hit. He alerted Tom Walker that they were ejecting and *bang! bang!* they both shot through the Plexiglas canopy of the OV-10, still at a very low altitude. Both chutes deployed correctly and they drifted to earth. Unfortunately, there were at least two companies of enemy all around down there. It just happened by luck that Major Curt Cassen, Hostage Smoke, was flying by Hill 55 in his Huey gunship when he saw the smoking OV-10 crash and sighted the two parachutes descending. Old Smokey Cassen, my tentmate from my first combat tour, dove his UH-1E chopper down and not too soon. The NVA were coming at Joe Rock and Tom Walker from all directions, firing their AK-47s. There was no time for either of them to get into the helicopter, so they both jumped onto opposite skids of the Huey and hung onto the forward-mounted M-60s. The two side gunners were firing all over their heads as they hung on and Smokey Cassen climbed the hell out of there. They made it and told us their hair-raising story that night at my little bar in my Quonset hut.

Our noncommunicative CO was transferred back to CONUS and we got a new CO who communicated with everyone, even me.

Shortly afterwards, we received our first AH-1G Cobra attack helicopters. We received eight of these slick Bell Helicopter Company helicopters that were designed and built specifically for attack of ground targets. Their mission in VMO-2 was for escort of medevac and supply helicopters and for reconnaissance. It was armed with four rocket pods and a front gun turret that could fire 40-mm grenades and 7.62-mm miniguns in an arc about the front of the thin fuselage. It was powered by a single jet engine. The crew consisted of a pilot in the rear seat and another pilot in the front seat acting as the gunner of the front-turret machine gun. It was determined that we pilots in VMO-2 would not switch back and forth flying the OV-10 airplane and the AH-1G Cobra, because we were in combat and we wanted maximum flying efficiency. Years before, when I was in VMO-2 and VMO-1, I flew both the OE-1 Bird Dog spotter airplane and the HOK-1 utility helicopter daily. So the CO offered the choice here to the pilots. If you decided to fly the new Cobra helicopter, that is what you would fly the rest of your combat tour and not switch back to the OV-10 airplane. To determine what you wanted to continue to fly, all the pilots were given a few flights in the new AH-1G. Since the first eight Cobras were turned over to our maintenance division, naturally the first pilot to fly this new attack helicopter was our hard-charging maintenance officer, Maj. Frank Dews—Hostage Uncle—who would later become a major general. The next pilot to fly it was Major Bart, the former maintenance officer and now our operations officer. My turn came to fly it, and Major Dews had me get into the front gunner's seat while he flew the machine from the rear, elevated pilot's seat. We took off and headed for the free-kill Arizona area near An Hoa. Within minutes we caught two NVA troops drinking water at a well in the village of An Phu. As they looked to the sky, Major Dews was already in a dive to demonstrate the speed and firepower of this slick chopper.

"Frank, should I shoot this front turret gun at 'em?" I asked.

"No. Let me demonstrate the stability of this airframe to you. I'll just fire a single rocket at them."

Frank Dews fired and we pulled off left. I watched the rocket impact next to the water well and both NVA were vaporized. I was impressed.

My next flight in the AH-1G had me in the rear seat as the pilot and Major Bart in the gunner's front seat. It was a medevac escort mission at night and we raised all kinds of hell with that Cobra. The CH-46 we were escorting was taking lots of .50-caliber machine-gun fire. I got one .50-cal gun with rockets, and Benny exterminated the other .50-cal with the high-powered front gun turret. I loved this attack helicopter. However, since my previous combat tour had been flying helicopters, I decided to stay with the OV-10A airplane after flying only twenty more Cobra missions.

One afternoon, I was seated in my S-1 personnel administrative office doing volumes of administrative paperwork when I heard that my old friend, whom I flew with in HMM-161 in Hawaii from 1962 to 1965, had just been killed. It was Capt. Ray Perry, who had, on his previous combat tour, earned a Navy Cross for his daring exploits of repeated rescue trips in his HUS helicopter into the falling Ashau Special Forces camp on March 10, 1966, until he was shot down. Ray Perry had been a warrant officer then and had worked his way up to captain. I knew he had been assigned at Chu Lai this tour, but I didn't know exactly what he was doing down there. This particular day, he had been flying a C-117 Hummer. This was the lengthened version of the old C-47 transport. We used them for years for logistics in the Corps (MARLOG flights) and also for night flare drops when the air force C-47 (Douglas DC-3) "Puff the Magic Dragon" or "Skytrain" wasn't available with its miniguns and night flares. From what I heard that fateful morning in my office, Ray had been flying the C-117 in the soup, and radar at Chu Lai guided him into a mountain top about fifteen miles west of the Chu Lai field. Apparently it wasn't radar's fault. The maps of that area were found to have erroneous readings of the altitudes of the larger mountains. So both Ray and the radar operator believed that he had proper altitude separation from the mountains.

I thought of Ray and his telling me of his encounter face-to-face with a tiger, after his being shot down in the Ashau jungle area in 1966. I knew that when I would write to my wife, Eleanor, about the loss of Ray, she'd well remember him and his wife, Cathy. What hurt now was that I recalled that Ray and Cathy had been married seventeen years and had no children. Then, magically, the good Lord gave them a child and now He took Ray in this terrible place called Nam.

As I sat there putting things in perspective, Capt. Joe Rock came into my office.

"Major, I'm assigned to put together a '68–'69 Vietnam cruise book of this squadron, with pictures and so forth. I need some words, some sayings besides the pictures we're taking."

"Why are you telling me this, Joe?"

"Because you're in here day and night writing and shuffling papers, when not flying. Maybe you can write something up for the book. I've asked a dozen guys and nobody wants to write anything."

"I'll think about it, Joe. If I come up with something, I'll give it to you. Where are you going to get a book published here in the middle of a war anyway?"

"I'm going to assemble it all here and then take it to a publisher, Sanyo Printing in Iwakuni, Japan."

"You're shitting me. You're going to get the CO to approve you to leave this hellhole to go to Japan for a few days to get a book published?"

"Yes, sir. I already have his approval and the wing's approval. But I must hurry up and finish this cruise book."

"Joe, I'm so goddamn envious of you getting out of here. I don't think I'll write you anything for this damn book. In fact, I won't write your orders to Iwakuni. You realize that I write the orders, don't you?"

"Major, you'll write those orders when the CO tells you to."

But that night at my homemade bar in my hootch, I wrote something for the last page of the book that Joe was putting together:

> The dawn burst forth into a new day.
> And despite last evening's rockets' red glare,
> hope rises for all, that in some way,
> this beaten ravished land,
> with more than its painful share,
> can find that sought-after peace.
> As the sunlight widens its path
> over villages and hamlets,
> some VMO-2 crews are retiring from last night
> and now crews that keep 'em flying are
> up at first light.
> The drone of the OV-10 and hum of Cobra is heard
> above the sky, whether it be sunny
> and clear or weather not fit for a bird.
> These Brave Men, with their own sweat and blood,
> have sacrificed so much for these people of South Vietnam.
> Through mortal combat and separation
> from Loved Ones, they have prevented the Flood,
> the disaster and death, of a people's cherished Freedom.

The next morning, I gave this to Joe Rock. He didn't even read it. He was just elated that someone gave him something written

to end his cruise book. Later, I had to cut him a set of orders at
the directive of the CO to send Joe to Iwakuni to get the cruise
book published.

On April 21, 1969, First Lieutenant Lane, Hostage Penny, was
the pilot of one of our new AH-1G Cobras. His copilot and
gunner was Captain Johnston. They were out on a routine medevac CH-46 escort mission: the CH-46 was to pick up three criti-
cally wounded marines located two thousand meters northwest
of Liberty Bridge. Liberty Bridge was a structural steel bridge on
the only railroad that ran north and south along Highway 1. The
bridge had been destroyed by the Viet Cong back in '65. It was
about seven miles northeast of An Hoa, near Ky Lam village.
Several attempts to get the seriously wounded out had failed.
One CH-46, Swift One-One, had been shot down, and another
CH-46, Lady Ace, was forced to abort the medevac mission
because of very intense NVA fire of small arms and .50-cal
machine guns. The ground unit, Latin Rebel Bravo One, was
under heavy fire from the northwest and southwest. Lieutenant
Lane in his Cobra directed the CH-46 medevac crew to make a
very low-level flat approach to the LZ to pick up the wounded.
As the CH-46 made his fast, low approach, the enemy began
pouring heavy volumes of fire at the medevac chopper. Lieutenant Lane attacked the dug-in NVA with rockets. The enemy fired
back heavily at the Cobra, but Lane returned for more attacks
upon them. The CH-46 landed, loaded the wounded but was hit
numerous times while in the LZ. One medevac navy corpsman
crew member was wounded. Despite hits upon the Cobra, Lieutenant Lane and Captain Johnston pressed their covering attacks
and escorted the CH-46 out of the zone and to the navy hospital.
Lieutenant Lane then had to land his battle-damaged Cobra at
Marble Mountain Airfield. While there, he got another medevac
escort mission call from a ground unit named Latin Rebel Two.
There were no other AH-1G Cobras available and his was damaged so badly that he and his copilot took a UH-1E gunship and
launched to escort the new CH-46 medevac bird. Again he covered the CH-46 under heavy hostile fire. He then returned to
refuel at An Hoa and while there received a third emergency
medevac escort mission. Latin Rebel Two had two wounded and

five KIAs to be removed from the same LZ. This time the NVA took up positions in a village and raked the CH-46 on final approach, wounding one of the CH-46 gunners. Lieutenant Lane attacked the village, silencing the enemy, although he received a hit on his lap belt, narrowly missing him. They got the CH-46 safely back to the hospital with the WIAs and KIAs.

Two days later, on April 23, 1969, First Lieutenant Lane was killed in his AH-1G on the side of Charlie Ridge southwest of Da Nang.

The same afternoon of April 23, 1969, I was a tactical air controller airborne in my OV-10 and was told by Da Nang DASC that there was an eight-man reconnaissance patrol, Asparagus Two, cut off by the enemy on a slope of a densely vegetated mountain about six miles southwest of An Hoa. When I checked in down there, Major Dews, Hostage Uncle, was piloting an AH-1G Cobra, and in his front seat as gunner was our new CO, Hostage Six. Major Dews was the emergency-extract commander at the time, and he briefed me on the situation. Asparagus Two was surrounded by a very aggressive NVA force, and Asparagus Two Leader, a first lieutenant, was killed plus two other team members were wounded. Major Dews had already requested an extract CH-46 section. I quickly requested a flight of jet bombers from Da Nang DASC. The recon team was about a half mile north, up a steep slope, from a possible LZ. Our job was to get them safely down to that LZ. Major Dews directed the team members to get the dead lieutenant. They could not, because of the heavy enemy fire from all around them. The Cobra ran low on fuel, so Major Dews turned the situation over to me and headed for An Hoa to refuel and rearm. I ran many rocket attacks close in and then ran several flights of F-4s, both air force and marines, in a circle around the surrounded recon team. I had gotten the team to move about 175 meters downhill when the NVA again increased fire and began a heavy volume of fire at me. A rain storm came through the area with showers and lightning. I couldn't see the ground, so I just kept talking to the recon team to assure them that we'd get them out of there, no matter at what cost. The storm passed, so I made a few more strafing runs and then brought some marine A-4s in with napalm to the west so it wouldn't roll down the hill on our trapped team.

In the meantime, Major Dews, while refueling and rearming at An Hoa, ordered two Huey gunships parked there to join him in his return with the two arriving CH-46 extract choppers led by Lady Ace Nine-Three, commanded by Major Roth from HMM-165. When he returned with his little air force of two UH-1Es and two CH-46s, I was also joined by another OV-10. Finally, after much close-in heavy fire support, including knocking out the enemy .50-cal gun that had killed the team leader, I fired white phosphorus rockets to create a smoke screen as the team retrieved the dead lieutenant's body. The team then moved quickly down the hill, fighting off attackers as they carried the dead lieutenant and helped two wounded. There was a fast-moving stream on their west flank. I led the other OV-10 on attack runs on the western flank along the stream, while Major Dews, in his Cobra, followed by two UH-1Es firing, attacked the east side of the retrograding team. As the recon patrol got close to the LZ, I broke off and ran an F-4 bombing strike to the north and northwest to stop NVA reinforcements from getting too close to the LZ pickup point. The CH-46, Lady Ace Nine-Three, came into a hover and dropped a ladder as it hovered above the LZ and jungle. The team members attached the body of the dead lieutenant to the bottom of the ladder, helped hook up their two wounded, and then the rest of them climbed up above and hooked onto the ladder. The CH-46 climbed out as all of us laid down rockets, bullets, and grenades. The satisfaction of being able to save this surrounded recon team by our low-flying lethal aircraft was worth an excuse to have a few rounds of beer that night.

By now the war had been allowed to go on for too many years. Congress never backed any of our presidents. Jane Fonda and Dr. Spock had our college campuses in an uproar. Many of our draftees were fleeing to Canada to wait out the end of this feeble attempt to stop North Vietnam from taking the South. The son of one of my best friends also fled to Canada. When this major in Vietnam read the letter from home about that incident of his son, he was devastated. I expressed my feelings to him. They were simple. Since none of the presidents could get the backing of Congress to wage a winning war, all stops pulled, then it was immoral to draft young Americans to fight a war that was not declared a war by Congress. So I felt that it was not immoral, just shameful, for those who fled the draft and ran to Canada. This conversation somewhat sedated my major friend, and he agreed with me.

These feelings of a lack of desire to win the war and allowing the war to drag on for years, crossed seven thousand miles from CONUS to Vietnam and to the troops and officers. Many a pilot who had too much to drink in the evening after a bad flight, had those drinks not because of his fear of the daily flight battles, but simply from despair brought on by lack of both governmental and citizen support of his monumental efforts. It was common international knowledge about the extensive drug use by the troops who tried to rid themselves of this despairing no-win attitude back in the States. Everything was affected.

The local black market in Da Nang flourished. Even some Red Cross girls in the White Elephant Hotel in downtown Da Nang sold themselves nightly for a fast buck. Several Red Cross men were caught trading Vietnamese dollars from the locals for American greenbacks for profit. The "I don't care" attitude was well established. The whole issue became deeply tainted and gloomy. It didn't have to be that way. But the stage was now set. Russian allies could move against Third World countries in the future without the strong American nation running to the rescue. The American presidents, Democrats and Republicans alike, got their fingers burned during this period. So did the fighting troops, as Congress did nothing year after year.

It was a nice sunny afternoon. The last weather front passed through our area that morning. It had rained all the night before, and so I was enjoying my flight in the now clear blue skies. I was flying a routine reconnaissance mission and I had just crossed a mountain peak over the Coal Mines southwest of An Hoa. I heard a familiar voice broadcasting over the UHF guard channel: "This is Lady Ace Two-Zero in a CH-46. I'm hit. I'm going down in Antenna Valley. I'm goin' in!"

Then there was silence. I knew that voice belonged to Len Bland. I was very close to Antenna Valley so I went to military power and covered the short distance of four miles in seconds. I saw one CH-46 circling over the valley and I looked down through the valley for a downed CH-46. I came up on guard-channel frequency and asked the CH-46 pilot that was still circling what was going on. He quickly told me that he was a wingman to the other CH-46 that had crashed. He said that they were crossing the valley when several .50-caliber machine guns fired at them and hit the lead aircraft and it went down smoking. I told him to climb to five thousand feet and stay in the area to the west over Dai Binh and to switch over to my assigned UHF tactical frequency. Maybe I could use him to get those downed flyers later. I looked below and saw our CH-46. It was upside down, nose down in a bomb crater and next to the village of Dai Phong. I saw some of the crew members crawling out of the wreckage. I called Da Nang DASC for a medevac package and two sections of jet attack aircraft. I got down to about one thousand feet and a heavy volume of fire was directed at me from three .50-cal guns. I rapidly climbed for a roll-in altitude and attacked one .50-cal gun, and it stopped shooting. Antenna Valley is a flat valley that had Highway 14 running east to west through the middle of it. To the north are the notorious Que Son Mountains. To the south are the Nui Chom Mountains. This valley was a known NVA staging area and infiltration route from the western mountains. It was called Antenna Valley because the NVA had so many radio antennas sticking up all over the valley. There were the four large villages of Phuoc Binh, Dai Phong, Trung Loc, and Tan An. I was worried about Len and his crew down there. There were NVA all over those villages.

I rolled in and strafed in the areas where I saw NVA moving toward our crashed CH-46. I saw our downed crew setting up one of their side-mounted .50-caliber machine guns in a defensive position beside their overturned CH-46. My first two attack aircraft arrived, two F-4s from the Gunslingers hot pad out of Da Nang, some thirty miles to the north. As soon as I worked the F-4s down to an attack-altitude orbit, the hundreds of villagers and NVA disappeared. They probably all went underground. I had the air force F-4s drop their thousand-pound bombs on the southern edge of the town of Phuoc Binh to let the NVA know we were here to stay and that we'd be bombing them until we got that downed crew out of there. As I worked the village over, four more .50-caliber machine guns began firing at both the F-4s and me. They were spread over a large area located on ground knolls north of Dai Phong and directly north of the crashed helicopter. I marked one of them with a WP rocket and then ran another section of air force F-4s on that gun, destroying it. I then had the F-4s get the other three guns. The pilots were sharp. I didn't even have to mark the last two gun emplacements. I simply described to these air force jet jocks where the guns were located from the last one that we destroyed. They visually picked up the guns despite their speed and altitudes and got 'em. The NVA .50-cal antiair guns were generally fairly easy to see from the air. Charlie usually had them on the high ground, and the gun emplacement was built like an anthill, except that a deep hole was in the center. The gun was located in the center of the hole. On most of them, they had a trenchline, or two, entering the center hole for fast access to the gun.

As I was running the second section of F-4s onto a group of NVA just to the south of the downed chopper, our extract medevac package of helicopters arrived. Two CH-46s, escorted by two AH-1G Cobras, began to try to get into the area. It took me another section of attack aircraft, marine A-4 Skyhawks dropping napalm, to fend off the aggressive NVA, who were attempting to kill the downed flyers. Finally, I was able to work two Cobras down close inside the bombings and burning napalm drops, and the two CH-46s both got the downed crew members. I did not use the extra CH-46 that I had holding over Dai Binh, so I had him come over to join the others en route home. I passed by the choppers in my faster airplane and was parked on our parking apron when they all came in for a landing at home base. I quickly got out of my aircraft after dearming and walked down to the CH-46s to see Len. I was devastated. Len was dead. So was 1st Lt. Randy Shell, the copilot. The other crew members were uninjured. What had happened was that a .50-caliber machine gun had shot their helicopter out of the sky. The bomb crater they had crashed into nose-first and inverted was filled with water. Len and the copilot were trapped upside down still strapped in their seats, under water. The other crew members tried but couldn't get Len and Lieutenant Shell out in time, and they both drowned. Our flight surgeon on the flight line examined Len and did not find any wounds or injuries from the crash. He had drowned. All my flights with Len in HOK helicopters and OE-1 Bird Dogs in the Caribbean, in North Carolina, and in Okinawa raced through my mind. I cursed this war and then withdrew from everybody except George Gross for days.

But, the very next day, I was airborne over Antenna Valley. I asked DASC for four flights of available attack air and received them. I stacked them up to twenty thousand feet and then worked each section meticulously. First I had them blow away every manned and unmanned .50-cal gun position that I could find. Then I started on the southeastern village of Tan An and worked the attack aircraft's five-hundred- and one-thousand-pound bombs up the valley. When I was finished two hours later, I was shocked to see the numerous large tunnels connecting all of the villages that our bombs had uncovered. I made the NVA pay for the loss of a very close friend. I made it a matter of principle to pay them a visit once a week during the rest of my tour of duty. I never did get over the loss of Len. He was special. He was vibrant and jolly at all times. He wouldn't hurt a fly or injure anyone's feelings. He simply was a happy pilot who loved to fly. George Gross and I talked several times about the night, my first night here on this second combat tour, that Len mentioned to us that he felt that he wasn't going to make it this tour. He was right.

One afternoon our XO came into our pilots' ready room and asked, "Who here personally knows Major General Thrash, our new wing commander?"

"I do," I promptly said. "I worked for him at Santa Ana and El Toro as a special-plans officer on airfield peripheral-land problems."

"Good. You're flying the general in the backseat of an OV-10 tomorrow."

"What's this all about, XO?"

"Tonight is a briefing for a large helo-assault lift into the south side of the Que Son Mountains. You attend the briefing. We'll also have three TACAs attend, since we'll have all-day OV-10 FAC coverage of this large troop movement. You will fly the general for the assault phase of the operation. He hasn't seen any helo-lift assaults yet in Vietnam and has asked to fly in an OV-10 to watch one. Take him a helmet, G suit, and torso harness. You will pick him up promptly at 0830 at MAG-11 flight line at Da Nang."

The next morning at 0825 I touched down on the Da Nang 36 runway and taxied up to the MAG-11 jet flight line and shut down both engines of the OV-10. I climbed out of my cockpit and watched Maj. Gen. William G. Thrash approaching with his aide. Here was this tall, distinguished-looking, gray-haired, two-star general in a green flight suit. He personally was carrying his own torso harness and helmet with oxygen mask. His aide carried only his kneeboard for note taking. I wouldn't need to use the helmet and torso harness that I'd brought for him. All I had to do was attach to his helmet a boom mike to allow the general to speak from the rear cockpit. The general wouldn't need his oxygen mask down at the one thousand to three thousand feet of altitude that we would be operating at today. As he drew closer to my aircraft, I recognized that glint in his blue eyes and the smile that I'd gotten used to when I worked for him at El Toro. His Georgia-Southern, slow-talking accent always projected the accurate facts, which he usually delivered with an exceptionally sharp sense of humor. Here was a true walking legend. He did things in the Corps that John Wayne made a fortune portraying on the silver screen. During WWII, he flew in the Solomon Islands, and then as the CO of MAG-5, he flew operations from the aircraft carrier *Salerno Bay,* (service for which he earned the Distinguished Flying Cross and five Air Medals. As a lieutenant colonel during the Korean War, he had command of MAG-12 and earned the Silver Star, the Legion of Merit, and the Purple Heart. In December 1951, he was shot down by the Communists and held as a POW until September 1953. Now he was here in Vietnam as commander of the entire 1st Marine Aircraft Wing. He didn't have to be here. He could have retired years ago. He sure as hell didn't have to be climbing into the back cockpit of my OV-10. But this was his lifestyle. He wanted to see, first hand, his air-wing support of the ground assault this morning.

We climbed out of Da Nang to about three thousand feet and were over the area of the LZ within minutes. The LZ was on an 845-meter-high mountain, Nui Chom, directly south of Antenna

Valley and to the southwest of the Que Son Mountains. As I crossed Antenna Valley, I looked down at the destroyed villages and large open trenchlines and tunnels that I had opened up by controlling bombings as a result of Len's death down there. I described all that below us to the general in the rear seat. I then spotted our OV-10 with the FAC aboard. It was Maj. Tom Watkins, Hostage Rifle. He would be the TACA and coordinate first an A-4 Skyhawk smoke-screen bird, then the troop-carrying helicopters with their Cobra escorts, and then the attack bombers simultaneously. He had 1st Lt. Bob Parks, Cowpoke Thirty, in his rear seat. I checked in with him and told him that I had "Actual" aboard, meaning that I had the general. I told him that I'd fly around over Antenna Valley until the smoke bird arrived and the assault started. Smoke time was scheduled for 0900 and it now was 0855 and still no A-4 smoke bird checking in. Both Tom Watkins and I saw the twenty-eight helicopters inbound, crossing the Korean-held area near Hoi An. When the lead chopper pilot checked in with Tom Watkins, he had them orbit over Hoi An until the A-4 smoke aircraft got in for dropping his smoke-screen canisters. The general was now very uncomfortable in my backseat and said, "Where the hell is my A-4 smoke bird?"

"I don't know, General. But it's now 0900 and he still hasn't checked in with our TACA in that OV-10."

Tom Watkins had shifted his UHF frequency to check in with DASC to determine where the A-4 was. He quickly came back up on our frequency and said to me, "Hostage Uniform, be informed that the A-4 smoke bird has not checked in with DASC or me. I've delayed the incoming helicopters."

"Roger, Hostage Rifle. I'll call home plate for our standby OV-10 smoke bird."

"Hostage base, this is Hostage Uniform with Actual. The A-4 smoke bird was a no-show for LZ prep. Request you send our smoke bird out here ASAP."

Capt. Don Kapon answered me, "Roger Uniform, this is Hostage King at base. That smoke bird will be airborne with Hostage Fox in seconds."

By now the general was very angry that one of his A-4 attack jets had not arrived precisely on time over the smoke target. He expressed a few strong words about it and commented that he'd raise all kinds of hell with that Chu Lai–based group commander when we landed back at Da Nang.

In fifteen minutes, the smoke OV-10 aircraft came flying into the area. He had aboard four nineteen-shot rocket pods filled with seventy-six 2.75-inch white phosphorus rockets. He checked in with Hostage Rifle and did not require a briefing, since he had been briefed on the LZ the night before. He rolled in and fired all of the seventy-six rockets. It was a fantastic smoke screen, masking the LZ from Antenna Valley enemy firebases. As soon as the CH-46s with Cobra gunships were on final approach, Tom Watkins had two F-4s dropping bombs around the LZ. It all worked like clockwork, and was very fast.

"I didn't know that the OV-10 had such a fine smoke-screen capability," said General Thrash.

"Yes sir. We use it quite frequently to help CH-46 medevacs get in and out of hot zones."

More and more helicopters landed and took off, as swarms of marines took all of the surrounding high ground for an eventual sweep north, down into Antenna Valley. Soon the CH-53 Sea Stallion heavy haulers arrived carrying internal and external logistics loads of ammunition, food, and water, and 105-mm howitzers for firebase operations. The whole helo-lift operation was over in minutes, and I asked the General, "Sir, would you like me to show you an enemy triple-A gun to our southeast, or would you rather head directly home now?"

"Why do you want to show me an antiaircraft gun, Major?"

"Well sir, it's a large Russian gun sitting under a camouflage net and protected by three .50-caliber machine guns triangulated around it. I've been reporting it for two weeks to intelligence, but it's still there. I've tried to get clearance to run bombers on it, but it's in the Americal Division area of responsibility. When I try to coordinate destruction of it, the army always says that they know it's there and that shortly they'll run a ground sweep through there and capture it. Unfortunately, the army's taking too long to knock out that damn gun. I'll show the general one of our CH-46s that the gun apparently shot down about a week ago."

"Yes, Major, I'd sure as hell like to see that gun and circumstances."

I turned east and flew over Highway 14 and through the pass that the highway bisected between the Que Son and Nui Chom mountains.

"General, the only way you can see this big gun under the netting is to get down on the deck and look under the netting. I'll stay well clear of it and we'll be in and out of there before they can track us."

I dove to pick up airspeed and flew along the north side of the river that paralleled Highway 14, staying on the Marine Corps side of our TAOR. I pointed out the three .50-cal machine-gun sites, and then the general saw this big AAA gun under the netting. I then showed him the burned-out shell of a shot-down CH-46 helicopter. We zoomed by and headed for home. I knew that if anybody could get something going for coordination with the army to get that big gun vaporized, it would be General Thrash.

En route to Da Nang to drop off the general, I thought: I sure as hell would not like to be that group commander at Chu Lai on the receiving end of the general's telephone call shortly, as to why that A-4 smoke bird didn't show up for helo-assault support.

Weather still played a factor with our air war in both the north and the south. We were missing Capt. Bob Story, called "Wimpy." He and his AO did not return from a very late afternoon OV-10 mission. While doing our regular missions, we all searched for Wimpy for three days. On the morning of the fourth day, we found his aircraft on the side of a steep canyon in the mountains northwest of Charlie Ridge. Our helicopter crews got both of these dead airmen out of the wrecked OV-10 and back to base. The aircraft was too smashed up to determine whether Wimpy had been shot down or had crashed into the mountains because of the low clouds. Knowing Wimpy, he probably was out there fighting with some NVA and got caught in the low clouds and could have been hit by gunfire or trapped in the canyon during the heat of the battle. A part of VMO-2 went with Bob Story. He'd been in VMO squadrons most of his long career in the Corps. I flew with him years before in VMO-1 in North Carolina and prior to that in VMO-2 in Okinawa. During my first combat tour, I flew several Huey gunship flights in VMO-2 in Vietnam with him. He had been one heck of a serious gooner killer, but now he had stopped chasing communists for good.

While standing the midnight to 0600 night-emergency-crew watch one night, we received a call from group operations. Da Nang DASC reported to them that a CH-46 had been shot down in the Arizona area during a medevac. It was reported that there were several active NVA .50-caliber machine guns in the immediate area. DASC wanted an OV-10 to go out and search for the .50-cal machine guns and neutralize them in the event that another medevac chopper had to go into that area this night. My AO, Cowpoke Sixty-seven, and I launched at 0200. It was an extremely black night. It was moonless with a solid overcast of about three thousand to four thousand feet. We arrived over the dark Arizona area at about 0230. It wasn't very difficult to find the general area where the .50-cal machine guns probably were. There in the middle of this dark, flat Arizona area lay a still-burning CH-46 helicopter. I flew directly over the burning wreckage to see if there were any survivors around it. I never did find out if there had been survivors, and if any other choppers had gone in there to get anybody out of the crashed helicopter. As I passed over the downed bird and circled north, a single .50-caliber gun opened up on me out of the blackness of an area directly to the north of the burning magnesium fuselage on the ground. The light from the burning chopper lit up the bottoms of the three-thousand-foot overcast silhouetting the dark green bottom of my OV-10 aircraft against the grayish white cloud bottoms. As the .50-cal gun's tracers arced through the night at me, it was a real play of lights. The whole countryside was pitch black, except for the fire below and Da Nang city about thirty miles north. With the bright, singular light of the fire glaring there and the total blackness all around, the only time that I could see the location of the NVA gun was when he fired his tracers at me.

I needed him to continue firing at me, but I didn't want to stay silhouetted against the overcast. So I dove straight at the .50-cal gun and fired two HE rockets to let him know that I was going to fight with him. That got his attention. He kept firing until the rockets exploded. My hits were way off. I couldn't achieve an optimum 3,500-foot roll-in altitude due to the 3,000-foot ceiling.

So I decided to roll in at a low 2,500 feet and use a dive angle of only twenty degrees. I quickly set my gun-sight setting for forty-seven mils. As I came around a second time the NVA gun did not shoot. I crossed him at 2,500 feet and as my tail was to him, the fool opened up again—a mistake. I immediately rolled inverted and turned toward him as his tracers came in at me. The tracers gave me a constant sight picture out of the black area in which he was located in reference to the burning chopper. Not losing that sight picture on my gunsight, I rolled back out, wings level, and set my twenty-degree dive. The maximum airspeed that I could pick up was 240 knots. I flipped on four of the rocket pod switches and then punched the rocket pickle button on my control stick with my right-hand thumb. *BBBWOOMM!* All four rockets fired, lighting up the black sky ahead of me as I pulled up carefully avoiding going up into the base of the overcast above me at three thousand feet. I looked over my left shoulder. All four rockets saturated the specific dark area that I had aimed for. Four little fires ignited from the massive explosions of my high-explosive rockets. I dove back down, picking up 250 knots and crossed the NVA gun site at one thousand feet. I was easily visible against the light gray of the base of the clouds as the CH-46 was still burning. The NVA gunner did not shoot at me. I turned 180 degrees and returned at the same low altitude. He again did not fire. I knew that I had gotten him. I crossed over the CH-46 for another last look for survivors. I didn't see any, so I told my AO, "Mike, let's go home. Nothing else that we can do out here tonight."

Just then, a volley of tracers arced at us from another .50-cal gun, one located on what we called Football Island, just on the eastern edge of the Arizona area on the Song Thi Bon River.

"That bastard! That shitbird! I was ready to go home, Mike."

As I added power and banked away from the tracers and Football Island, the tracers stayed with me. The sonuvabitch kept moving his machine gun as fast as I could roll and climb the aircraft. The reddish white tracers were now arcing about two feet from my Plexiglas canopy and staying with me.

"Mike, the bastard has us bracketed. Expect some hits."

"Major, those big bullets are awful close," responded Mike in the rear seat.

Then, abruptly, we were nose-high, climbing into the base of the overcast. The tracers were right there with us, lighting up the dark interior of the clouds. . . . an eerie sight of moving patches of white glowing spots moving with me in the clouds. Then the tracers stopped and it was all black except for the red lights of my instrument panel. Shit, my airspeed had bled down to 102 knots and my gyro horizon instrument was tumbling. I couldn't tell if I was inverted, straight up, or what my position was in the black clouds, due to having unexpectedly entered the clouds at an unusual attitude. I glanced at my rate-of-climb indicator. I was still in a thousand-foot-per-minute rate of climb. I glanced back at my airspeed—ninety-eight knots! With a load of ordnance aboard, I was ready to stall the wings out and spin in.

"Mike, hang onto your ass. I've got vertigo and we're near stall."

"I've got vertigo also, Major. I'm standing by for whatever."

I instinctively kicked left rudder and pushed the control stick forward, while still in full military power. We arced over in an apparent wingover, passing through zero gravity at a mere ninety knots of airspeed. Passing through the no G situation, something went by my nose. It was my AO's kneeboard. It had ripped off of his right thigh, floated up past the back of my ejection seat and slowly floated past my face. Just then my gyro horizon returned to usefulness, after it had made a few last tumbles. I saw that we now were in a deep dive, rapidly building up airspeed. Out of the clouds we came in a screaming dive . . . and would you believe, that sonuvabitch of an NVA gunner picked us up immediately against the cloud base and the .50-cal tracers were on our nose area. At that point, I didn't care if I was going to get shot or not. All I could do was to concentrate on our flight predicament. We were nose down, out of the soup, but with the airspeed climbing through 280 knots. I began a smooth steady pull of the stick, after pulling off both power levers back to flight idle. I pulled on the stick until I got a steady six-G pull on the G meter. The airspeed continued to increase as I slowly pulled the nose upward. We were passing 325 knots of airspeed.

"Mike, get ready. If we're not level at five hundred feet, I'm ejecting both of us."

"Okay, Major. I'm ready to go."

I had both hands on the stick pulling back like crazy and that dedicated NVA's gun tracers were still arcing above my canopy, just above my tall twin vertical stabilizers. He was moving his gun as fast as he could. However, I was still out in front of the bullets. Finally, at about six hundred feet, I leveled and then relaxed the stick and added full military power to get distance from the NVA gun.

I had two thoughts: one, go home and call it a night; two, get this rotten NVA gun now. I owed it to him for picking me up so fast after my uncontrolled dive out of the clouds. I thought about it a few seconds and then picked a third option. Get him with attack bombers. I called Da Nang DASC and asked for a section of attack jets. In fifteen minutes I got a call from the lead pilot of a section of air force F-4s. I explained to them that at this time there is only one .50-caliber machine gun out here and really not worth dropping bombs on. But I added that a .50-cal gun here did shoot down a chopper and almost got me and we have to get these NVA gunners to understand that when they shoot down a chopper, they'll pay with their lives. These air force jet jocks were more than willing to come down through the clouds and get this guy. I also added that they should be aware that there is never a single .50-cal gun. The NVA usually set them up Russian style: three triangulated. I briefed them on the fact that the bottoms of the clouds were only at three thousand feet. So they really had no dive angle for fast-moving jets. They responded with an estimated six thousand feet for the tops of the clouds based upon their climb-out from Da Nang. I had to brief them very thoroughly on the mountains just five miles to the west of the target area. I gave them a 360-degree simple run-in heading and a pull to the right (east), away from the mountains that none of us could see at night. The leader reported that he had broken out of the overcast at 3,100 feet and saw the now not-so-bright but still burning helicopter on the ground. It was an excellent reference point for these jet jocks.

"What the hell was that, Major?"

"Jesus, Mike! It was Dash One going right below us!"

"Dash Two. Watch out for the OV-10. Dash One just went right below me and heading west, the wrong heading," I screamed over the radios. It was too late. The second F-4 zoomed below me at about a hundred feet to join his leader. They both still had their night running lights on. I told them to take it around again and recheck their compasses for a 360-degree run-in. I then explained that I'd be at their same altitude of 2,800 feet, but I'd be on the west side of their attack orbit and out of their way. I told them to turn off their running lights or they'd get shot down. They did so and then I lost them in the darkness. I told them to make sure that they are set up on 360 degrees roll-in heading and to drop two thousand-pound bombs from where I tell them based upon my marking rocket hit. I rolled in and fired a single Willie Peter rocket. Its white puffy smoke was easy to see in the ever darkening black night as the CH-46 wreckage was now almost burned out.

"I'm in hot, Hostage."

"Roger, Gunslinger. I don't see you. If you're on a three-six-zero heading for my mark, you're cleared hot. . . . Shit! I've got you Dash One. You're in on a wrong heading. Turn zero-two-zero degrees immediately, mountains ahead. You must have been coming in on a two-eight-zero so . . . straight for those mountains to my west. Dash Two, do you also copy? Break it off and rejoin Dash One."

"Dash One off cold. Turning zero-two-zero. No drop."

"Dash One, what's the problem with your headings?"

"Hostage, I'm experiencing difficulties with my magnetic compass."

"Roger, Gunslinger. You're cleared to RTB. These mountains out here in the dark are nothing to fool with. Thanks for coming out. See you tomorrow."

"Roger. Good night, Hostage. Break . . . Dash Two, come up on my right. My lights are going on now. Take the lead home. My headings are all off on this bird. Let's keep it right below the undercast at three thousand feet or below and head straight for Da Nang. I don't want to climb back up through the soup with a nonfunctioning compass."

The F-4s were gone as fast as they arrived. I was still pissed off at the one NVA gunner down there. So I called Da Nang DASC for another section of air. A section of A-4E aircraft arrived from Chu Lai. They punched down through the soup and to my surprise, the lead pilot was Capt. Mike Dickerson, who had worked for me in 1st ANGLICO in Hawaii some years back. Mike was flawless and after a little cat-and-mouse game with that .50-caliber machine gunner, I marked the general area of the gun and Mike and his wingman dropped a total of four five-hundred-pound bombs on him. That NVA gunner met his ancestors at about 0345 that morning. Mike Dickerson and his wingman departed the area with a bona fide BDA of a .50-caliber machine gun to their credit.

It was late and we were low on fuel. Time to go home.

"Mike, let's head for home."

Mike, in the rear seat, responded, "I'm ready. It's been a long night out here, Major."

I flew straight for Marble Mountain when a third .50-cal gun opened up on us. I jinked a lot until I got well clear of Football Island and continued heading north for Da Nang.

"I'm too tired to fight with that son of a bitch, Mike. Let's look for him tomorrow afternoon."

"Roger that, Major. No sense in carrying on this whole war out here tonight by ourselves," he chuckled.

It sure looked quiet and peaceful as I made a long approach for landing on runway 35 at Marble Mountain Airfield. I landed and taxied into the dearming area. Just as our ordnance men began dearming our guns and rockets, an NVA rocket landed directly behind us and into a CH-46 helicopter in a parking revetment made from sand-filled fifty-five-gallon fuel drums. The chopper blew up in a mix of red, orange, and yellow colors. I quickly shut both engines down as our ordnance crew ran for a nearby bunker at the dearming site. A second incoming rocket impacted about fifty yards to our right out on the western taxiway. Mike and I were now out of the aircraft and running to the nearby bunker, when a third rocket exploded down near our crash crew. While we were in the bunker, four more rockets exploded out on the flight line.

Mike and I waited a good fifteen minutes in the bunker before we climbed back into the aircraft. I started it and the ordnance crew finished dearming the bird. I then taxied back to our OV-10 parking apron, a very tired pilot. It had been a long night. Mike said, "We didn't destroy much. But we did let the NVA know that there would be some response to their shooting a chopper down no matter what time of the day or night."

By the time we finished our debriefing with intelligence, it was about 0515. I drove Mike to his hootch in my jeep. I then parked my jeep at my hootch and walked next door to George Gross's hootch. I walked in and woke George.

"Goddamn it, Bob. What the hell time is it?"

"It's zero five forty-five, George. The sun is coming up. It's been one hell of a night out there. I need some rum and Coke, George."

I had a few drinks and talked with a sleepy George. He was now up for the day and soon would be going to fly his CH-46 helicopter. So I just hit his rack for a sound sleep.

(Several months later, Mike the AO had received notice that his application for flight school at Pensacola, Florida, had been approved by Headquarters Marine Corps. I thought, After that crazy night of duking it out with .50-caliber machine guns and then getting inverted in the soup and experiencing vertigo and then coming out of it into another .50-caliber gun shooting at us, that Mike must be nuts wanting to be a naval aviator. But Mike did go to Pensacola and a year and a half later was a pilot. His first squadron was a VMO squadron of OV-10As.)

The next afternoon, I got the word that Maj. Bernie Bronson had gone down in his CH-46 near Phu Thuong just twelve miles west of Da Nang. He and his whole crew got killed. Bernie had lived right next door to my hootch for the last four months. We often shared a bunker when NVA rockets came into our living area. He was a real professional Marine Corps officer and a very experienced pilot. He could not be easily replaced. It was during times like this, when we lost good people, that the antiwar groups back in the States most disturbed us. Tom Hayden was running around the country undercutting everything we were trying to accomplish at that time. His name as used in Vietnam during this period is not fit for print. But his name came up almost daily. Tom Hayden was a student radical who was quoted as demonstrating to "free the leadership of the revolution from U.S. prisons," and vowing to embarrass and destroy the authority of the government.

Several days later, while flying a routine reconnaissance flight, I came upon about 250 North Vietnamese out in the open. They apparently had just come out of a deep valley trail on the north side of the Que Son Mountains. They were heading across the open flatlands. They would eventually cross the railroad toward the Son Ba Ren River near the Korean Marine Corps TAOR. I'm sure that they heard and then saw me at my four thousand feet of altitude. I could have rolled in and got a lot of them right then. But I decided to see if we could get most of them in an attack that would not permit too many to scatter and run for it. I called Da Nang DASC and asked if they could, within thirty minutes, get me a flight of marine air loaded with antipersonnel canisters called CBU-24. This SUU-30/B (CBU-24) ordnance was a canister bomblet unit. Each can contained more than a hundred grapefruit-sized bomblets made up of flechettes (little steel darts) and ball bearings packed in explosive powder. The canister is preset to open at a predetermined height above the ground or target. When the can opens up, these hundred-plus round bombs fall the remaining distance dispersing in the air. Upon impacting the ground, they explode, sending the numerous steel flechettes and ball bearings out to about forty meters away. It is a very lethal, but expensive bomb package against large troop concentrations.

I asked Da Nang DASC to have ordnance at Chu Lai set the opening height of the canisters for one hundred feet, for large dispersion. DASC acknowledged my request and called Chu Lai's MAG-12 operations. I knew that MAG-12 had a lot of CBU-24, MK-20 Rockeye, and CBU-49 cluster bombs stored from the preparations for the Tet holiday offensive that the NVA never achieved this year. On the other hand, I had never requested any of these because of their high cost—about $40,000 per bomb canister. But here I could stop at least 250 NVA from getting out of the mountains and closer to Da Nang. As I waited for the DASC response to my request, I flew away from the NVA to fake them out and let them think that I didn't see them. I flew over toward An Hoa and orbited there where I could still see them moving in a tight formation, wearing bushes on their backs.

"Hostage Uniform, this is Da Nang DASC. Chu Lai says they'll have two A-4s up here for you within two-five minutes."

"Roger, DASC. I'll wait for 'em. These guys will be in the open for at least that time." The NVA were moving slowly. They then changed directions from northeast toward the north directly for the village of My Hoa. The north-south railroad traversed these flatlands and ran directly across at an angle from northwest to southeast. Due to these lands being low, marshy, and susceptible to flooding, the railroad was well elevated up on about a twenty-foot mound of dirt for about four miles. I watched the NVA approach the elevated railroad and stop. They held up on the south side of the railroad berm. It made me think of the Great Wall of China holding back the hoards of attackers from the north moving into China proper, centuries before. Of course, the NVA here could easily have climbed up this twenty-foot incline and crossed the railroad track. They were all in a group. Apparently they were getting some instruction, when my A-4s checked in with me.

"Hostage Uniform, this is Hellborne flight Four-Zero with a flight of two Alpha Four. Over."

"Roger, Hellborne Four-Zero. What's your posit, angels, and ordnance lineup?"

"We're inbound at angels one-two, descending for niner on the Da Nang one-seven-zero at four-zero. We just passed over Tam Ky city. Lead aircraft has two Delta One-two. Wingman has six Delta One."

"Roger, Hellborne Four-Zero. Meet me at the Da Nang one-eight-zero at two-zero miles."

The lead A-4 had two CBU-24 cluster bombs and his wingman had six five-hundred-pound general-purpose bombs. I didn't move near the NVA until the A-4Es were over the Que Son Mountains. I set them up for an orbit over the mountains, not over the concentration of NVA troops. I then told the lead A-4 pilot to drop both canisters of cluster bombs on the first run on target and his wingman to drop all six general-purpose bombs on his first run. I had them come out of the sun on a 360 heading. When they were set up and had the general area of the target in sight, I rolled in on the NVA from the southwest, also out of the sun, and fired a single Willie Peter marking rocket. As I pulled up to see my rocket smoke rising from the middle of the enemy concentration, the NVA began to scatter. But it was too late. My prebriefed flight of A-4s were in on the target with a five-second interval between aircraft. As I stopped my climb at one thousand feet just to the west of the disorganized NVA, the two white canisters fell from Dash One A-4 and he pulled off target. The cans descended about four hundred feet, then one opened and then the next. I saw nothing for a second. Then black and white puffs of smoke started exploding all over the ground throughout the semidispersed NVA forces. It was unbelievable, with several hundred explosions going off all over the place. The Dash Two A-4 was in at a steeper dive angle and I saw six black five-hundred-pound bombs descending into the North Vietnamese infantry. I then had the two A-4s make two 20-millimeter-gun runs on the edges of the destruction. I then came in low looking over the target area. Some of the NVA made it out of there, but not a hell of a lot of them. I gave a bomb-damage assessment of a probable 180 killed by air (KBA) to the departing A-4E aircraft crews. It was time to go home. I called DASC to send a relief OV-10 down to my area so he could clean up what was left running around out there on the flatlands with their bushes and branches on their backs. What I didn't know at the time was that the railroad dirt trestle was full of caves and honeycombed with tunnels under the railroad tracks. Apparently, the NVA moved large numbers of troops across the flat land at night from the Que Son Mountains and they stayed in these caves during the day. Then they would make another move from the railroad area the next night up toward the lightly vegetated fields and rice paddies south of Da Nang. For some reason, today they moved too many troops in broad daylight. That was one company of NVA that never would meet the "sting" of our marine infantry waiting for them.

Over the next several days, our OV-10 pilots and AOs killed a lot of the remnants of that large group of troops. They were finding them mostly trying to head back up into the Que Son Mountains. So there were a lot of reports to intelligence of "marking targets."

Late one morning, while in my S-1 office, I heard the meat wagon siren coming up the dirt road from sickbay. It stopped in front of our building. I went out to see what had happened. The corpsmen then escorted our XO and an AO from one of our OV-10s that had just returned from a mission. The crew members got into the ambulance and it took them to sickbay. Since I ran the personnel office and casualty reporting was one of the many divisions under it, I waited a while and then called to see what had happened to our executive officer, Hostage Papa, and his AO, Cowpoke Nineteen. The flight surgeon said that both were okay and were now on their way back to the squadron area. The major had been hit in the side of the face and had been bleeding a lot, but it was a minor wound. The AO had been hit in the front teeth and only received a slightly loose tooth and no open wound or bleeding.

Shortly, they both came into my office to report their battle wounds. I had my casualty reporting officer interview them to get the story of what the hell happened and to determine if they qualified to be administratively put in for a Purple Heart for wounds received in action against an enemy.

From what I was told, they were flying along when a .30-caliber bullet came through the side of the front cockpit. The impact upon the thick Plexiglas canopy tore the steel jacket covering off of the slug. The slug hit the XO in the face. Facial wounds bleed profusely, so he was bleeding like a stuck pig. The slug, after the jagged jacket tore off, flew back over the XO's shoulder and hit the AO in the partially open mouth, stopping in his teeth. He literally caught the slug in his teeth. My casualty officer reported this to me and then called sickbay for a "wounded in action" written report from the flight surgeon. Later that day, he received only one written report. That was on the XO because he was the only one that received physical damage and drew blood from the bullet. So my casualty officer wrote up the necessary administrative paperwork requesting a Purple Heart for him. The next day I heard an argument between the AO and my casualty reporting officer. I intervened and found out that the AO had not been put in for the Purple Heart. I called the flight surgeon at sickbay. He specifically told me the technical reasons why he did not consider a shaky tooth a wound. I lost the argument and told my casualty reporting officer that the flight surgeon will not document that bang on the teeth as a wound, so don't pursue it any further. The AO then approached me and asked me what I thought. Personally, I felt that he was injured, but I had no choice but to abide by the doctor's refusal to recognize it as a wound. So I told the AO that I'd write a news article for the 1st Marine Aircraft Wing newspaper titled "Marine Aerial Observer Catches Enemy Bullet in His Teeth." I did write the article and they published it as it happened. He showed me the slug. It had been bent in the middle at a forty-five-degree angle from impacting through the Plexiglas. He probably still has that bent bullet as a souvenir calling card from Charlie.

Not too long after that, the XO was transferred, and we had a new executive officer check into the squadron straight from CONUS. The XO promptly began flying our new AH-1G Cobra gunships. Only a few days after he checked in, several of us from VMO-2 were involved in a tactical problem with the enemy.

One of our battalions was engaged with an NVA force at the western base of the Que Son Mountains. The NVA had reinforced concrete bunkers built midway up a sheer cliff. The machine-gun bunkers apparently had deep tunnels back into the Que Son Mountains. These bunkers were firing down upon the battalion, which was having difficulty maneuvering under the hail of fire from the cliffs above. I was running attack jets with bombs and napalm against the NVA fortifications. However, it is very difficult to bomb the side of a cliff. Some CH-46 helicopters coming into an LZ in the battalion area drew heavy fire from these cliff machine-gun positions, despite our bombs falling on top of the caves and gun positions above. Our two helicopter-escort AH-1G Cobra gunships went right after those machine guns as their transport helicopters landed below the cliffs. As our two Cobras began attacking straight into the side of the cliff positions, the NVA shifted their fire from the battalion and the just-landed CH-46s below. The enemy fire began going after the attacking Cobras. On about the fourth rocket and gunnery run by the Cobras, I saw smoke pouring from the engine compartment of one of our Cobras. Then I heard our new XO in the smoking gunship say that they were hit and that they were going in. The other Cobra, flown by Maj. Steve Cross, Hostage Able, relentlessly attacked the hardened-concrete gun positions, but the NVA continued to fire on the downed Cobra, which landed safely but burning on the ground below the cliffs. I saw the front pilot/gunner jump out and run one way and the rear-seated pilot run the other way from the burning chopper. Unfortunately, one of them ran up a small incline in the terrain and the rotor blades, still turning slowly, struck him on his head and he fell to the ground. I called for more Cobras and more OV-10s and continued air strikes as we shot rockets straight into those reinforced-concrete bunkers.

Hours later, back in the squadron, I was told that our new XO had been killed. The still-moving rotor blades of his shot-down Cobra had killed him. This early version of the AH-1G Cobra did not have a hand-pull rotor brake on it like all previous helicopters. Had it had one, the XO probably would have pulled the rotor brake prior to exiting the burning chopper. A year later, I met the XO's wife, and she wanted to know exactly how he had gotten killed. I told her, and it was very important to her that she knew how it had happened.

One of our daily missions was different from a single OV-10 flying out over the TAOR and looking for NVA or adjusting artillery or naval gunfire. This particular mission was a two-plane formation of a deep reconnaissance flight west of Da Nang back into the mountains on the edge of Laos near the Ho Chi Minh Trail. It was conducted at very low altitude so that we could see down into the jungle. The lead OV-10 was flown at five hundred feet above the jungle canopies, while his wingman covered him from a stepped up and back position at about 1,500 feet above the ground. The objective was to look at the numerous trails coming out of Laos and the Ho Chi Minh Trail and report any heavy troop movements and to take pictures of them. Low-level visual navigation was extremely difficult out there over those numerous large mountains. They all looked the same. One afternoon, as my wingman and I approached what we thought was the border of Laos, I flew across a small open field in the middle of thick jungle. I saw five elephants grazing in the tall grass of the open field. But I also saw that the elephants had large boxes on top of them and also hanging over their sides. I crossed over them at about five hundred feet in a second and told my wingman. He also saw the elephants, but he had already crossed over too fast to fire at them. I jammed my two fuel condition levers full forward, followed by pushing both power control levers to full military power and climbed for a rocket run. In my climb, I saw North Vietnamese soldiers chasing, with long bamboo sticks, the fully loaded elephants out of the open field and into the jungle. By the time I was all set up for my attack dive, there was only one elephant left in my gunsight out in the clearing. I fired and pulled looking back for my single rocket impact. There was a small explosion followed immediately by several very large secondary explosions. My wingman was in on an attack and he rocketed the thick jungle, where the other elephants had been chased. There were several more secondaries. We both unloaded all rockets in there and departed for home, knowing that we got at least one heavy jungle truck full of NVA ammunition that would have soon made its way down to South Vietnam to be used to kill anyone who resisted the communist invasion from the North.

It bothered me for a long time after that to have shot an elephant simply because those North Vietnamese were using it for ammunition transportation. I didn't tell my wife, a staunch conservationist, about this unfortunate situation until about four years later.

On another mission outside of the TAOR, I was on a single-plane reconnaissance mission. It was a search for NVA on trails closer in, but still well west into the mountains. Just after dawn, I came across a long, snaking river coming out of the mountains near Bung Bac, about thirty kilometers west of An Hoa. I spotted four long sampans, or junks, heading east, downstream. I dove down and slowly passed the boats. They were loaded with boxes. As I went by, I could see NVA troops aboard, but they did not fire at me. They were wearing steel helmets instead of the jungle pith helmets. I circled and climbed to the east and then rolled in on the lead boat from the east, with the rising sun to my back. I threw my SUU-11 Gatling gun centerline pod switch on. I started firing the 7.62-mm Gatling gun. The extreme rate of fire cut the boat in half, as NVA soldiers jumped into the wide river. I continued firing into the second junk and it blew sky high with several secondary explosions, as I pulled back hard on my stick to avoid flying through debris blown into the air. I quickly turned 180 degrees and made an attack run from the west, coming downstream. A third boat was sunk, as secondaries exploded. By the time I rolled in from the east, out of the sun again, I saw the soldiers from the fourth junk jumping into the river. Holding my finger to the trigger on the control stick, I walked the Gatling-gun bullets down the long boat from bow to stern and it blew up almost instantly from my bullet impacts on the load of NVA ammunition.

On my way home, I flew down a valley above the Song Vu Gia River. I approached the end of the valley over the area where in my previous combat tour I had troubles with my collective stick on my HUS helicopter during Operation Orange. I decided to come down from about six thousand feet, since I would be out over the flatlands in seconds. Just prior to reaching the end of the valley, I leveled at two thousand feet. I no sooner leveled when I saw a silver U.S. Air Force FAC aircraft. It was the O-2 Super Skymaster, called a push-me, pull-you, or Mixmaster. This twin-engine Cessna was from an air force FAC squadron located directly across the runway from our squadron at Marble Mountain. The O-2 was crossing in front of me from right to left and was only about a half mile directly in front of me. I added power and began a climb so as not to fly too close to him. All of a sudden, he blew up below my nose. The explosion appeared to be in the rear of the cockpit, disintegrating the fuselage. The two wings and tail section fluttered to earth like an East Coast "pug nose" seedling from a tree. The burning cockpit and engine section fell faster to earth. I never saw any gunfire. I didn't know exactly what those air force FACs were doing there at the time. But I knew that now they were apparently dead. There were no chutes and there was certainly no time for either of the two crew members to use a chute. The O-2 has no ejection system. I orbited twice at three thousand feet looking for survivors, knowing that there were none from the exploded impact of the fuse-lage crash upon the ground. I looked for NVA guns or smoke from guns. I saw nothing. I called DASC and reported the plane being shot down. I asked for an OV-10 to come down and check the area out. I only had about twenty minutes left on my thirty-minute low-fuel-warning red light. The area was located on the extreme northwest corner of the Arizona area. We'd all have to look very closely at that area over the next few days to find out what had happened to that O-2 aircraft and crew.

I had the good luck to catch boats of ammunition on this river where I had been this particular day on six more flights out there during this tour of duty. These NVA sure were busy beavers using trucks down the large, six-lane Ho Chi Minh Trail, elephants through the jungle along with mountain tribesmen used as slaves, and numerous boats on the many rivers to move their Russian and Chinese ammunition south from North Vietnam.

On June 28, 1969, I was assigned as a TACA on a mission to support our recon unit located on the top of the Que Son Mountains, twenty miles south of Da Nang and four miles southeast of An Hoa. Our recon unit was up there counting and reporting the numbers of NVA moving through the mountains northward from the Antenna Valley area.

When I checked in with the recon unit, Hireling, they reported sighting 160 NVA troops with bushes and shrubbery on their backs, moving north in a deep ravine. My backseat AO, Cowpoke Fourteen, quickly called a nearby American army recon team, Cradle. Cradle reported to us that they were on the opposite side of the deep ravine from our marine recon unit and that they sighted and counted about the same number of NVA troops walking north, deep in a ravine. I asked our marine recon team if I was cleared to fire into that ravine. They said that there were no marines down there. But they could not vouch for the army. The army TAOR was on the other side of the east end of the Que Son Mountains. We received clearance from Cradle. The army recon team reported that there were no army friendlies down in that ravine area.

Because clouds were just five hundred feet above the Que Son mountaintops, I couldn't climb any higher than three thousand feet. Therefore I set up for a slant range and dive angle. I attacked with all four rocket-pod switches on and all four M-60 machine-gun switches on. I did not have a centerline Gatling gun aboard this flight and sure wished that I had. Coming out of the south with the NVA troops marching north, they never saw me until my four rockets impacted and then my four machine guns started ripping into their straight column. I quickly came around for a second pass. The back end of the column had been hit hard.

Bodies were lying all over the ravine bottom. The middle of the column was scattering frantically up both sides of the ravine. The front of the column was somewhat scattered. However, at least twenty NVA were running north still in the ravine. I put two rockets into their midst. Coming around for a third pass, I had a good look at them on my downwind leg. Most of the center group of the column were now up out of the ravine behind big rocks and I even saw some caves that they were running into. All I could do now was to strafe with my guns. There were no longer groups to fire rockets at. A couple more machine-gun passes and then it was a waste of time. It was also time to go home from my two-and-a-half-hour flight. Recon told me that they would go down closer to the ravine early that evening to get a body count.

The next morning, on an early launch while checking in with Da Nang DASC, DASC congratulated me for one hundred KBA. They had gotten a call that night from our recon team Hireling that their body count totaled a hundred. I flew down there and looked down the ravine and on the hillsides and my AO counted fifty-five NVA bodies still there. The next day, while working in the area, we sighted only twenty-five bodies. The NVA must have been pulling those dead bodies out a few each night.

Another type of mission that we flew in VMO-2 was a support mission to cover U.S. Navy gunboats along the Truong Giang River. This river forms at the intersection of the eastern end of the Song Thi Bon River where it runs into the Song Cua Dai exit into the South China Sea. This northern start of the river is only two miles south of the city of Hoi An on the coast, and it runs parallel to the coast and southeast past Tam Ky city to another outlet to the South China Sea, just north of our marine Chu Lai air base. It's very similar to our East Coast inland waterway, except that on the western bank it is very heavily vegetated and has numerous villages along the approximately forty-five miles of river.

My AO, Cowpoke Twenty, and I flew past Hoi An and checked in on the assigned FM frequency, as we picked up visual sighting of the river.

"Jasper Three, this is Hostage Uniform. Over."

"Hostage Uniform, this is Jasper Three. We've been expecting you. We are taking heavy .50-cal fire from a vil down here on the river. Where are you?"

"Jasper, this is Hostage Uniform. I'm inbound about five miles south of Hoi An and over the river. How far south are you on the river?"

"Hostage, we're about eight miles south of Hoi An at Bravo Tango two-four-three, four-three-zero. The village that we're taking fire from is Van Doa Tay. Hurry up and get down here. We could use some air cover. There are several .50s raking us. We may have to back the boat up and withdraw. The fire is heavy."

"Okay, Jasper Three. We have you in sight. We see your boat now and the gunfire exchange. Where is most of the gunfire coming from?"

"Most of it is coming from behind trees along the river's edge in the east end of the village."

I orbited once around at 1,500 feet, getting the lay of the land. I could see the backs of some of the NVA gunners on the west side of the river.

"Jasper Three, keep firing at those guns. I'm coming in from the rear with a few rockets. We'll teach those suckers to shoot at navy gunboats."

I rolled in from the west and put four HE rockets into the backs of two NVA machine gunners. While in on that run, I saw two more .50-caliber machine guns. I came around again and as I was rolling inverted, I saw our gunboat coming very close into the edge of the river, firing its high-mounted .50-cal gun into the same treeline. After four more of my rockets exploded, it all seemed quiet down there, as I orbited the village. Then I saw all of the villagers, who had crowded on the west side of the village, leaving the village to the west through a thick treeline.

"Jasper Three, this is Hostage Uniform. There's about one-two-zero people departing the west side of the village now. Are you still getting any fire from the village?"

"Roger, Hostage. No more fire at us from the vil at this time. Understand one-two-zero villagers leaving to the west. You are cleared to attack them. Do you have jet bombers with you?"

"Affirmative. I have bombers up here with me. But I don't have any good targets for bombs."

I switched on my tape recorder that all FACs in the OV-10s could carry with them for radio conversations to give to intelligence for information gathering and for recording any heated close-air-support discussions between the air and ground units. I began recording all of our radio conversations between the gunboat and me.

"Well, bomb those villagers, Hostage."

"That's a negative. We don't bomb villagers."

"Hostage, those sonuvabitches were just shooting the hell out of us. You're not going to let those NVA get away with those villagers are you?"

"Jasper Three, there may be some NVA regulars mixed in with the villagers but I can't tell from up here. The mass of people is now leaving the treeline that is on the western part of the village. Looks like they stopped along a rice-paddy dike. Looks like someone, maybe the village elder or chief, is talking to them."

"Hostage Uniform, those people are all NVA supporters. Go ahead, kill them with your own guns, or bring in the jets."

"Jasper, I can't do that. They're civilians with possibly a few NVA hiding mixed in with them."

"Hostage, the province chief said that you have his permission to kill them all. He said that this particular village has been a VC village for years and has fully supported the NVA regulars for the last two years. Plus, all the young men are draft dodgers who joined the VC."

"Jasper, I understand that the province chief wants all those people killed. What province is the chief from?"

"He's the province chief from this province. He says that all those people are communists who are responsible for killing many village chiefs along that river."

"Understand that he is the local province chief. Where is he now?"

"Hostage, the province chief is right here on the gunboat. He's standing right next to me. He came along to show us which villages were under the NVA control. This is one of them."

"Okay, Jasper. I understand that the province chief is aboard and that he wants all of those people killed. I can't make those judgments from up here from what I can see. I'm going to fly very low over those people to see if there are NVA in with them. I'll let you know what I see."

I got down to three hundred feet and came by the crowd in the rice paddy, flying north to south. The sailors on the gunboat were right. I saw four regular, uniformed NVA troops, each carrying an AK-47 assault rifle. Then, by luck, an army O-1 Bird Dog observation plane was going by at about two thousand feet. I called him up on the common emergency frequency of the guard emergency channel and told him to come up our frequency on which the gunboat was up on FM.

"OV-10 south of Hoi An. This is Blue Lightning. Over."

"Blue Lightning, this is Hostage Uniform in the OV-10, below you to your east. Do you have a few minutes of fuel to work with me?"

"Affirmative, Hostage Uniform. We have two-zero minutes to dedicate to your activities. What do you have in mind?"

"Blue Lightning, do you see that crowd of people gathered on the west side of the vil, off my right wingtip?"

"Affirmative. We see those people."

"Blue Lightning, I want you to go very slow and very low past them. I saw four NVA with weapons mixed in with them. I want you to fire your pistols at the NVA, as you go by. Maybe we can get the crowd away from the NVA."

I gotchya, Hostage. Cover me. I'm in. Both my rearseat AO and I will pick away at 'em with our .45s."

"Great; I'll climb to three thousand feet and orbit you, as you make your several low passes. If you get a single shot, let me know. I'll dive right down and shoot my machine guns."

The army Cessna O-1 went right down on the deck and came by the crowd. Then I saw both handguns firing from front and back cockpits. The crowd below dispersed in panic. Some ran back toward the village and immediately the gunboat opened up at them and they quickly ran back through the treeline to the open paddies. The rest of the crowd ran in four directions, all over the rice paddies to the west. The four NVA stuck together and headed due west through the rice paddies and then up onto flat, dry land.

"Hostage, your idea worked. We have those NVA all alone out there. We'll get 'em with our .45s."

The O-1 aircraft came alongside of the running NVA and I saw puffs of smoke and flashes from both of the O-1 cockpits. Then I saw one NVA fall, apparently hit by a couple of .45 slugs. Immediately, the three remaining NVA hit the ground and began firing their AK-47s at the passing O-1 Bird Dog.

"Hostage, I'm taking some rounds. These guys now want to fight it out. I'm out of your way to the west now."

"Thanks, Blue Lightning. I'm in with four M-60s. You pull south. I'll be pulling off target to the north. Thanks a hell of a lot. I won't need you anymore. Have a safe trip home."

The three NVA, plus the apparent dead NVA, were lying right out in the open as my M-60 slugs dug dirt from east to west through them. I figured that I killed them all in that run. I climbed and came back for a second run. One of the NVA wasn't hit. He got up and ran like hell into a nearby treeline. By the time I could maneuver into another gun run, he had ditty-bopped into the thick treeline. I sprayed the treeline with machine-gun bullets. Then I came back and fired four rockets with hopes of accidentally getting him. I knew that I had lost him. I came back over the other three NVA. They weren't moving a muscle.

"Okay, Jasper Three. The army Bird Dog got one NVA and I got two. One other might have escaped. I'm going to come back over the village, slow and low for another last look for NVA and guns."

"Thanks, Hostage. The province chief says that you did a good job. We're now moving on down the river to check out Ca Linh village."

"Okay, Jasper Three. My relief OV-10 is on its way over Hoi An now. He'll check in with you in five. I'm departing for home now. See you some other time. Tell that province chief that he can't kill everybody down there, or he won't have any people to be the province chief of."

I briefed my relief OV-10 crew and told them about how this province chief would have us kill everybody in the village, so they should exercise caution. Then I headed for home. I gave my tape of the conversations between me and the gunboat to our intelligence officer for his briefing future air crews going down to work that river area.

I mentioned to our intelligence officer that I wasn't going to play God from up in the sky and determine that all those villagers should die. Hell, as far as I knew, maybe the province chief just didn't like that whole damn village, long before the NVA took control of it. The bottom line was that I was not going to shoot unarmed villagers, just armed troops, no matter what the political situation.

Walking back to my hootch, I came across one of my old gunners from flying Huey gunships during my previous tour here. He was up on top of his rusty corrugated tin roof of his hootch. He was holding a paint brush and paint can. I shouted up to him, "Sarge, what the hell are you doing up there? Painting the roof?"

"No, Major. I'm painting a big bull's-eye on the center of my roof. Then I'm going to paint a sentence: 'Gooners can't hit shit!' "

I shook my head and with a smile said, "If Charlie sees that, he may try to blow you away."

"Major, those assholes fired mortars at us the last tour and now rockets at us this tour and they haven't hit me yet. I may as well give them a target to shoot at."

I crawled up onto the side of the roof. Sure enough, he had a very large bull's-eye target painted on his hut. This guy had a sense of humor and now had a sense of satisfaction.

chapter 7

Killing Is Now Routine, 1970

On one of my routine responses to a ground unit in contact with the enemy, I arrived over a company that had elements trapped under heavy fire. The location was on the northern end of the Arizona area. As I crossed over their firefight, I looked down and saw parts of the air force O-2 Super Skymaster Cessna that had exploded right under my nose, sometime back. This was always a hot area. In this case, the NVA held a large village and had been hiding in a typical treeline waiting for one of our marine companies to advance in the open toward that village. When the marines were in the open, the NVA opened fire, pinning the lead elements out in the open rice paddies.

I didn't waste much time and got a section of marine A-4E aircraft in there to drop napalm tanks on the treeline. As the A-4s left the burning treeline, the marine lead elements got up and began to attack the enemy in the burning treeline. I thought that I'd roll in and put some more rockets and then bullets into the NVA defense line to assist the now attacking leathernecks. As I came down in my thirty-degree dive, with both guns and rocket switches on, I saw this one NVA get up out of the burning timber and smoldering rubble. He stood straight up and held his AK-47 right at me. He completely disregarded the incoming bullets from the attacking marines who were now charging the smoking treeline. I couldn't believe this guy. He was going to take me on, with an assault rifle, all by himself. I was still too high to fire my rockets. As I continued to dive at 250 knots, passing through 2,200 feet, this crazy NVA began shooting at me. His tracers were dropping way off below my nose, but he kept standing there, apparently in great anger. I stared through my gunsight at him and glanced at my altimeter unwinding. He kept firing, challenging me. At exactly two thousand feet AGL, I punched the pickle button on the stick and a single rocket went straight for him. As I pulled and looked back, he continued firing at me and then disappeared in a cloud of black and white smoke. He apparently had been crazed by the napalm burning all around him. He must have known that he was going to die if he stood up. Yet it made no sense to stand up and fire at an attacking aircraft, while under ground attack. Maybe he did it for Ho Chi Minh or even for Karl Marx.

On a sunny afternoon, I checked in with a battalion called Snap Dragon, located near Chu Buai, fifteen miles south of Da Nang. They had just begun receiving incoming mortar fire from the north. As I discussed the situation on the FM radio with them, I received a call from Da Nang DASC on the UHF radio. DASC told me to report to a battalion with the call sign of Flash Back. I told DASC that Snap Dragon was receiving incoming and that I'd begun a search for the mortar position. I would soon call Flash Back.

As I flew over the positions of Snap Dragon, I saw that they had received casualties and that there also was a marine who appeared dead lying on the northern end of a wooden footbridge that crossed a narrow river. He must have been hit by the mortar frags, since the bridge was still intact. Snap Dragon was calling for a medevac chopper, as I flew north to locate the NVA mortar position. I descended to one thousand feet, and my AO and I scanned the village treelines and rice paddies.

I called Flash Back on the FM radio and they reported incoming mortars from the south. I told the Flash Back radio operator to get their battalion commander, Flash Back Actual, up on the radio.

"Hostage Uniform, this is Flash Back Actual. We are taking incoming from NVA mortar. They are coming in from the south."

"Roger, Flash Back Actual. I'm over your area now. Be informed that companies from Snap Dragon are to your south and that they also are receiving mortar incoming, but from their north. That's from your south. Over."

"Roger, understand. We know that Snap Dragon is somewhere to our south. That's why we didn't fire southward."

Just then, my AO, Cowpoke Sixty-three, said, "Major, I've spotted the gooner mortar at our four o'clock on that mound near those three hootches."

I looked downward to my right rear, and sure as hell, there were four NVA dropping mortars into two mortar tubes. One tube was firing south toward Snap Dragon companies and one was firing north at companies of Flash Back.

Both Cowpoke Sixty-three and I realized, at that moment, that these smart bastards had deviously established themselves right in the middle of the two battalions of U.S. Marines. The NVA obviously figured that in the confusion of their firing at both marine companies, the companies would immediately return mortar fire. If just a little long on their shots, the companies would soon be firing at each other, taking casualties before realizing that they were both firing at friendlies.

I quickly called both battalion commanders to pass the word to their companies not to return mortar fire. I fully explained the NVA trick.

I then climbed to 3,500 feet and rolled in firing two HE rockets. One rocket impacted close to one mortar tube and threw the two NVA gunners into the air in a cloud of dust. The other two gunners quickly abandoned their tube and ran into a thatched hut.

I came around again and fired a single HE rocket into the thatched-hut roof. As I pulled off target, I saw the grass roof burning from the explosion inside.

On my downwind leg, I saw four NVA running out of the burning hut. There must have been a group of NVA in that hootch. How any survived my rocket explosion in there amazed me. I watched them run directly to a hole in the ground. It must have been an entrance to a hole or a tunnel complex. If it was a bunker, my 2.75-inch high-explosive rockets would only dust off the sand from the large timbers that the VC and NVA used for bunker roofing.

I quickly called my friends at about eighteen-thousand feet above me. As a FAC, I always had at least a section of two jet attack aircraft with me to use on hard targets.

I briefed the flight of marine F-4 pilots and then rolled in and marked the bunker target with a Willie Pete marking rocket. It hit about ten meters from the entrance of the bunker or tunnel.

The lead F-4 dropped a pair of five-hundred-pound bombs. One blew away the entrance to the bunker. The other impacted about fifteen meters to the left of the target.

His wingman, Dash Two, dropped a pair of five-hundred-pounders. One missed to the right and the other was a bull's-eye.

"Good hit, Dash Two. Direct hit. Dash One, I'll give you a quick BDA and adjustment as soon as the smoke and dust move off the target. Extend your downwind a little for me and stand by," I directed.

"Roger, Hostage. Dash One and Two extending."

As the smoke drifted to the west from a gentle breeze, I was shocked. The roof of a bunker had been blown off from the single hit. What I saw made me sick. There, among the smoking timbers and dirt, were at least twenty people. Only a few looked like NVA. The rest appeared to be women and children.

"Dash One. Take her around for an orbit and go switches off. I think I have a problem with our target. I'm going down closer to look over exactly what we uncovered."

"Roger, Hostage. We'll take our orbit up to about six thousand feet and stand by ready."

I dove down toward the uncovered bunker, machine-gun switches on. I aileron-rolled the aircraft on its side and looked into the debris, passing overhead at about five hundred feet. It was a gruesome sight. All huddled together, some obviously injured, black-pajama-clad villagers sat expecting to die. The NVA stayed right in there with them, as I zoomed aloft to three thousand feet. I slowly circled the village and saw no more NVA.

I called both Snap Dragon and Flash Back to inform them of the exact location of the NVA and told them that I would continue to orbit over the NVA and villagers, as the marines coordinated sending an assault company up the ridgeline between the two battalions to capture the NVA troops.

I sent the two F-4s home. Twenty minutes later, I carefully watched our grunts encircle the village. Then they were upon the still-smoking opened bunker pulling out the wounded NVA and villagers.

I sure was glad that none of the villagers died from my directed bomb blast. But I was really pissed off at those NVA for running into the villagers' cowering bunker, causing them to be my target.

One early afternoon, I was assigned on a mission to try to locate a reported NVA regimental headquarters. The grid coordinates given to me by intelligence were AT 820895. This was about twenty miles northwest of Da Nang in the mountains. After looking over the specific area for an hour, my AO, Cowpoke One, and I couldn't see anything but jungles. Out of desperation, I got down right over the jungle canopy and slowed to about 140 knots. We made numerous turns over the hills, when my AO said, "I saw a corner of a concrete bunker. Did you see that, Major?"

I hadn't seen it. He then directed me over that area again. Sure enough, under the trees we could see the corner of a massive concrete structure. But in addition to that, we both now saw a steel-helmeted NVA, with rifle, standing outside of a doorway. He was looking right up at us, but didn't run back inside the doorway. I went by again and I couldn't slow the OV-10 aircraft down below 108 knots because of my heavy ordnance load. I wanted to see more. My AO then told me that an army Loach helicopter was going by the area. This was a small army helicopter built by Hughes Helicopter Company and designated LOH for Light Observation Helicopter. It could carry a crew of two and four troops and was nicknamed Loach.

I called the Loach's pilot to come up on my frequency and he did. I asked him if he'd go down slower than I could and lower to look at a concrete building for me. I needed a better feel for the size of that concrete structure. He obliged me and I covered him with my guns. As I watched him, I expected him to fly by slowly and look over the concrete building. Instead, this heroic army pilot came into a hover directly over the corner of the structure, just above the canopy of trees. The next thing I see is that his passenger is exchanging gunfire with that sole NVA at the entrance door to the bunker. He must have been hovering only twenty feet above that NVA. Then he quickly buzzed off. He climbed up and briefed me. He had seen a concrete building that was the size of a four-bedroom home. This sure as hell must have been the intelligence-reported NVA regimental headquarters. It was almost right on the grid coordinates on the map, but almost impossible to see from a few hundred feet above the thick jungle. I thanked the army Loach pilot, and we both flew back to Marble Mountain Airfield.

I briefed our intelligence officer, 1st Lt. D. Baker, Character Bravo, who worked in our pilots' ready room, but was from the 1st Marine Division intelligence, G-2 Department. Lieutenant Baker immediately passed on the information, and the III MAF and 1st Division coordinated a 1st Marine Aircraft Wing heavy bombing raid on this suspected regimental headquarters complex. The very next day, our VMO-2 squadron got a mission to mark the target for a six-plane A-6A Intruder attack-bomber mission at those grid coordinates. Since I barely found the target with the help of the passing army Loach helicopter crew, I was assigned to go find it again. Someone else might take too much time looking for it again. So I would go out and find it and mark it with my Willie Pete rockets for the A-6s. When I got out there, the marine A-6As arrived from Da Nang within minutes. The A-6, built by Grumman Aircraft, is an all-weather attack bomber

capable of carrying thirty five-hundred-pound bombs. Only the
B-52 could carry a bigger bombload. Instead of five-hundred-
pound bombs, the lead pilot of the A-6s reported to me that each
of the six planes was carrying six Delta Four bombs aboard, that
is, six MK-84, two-thousand-pound general-purpose bombs. I
quickly found the almost concealed bunker and marked it with
a 2.75-inch WP marking rocket. The six A-6 bombers unloaded
their total of thirty-six tons of bombs and departed. I had to wait
about twenty minutes for the smoke and dust to settle down
before I could fly in and make a bomb damage assessment. When
I finally looked over the target, I found that all we had done was
knock the jungle clear off of a massive complex of four large
concrete buildings. I got down low and saw cracks and gouges
out of the reinforced concrete. However, the structures still stood
intact. I did not see any enemy troops moving into or out of the
massive buildings. I RTB'ed and made my after-mission debriefing to intelligence. Three days later the air force ran a B-52 ARC
LIGHT raid upon this concrete complex. I returned up there the
next day and the thick concrete buildings had been crumpled into
heaping masses of concrete rubble and twisted steel reinforcing
bars. Whether there were an NVA regimental headquarters and
any troops still in those structures during the ARC LIGHT, I
never heard. How the NVAs were able to move such massive
amounts of concrete in bags and tons of steel reinforcing rods all
the way down from North Vietnam through those mountains
and across jungles and then were able to build such large structures in the jungle, just twenty miles from Da Nang city, baffled
me.

On July 16, 1969, I received an urgent call from DASC to
support an emergency extraction of an eight-man reconnaissance
team that was under heavy attack by NVA forces in mountains
four miles southwest of An Hoa. The marine recon team had
captured a North Vietnamese soldier in an operation called
Snare. This was to obtain intelligence information on the NVA
operating in that rugged area. A sheer cliff to the east of the recon
team had numerous concrete machine-gun bunkers that were
firing down on the besieged marine team. The recon team was in
a dense forest that had a dry riverbed to the south. The NVA had

enveloped the recon team on three sides. It was getting dark, so our CH-46 extract helicopter had to get those marines out quickly, or they'd never get them out at night. It took every HE rocket that I had aboard to fend off the attacking NVA, and then I used all of my white phosphorus rockets to create a smoke screen to cover the team getting to the open riverbed area for helo pickup. The Cobra escorts gave intense, close-in fire support, and the CH-46 got the entire eight-man team and the captured NVA soldier out of the trap. However, from that one-hour battle, I discovered just how many concrete caves were up on the sheer cliff overlooking that recon team. For the next several days we tried to bomb those caves and bunkers on that cliff. We couldn't hit them because of the sheerness of the cliff that they had built them into. Naval gunfire and artillery were miles out of range. What we did was unconventional and very dangerous. We had four CH-53 Sea Stallion helicopters hover on the very edge of the cliff. As they hovered, their crewmen opened fifty-five-gallon drums of JP-4 jet fuel and let it run down the sides of the cliff. As soon as the cliffside was saturated with jet fuel, we had an A-4 come in and drop a single napalm tank on the edge of the cliff. This thick fuel-and-soapsuds mixture impacted and exploded. As it slid burning down the cliff, all of the other jet fuel on the cliffside ignited. If the NVA weren't burned, then most of them were suffocated.

On July 22, one of our OV-10s was deep in a ravine in the Que Son Mountains marking targets on a large number of NVA. We then received a call from a helicopter that the OV-10 had gone down in those mountains. We launched a couple of OV-10s and Cobras and joined two CH-46 extract helicopters to go rescue the downed pilot and AO. As the rescue party approached the crashed OV-10, we heard the signal of one of the downed airmen's emergency radio beeper. Despite numerous calls on that frequency, nobody answered us. As the CH-46s landed down in the ravine, they came under intense automatic-weapons fire. Fortunately, the downed OV-10 pilot, Hostage Bravo, was able to get to the chopper and the helicopters had to lift off immediately.

After taking Hostage Bravo back to our base, several more attempts to land helicopters in that area were unsuccessful because of the heavy volume of enemy fire. For the next two days we kept hearing an emergency radio directional beacon beeper in those hills. And the directional beacon kept moving around. We saw Hostage Bravo's and the AO's parachutes lying down on the side of the ravine. We figured that the AO had been evading capture and was trying to lead us to him with his radio beacon and beeper signal. However, on the third day, we had a marine rifle company land in that area in several helicopters. The marines soon found a shallow grave. They dug it up and found our AO still strapped in his ejection seat. His .45 pistol and hand-held emergency radio had been taken by the NVA, who had buried him. There were no gunshot wounds on him. Apparently, the AO did not get seat-man separation during the ejection phase and the chute didn't fully deploy. He may have ejected and bounced off of a cliff, damaging the chute and the seat, preventing proper functioning of the escape system. The NVA apparently then removed the body along with the seat from the partially deployed parachute and took the body in the seat some distance away from the chute lying on the hillside. After burying the AO to prevent us from seeing or recovering him, the NVA played hide-and-seek games with the dead AO's radio beeper to confuse us. They probably figured on shooting down a helicopter or two during rescue attempts, while we were homing in on the beacon of the beeper radio.

During a routine flight, I checked in with a battalion that informed me that one of their companies was going to move through a Viet Cong–held village. North Vietnamese troops had been seen in this village on numerous occasions.

I quickly flew over to the village, called Havi. I checked in with the company commander and told him that I'd check the village over before he moved through it.

I flew low over the village, and it appeared devoid of inhabitants. Then I passed over the western end of the village and saw that all of the villagers had beat it out of the village to the west and were still moving westward. They obviously knew the marines were coming. As I passed back over the village, I saw a little old lady in black pajamas run up to the only well in the town. At about a thousand feet of altitude, I couldn't see what she was doing at the well. But it certainly was suspicious, considering that everybody else in town had gotten the hell out of there.

I quickly called the company commander.

"Lieutenant, this is Hostage Uniform. I'd advise your troops not to go near the village well in the open area at the middle of the vil. I saw a woman messing around the well before leaving the vil."

"Roger, Hostage. I'll pass the word on down. We're moving into the vil now. Keep us informed if you see any Charlie."

I circled around as the marines swarmed about the empty village, looking for weapons and excessive food for the NVA. As I was making a turn, a puff of smoke caught my eye. It came from the center of the village. It came from the well area. I flew directly toward the center of the village.

"Hostage Uniform, this is Blazer Actual. I have two casualties down here. Can you get through to DASC quicker than me, down here, for a medevac chopper?"

"Roger, Blazer Actual. I told you that an old woman was doing something near that well."

"Roger, but some of my men didn't get the word. I passed it down, but maybe somebody was awful thirsty."

"Shit. What's the status of the casualties, Blazer?"

"Hostage, it looks like one marine has lost both legs and the other is torn up pretty badly. There was an explosion set off next to the well by a trip wire."

"Roger, Blazer. I guess I should have blown that little old lady away. But how could I know, from up here, just what the hell she was doing?"

The CH-46 medevac bird arrived and took both seriously wounded marines away. These two young men wouldn't walk through this hell hole here again, or anywhere.

One day we got the word at VMO-2 that VMO-6 at Quang Tri had a disastrous OV-10A accident. The thing that all OV-10A pilots feared had happened. A fully armed OV-10A was taking off at Quang Tri Airfield and it experienced an engine failure. If the OV-10A had the power of the P-38 fighter, a similar-looking twin-fuselage aircraft of WWII some twenty-four years before, this accident and others would not have occurred. The twin-engine OV-10A had only 715 horsepower available on each engine. This was about one-fourth the power plant of the P-38 of a quarter century before. All of the OV-10 pilots were more than aware that the pilot's handbook specifically projected charts that reflected that if at gross weight and a single engine failure occurred, this aircraft did not have single-engine flyaway capability with the landing gear extended. It would be very marginal even if the landing gear had been retracted up into the wheel wells.

This unique observation aircraft was designed specifically for the Southeast Asian conflict. Additionally, it was to be a multipurpose aircraft at minimum cost, including not having anti-icing equipment installed. And that's exactly what we got: a minimum-cost armed reconnaissance airplane. When the Department of Defense contractors were evaluating bids for the aircraft, a Canadian firm offered a 1,000-horsepower engine. The defense contractors opted to keep costs down and also have the engine built in the U.S., despite the fact that the only engine available for it was an underpowered 715-horsepower engine. What we heard had happened at Quang Tri was that as the OV-10A had just lifted off the runway, and before the pilot retracted the landing gear, one engine failed. With only a single 715-horsepower engine, and fully loaded, the OV-10A rolled immediately into the dead engine due to the torque of the good engine and the aircraft being a two-engine-designed aircraft. The plane, slightly airborne and rolling inverted, barrel-rolled into the roof of a hangar. It then came through the roof and impacted into another OV-10 parked inside, and they both exploded, killing the air crew of the disabled aircraft and also several maintenance personnel in the hangar.

This lack of a single-engine-flyaway capability due to underpowered engines was only one aspect of the problem. Due to having only 715 horsepower per engine, the total of 1,430 horsepower available was totally inadequate for zoom power after a gunnery- or rocket-attack dive. Therefore, the air crews were not only exposed more to hostile fire on a pullout from an attack, but they also had to pull out at a higher altitude. They simply could not pull out with power. There wasn't enough of it. They required more airspeed to get out of trouble, since the engines could not haul them out of there. Prior to my joining VMO-2 this combat tour, VMO-2 lost one OV-10A on a rocket run, and the pilots in VMO-2 attributed the loss of this air crew to the lack of zoom power. The plane simply flew into the ground despite the pilot's apparently trying to pull up with full power applied.

The weather was now hot again. It was my seventh month of this second combat tour. The 105- to 120-degree days were unbearable on the ground for everyone. In the OV-10, it was hell. Most of our missions were flown at a thousand feet to enable us to see the enemy, and that's where most of the countryside heat was—from the ground up to a thousand feet. It must have been 130 degrees inside the big clear canopy of the cockpit. We took two canteens of water with us, and they were completely drained during each two-and-a-half-hour low-altitude mission. If there was no enemy contact out on the battlefield and if time permitted, a quick climb to ten thousand feet to cool off was like going to heaven. Unfortunately, there weren't too many times available for this luxury.

But rumor had it that because of our bitching, the Corps was evaluating placing air conditioners in the OV-10A, just like in the jets. To reinforce our request for this item, which would definitely increase FAC efficiency, our flight surgeon ran a three-month statistical study on our pilots and AOs. Each pilot and AO weighed in on a scale prior to flight and then weighed in upon his return to the ready room prior to debriefing. On the average, each crew member lost five pounds per two-and-a-half-hour flight due to excessive sweating. Flying two missions a day resulted in body-liquid losses of ten pounds per person per day. This was a staggering figure, but without long-term impact. Since it was only body liquids lost, drinking water and beer each night enabled most of the air crews to regain most of the lost weight.

However, the evaluation of a single air conditioner in a single OV-10A at the Navy Flight Test Center at Patuxent River, Maryland, resulted in termination of the concept, despite our need. The problem, as expected, was that the underpowered 715-horsepower engine became unacceptably underpowered if even a small air conditioner was mounted on one of the engines. So it never came to pass. I sure envied the jet jocks on those hot July and August days while I circled at one thousand feet over the NVA. I'd get a flight of jets on station and they would have fuel time on station for only fifteen to twenty minutes. So they'd arrive in their air-conditioned cockpits, drop their bombs, and get out of there in a few minutes and RTB. We'd stay out there in that heat for two and a half hours, twice a day.

Of course, again, life is all relative. If compared to my first combat tour flying my HUS helicopter or Huey, eating dust all day down at the most intense heat level with our lovable grunts and flying seven or eight hours a day, the OV-10 duty wasn't all that bad. But it was not as comfortable as our jet jocks had it in their air-conditioned cockpits and one-hour flights.

At the end of the summer, I got called up by the group commander. He had received directives to expand our base at Marble Mountain Airfield, despite President Nixon's "retrograde," the incremental withdrawal of troops from South Vietnam. As a matter of fact, it was *because* of the retrograding of units that we had to expand our base. The group commander had found out that I had been deeply involved in the supply and construction of Marble Mountain Airfield in 1965. Therefore, he figured that I'd make him a good base development officer for this required expansion. I fought the idea tooth and nail, but he simply had the group S-1 send me a set of orders assigning me as the group base development officer. Although I checked out of my S-1 job in my squadron, VMO-2, to join the group logistics department as a staff officer, I could still fly in my old squadron whenever I was able to get away from my new job. Well, that turned out to be mostly night flying from then on. As the group commander explained to me, we had to absorb two CH-46 squadrons and a CH-53 squadron from our northern base at Phu Bai. The Phu Bai base would close in three months. So I had to finish everything at Marble Mountain Airfield to fit in these new squadrons for one year, as we phased bases and squadrons out of country, per President Nixon's directives for "Vietnamization of the war."

I planned for several days and figured that I needed four buildings for the pilots, twelve more strongback hootches for the enlisted men, and an additional hangar and associated taxiways and parking apron, as well as expansion of the enlisted club, SNCO club, and officers' club. Not counting on it, but hoping for it, I also calculated costs to include large concrete arches, called wonder arches, for providing cover for some of the aircraft and to protect them against the constant rocket attacks. These wonder arches were common sights at Da Nang, Cam Ranh Bay, Bien Hoa, and Tan Son Nhut airfields. Until now, we at Marble Mountain Airfield only had fifty-five-gallon fuel drums filled with sand to provide lineal revetments for walled protection, with nothing over the top of the aircraft to protect against rockets.

My plan included removing these hundreds of rusted barrels of sand and replacing them with aluminum-walled lineal revetments. The plan was submitted to the 1st Marine Aircraft Wing at Da Nang and was quickly endorsed and forwarded to the staff of the commander, U.S. Military Assistance Command, Vietnam, in Saigon (USMACV). The plan submitted was a very detailed plan with a cost of material and construction of 3.8 million dollars. I was almost shocked when the request for approval of the plan and the full 3.8 million dollars were approved within a few days. I had to clear out old junk and make areas of land suitable for building rapidly. It all had to be completed within twelve weeks. I had to borrow heavy equipment from 1st MAW engineers to remove old pierced-steel matting that had been pushed off of the old five-thousand-foot runway two years prior, when the Seabees built a new seven-thousand-foot asphalt runway. The old steel matting had been pushed off the runway and rolled into a five-thousand-foot-long spiral of steel all welded into one long, rolled piece of steel junk. To remove this worthless steel located dangerously close to the runway, I had to employ several welders to torch-cut this mass of steel planking into five-foot lengths. My crane operators then loaded these pieces onto lowbeds to be pulled off the base by prime movers. The very day of operations to clean up the steel planking, I sent ten lowbed trucks full of this steel to a nearby army refuse base. I made arrangements for the army at that camp to pile the junk steel there, and then the army could do what it wanted with it as salvage steel.

My trucks all left our base fully loaded by noon. At 1700 hours not a single truck had returned for more loads of rolled-steel planking. I jumped into my jeep and drove four miles down the road to the army salvage base, which was located across from the

POW camp. I was shocked to see a line of army, navy, and my own trucks stretching about two miles along the dirt road. They were all loaded with junk—half-blown-up jeeps, broken truck parts, and rusty steel parts of mechanisms. I went into the army salvage base and asked what the reason for the long delay was. They responded that they simply could not offload all the junk coming into them in a reasonable period of time. I realized right then and there that if I were to try to get my five-thousand-foot old steel runway cut up into movable sections, loaded onto trucks, and driven here to wait more than half a day, I would never get my needed real estate cleared before my construction schedule start date in four days. There had to be another fast solution.

Then I thought, What about that civilian salvage ship sitting off the coast just to the east of the POW camp? I got back into my jeep and drove over to the beach just outside the POW camp. There I found a very large pile of salvage junk made up of everything from parts of broken-down tanks, generators, and trucks to Bay City cranes. In the middle of the junk pile was a skinny Vietnamese operating a crane and lifting junk from the pile and dropping it onto an old WWII LCM landing craft. The LCM then headed out to an old WWII LST. The rusting former navy landing ship also had a crane aboard it. I stood there and watched that ship's crane lift several loads of scrap steel from the LCM to the LST. I then tried to talk to the old Vietnamese crane operator on the beach. We couldn't communicate, so he used a radio to call the ship.

In half an hour, the LCM came into the beach from the ship. A Caucasian man came off of the LCM and waded ashore, and we met. He was the owner of the ship, the LCM, and the two cranes. He was a salvage operator from Wilshire Boulevard in Los Angeles. He told me that he goes wherever there is a war, large or small, to get scrap metal and parts of equipment very cheaply. He had been to the Egyptian-Israeli battles and had made a fortune in scrap-metal salvage operations. In this situation, he bought an old surplus navy ship and set up two repair and rebuilding plants in the Philippines. He then hauled scrap and junk from Vietnam to the Philippines. There his two plants went through the salvage piles and separated steel from aluminum, and also junk from useful component parts. He then sailed the scrap steel to Taiwan and Korea, where he sold it.

He said that he was averaging two large cranes in reconstruction for sale monthly along with his scrap-steel sales. It generally took ten beat-up cranes to get one good crane from them. He sold the cranes primarily in Korea. He said that he paid a penny a pound for scrap steel. I told him that I had tons of steel, damaged trucks and jeeps, and rusty fifty-five-gallon steel drums. He said that he'd buy everything, except that he had no use for the rusty steel drums. I told him that I can't sell him anything or I'd probably break some kind of regulation. However, I told him that I couldn't possibly get ten trucks full of junk steel out through the army each day and I didn't think that I could bury that much in the sand each day. Therefore, if he wanted it free, I'd be glad to unload my trucks there on the beach every day for about three days. He smilingly agreed and insisted that he'd be glad to pay me for it. I said I'd be thrilled just to get the junk off of our base, and I left it at that.

The next three days my trucks convoyed down to this salvage location to quickly solve my compressed-time problem. With all of the tons and tons of scrap metal that this guy was hauling out of there, my monumental pile was nothing next to his pile on the beach. However, this did not solve my problem of getting rid of the fifty-five-gallon drums full of sand. So I borrowed three army bulldozers and operators, and they daily dug very deep holes and trenches in the few vacant pieces of sandy real estate that I had left on the base. Then, with three crews of three men each and three dump trucks, we loaded the barrels onto the trucks each day, dumped them into the deep holes, and buried them under the sand.

With tons of steel drums buried, I began jokingly asking some of our pilots how their radio directional instruments worked when coming in directly over the airfield—whether there was some magnetic pull of the tons of steel barrels piled and buried under the sand. I also thought, Hell, years from now, when the locals here start excavating for building a Da Nang Hilton hotel on this beautiful beach, they'll wonder what the hell all those tons of rusting steel are doing way the hell down there under the sand. But burying the drums did the job and was better and much safer than the alternative of dropping them from helicopters out over the South China Sea.

As the Seabees began building strongback wooden-decked hootches for our enlisted men coming down from Phu Bai, they ran into a problem. Their commander came to visit me to tell me that each night someone was stealing loads of their plyboards that they had stacked for the wooden deckings of the strongbacks. They suspected the marines. I told them that I suspected the army because they were located right next to the new construction. We both toured the entire marine eastern side of the airfield and were unable to find any fresh-looking four-by-eight sheets of plywood. We then asked the army lieutenant colonel in charge of the army section of our base for permission to look in the army compound. He gladly toured his section with us and he was relieved not to find fresh plywood sheets. I thanked them both for their search efforts and left them, telling them that I would personally look in the last logical place, the nearby Republic of Korea marine aviation detachment. This detachment was located on the west side of our runway and north of the construction area. They had a single prefabricated hangar, three metal buildings, and a number of tents. Along the taxiway they had twelve OE-1 Cessna Bird Dog observation airplanes. About thirty yards to the north of their hangar was a large bunker. The bunker was built up on about a twenty-foot-high sand dune or hill.

As I drove into the ROK aviation area, what caught my eye were the OE-1 Bird Dogs. Although the aircraft were painted a different green color from our old Marine Corps Bird Dogs and also had ROK flag symbols painted on them, I looked at familiar bureau numbers painted on the vertical stabilizers. The first three serial numbers were very familiar—133813, 136888, and 136894. They were indeed the very same OE-1 aircraft that we had flown in VMO-2 back in Okinawa in 1959. I had then taught some of the Korean marine pilots how to fly our Bird Dogs during that period. And now, exactly ten years later, the ROKs had these still-flyable observation aircraft that we used to own. I walked closer to the aircraft and asked a mechanic, "Where is your commanding officer?" He didn't understand me. So I asked,

"Where CO?" He smilingly pointed to the large bunker located up on the sand mound and said, "CO, CO."

I climbed up the sand mound toward the bunker. It was very strongly built and fashioned after our MAG-16 command bunker that was built down into the ground. This, however, was built up on the sand mound. It was constructed of very long one-foot-by-one-foot-square timbers, and it had steel planking on the roof with many rows of sandbags on top of that. It obviously could sustain a direct hit by a Russian rocket. I knocked on the thick door, and a Korean lieutenant colonel opened it. He was in his flight suit and was obviously the CO.

"Colonel, I'm the base development officer and I must talk to you."

Yes, Majo. Pwease come in."

I entered and commented, "Colonel, this is a helluva strong bunker."

"Yes, Majo. This is my home. It vewy stwong. NVA wockets no howt it."

"So, this is home. Hell, you don't have to run for a bunker when the rockets come in at night. You're living in one. Also, on this hill, you can see your entire flight-line operation."

"Oh yes. Wewy good setup. What you want?"

"Colonel, I came to talk to you about some missing Seabee lumber."

"Missing rumbew?"

"Yes sir. The Seabees are missing many sheets of plyboard. The U.S. Marines don't have it. The army doesn't have it. Would you give me permission to look around your section of the base for the missing plyboard?"

"We no have missing pwybode. I rock all ovew my camp this mowning. No see pwybode."

"I'm sure it's not here, Colonel. But can I have your permission to look down inside of your tin buildings and hangar?"

"No. No pwybode there. No need for permission. If I find, I call you at MAG-16."

"Okay, Colonel. If you see any, call me at MAG-16 logistics. Incidentally, those OE-1 Bird Dogs down there are the very same ones that I trained Korean Marine Corps pilots to fly on Okinawa."

"Ah. So you maybe twain me. July 1959."

"Yes sir. By God. You're right. It was June and July of 1959 at the Sukiran coral airstrip."

He was impressed and shook my hand and then let me out of the heavy door. I drove out of his flight-line area and went over to the Seabees constructing the enlisted hootches. A Seabee chief came over to me and said, "Major, my boys tell me that the army guys here told them that they saw the Koreans stealing the lumber about 0230 this morning."

"I'll be a sonuvabitch. And their colonel told me that they didn't have it. I'm going back over there and look around again."

I drove back over to the ROK flight line and parked right in back of their hangar. I opened the back hangar-personnel door and walked into the hangar. There were about twenty ROK enlisted men sawing fresh new plywood and hammering the sections together to form large boxes. Finally, one of them saw me and saw my golden major's leaf on my cap. He hollered, "Attenon!"

They all stood smartly at attention. I walked over to my obviously stolen plywood. They just stood there, hammers and saws in hands. Then I saw a lieutenant.

"Lieutenant, what the hell are your men doing with my construction wood?"

"Solly, Majo. I go get conol to talk with you."

The lieutenant dashed out of the open doorway and I saw him running for the hill and bunker. Then the CO was soon on his way down the sand mound, heading for the hangar and me.

"What matter, Majo?"

"Colonel, I've found my missing plyboard."

"Ah. Let me talk with rootenant."

The ROK CO turned to his lieutenant and they had a long Korean discussion with much hand waving and gestures. Then the CO turned to me and said, "I solly, Majo. Some of my enristed men take wood to build boxes."

"I see that, Colonel. What kind of boxes are they?"

"They go-home boxes."

"Go-home boxes? What do you mean?"

"We go home in one month; back to Kowea. Yow Pwesident

have wetwogwade of aw twoops. We need boxes to ship equipment to Kowea."

"Hell, Colonel, all you had to do was ask our logistics section for wooden mount-out boxes. Our group commander would have had our utilities section make them for you."

"Solly. Yow can have plybode back. Mistake."

"I can't use boxes, and the other four-by-eight sheets have been cut in half. You keep it now and continue making your go-home boxes. But don't take any more of my wood. If you need more boxes, call our logistics section at MAG-16."

I left and told my group commander about the incident.

On one of my night flights, after all day out in the hot sun supervising earth movement and new construction, I teamed up with the VMO-2 operations officer, Hostage Jim. It was a TACA night mission using our own flares from our OV-10 aircraft. We briefed at 2200 for a midnight launch. I was the TACA, and Hostage Jim in the second aircraft was the flare-drop bird. Ironically, the area that the mission was to be flown in was the exact area in which, back in 1965, I participated in the first night HUS helicopter assault. It was in a mountain pass near the village complex of Ho An Thong at AT 875865 grid coordinates. We had gotten sophisticated since 1965. Our OV-10s had the capability to drop intrusion-detection devices. So at dusk, 1800 hours, Hostage Yoke flew into the targeted area in his OV-10 and dropped the sensors, which imbedded themselves into the ground in the base of the ravine. As suspected, our recon team in the high ground in that area reported heavy NVA troop movement, which was picked up by the sensitive devices at 2315.

Upon our arrival over the area, Hostage Jim broke off from our two-plane formation and got ready for his flare drops and my control of two marine F-4 attack bombers. Each F-4 carried five-hundred-pound bombs. As soon as the flares lit up the ground while descending by parachutes, I could see at least fifty NVA troops right out on the trail. It seemed like they simply stood there and looked at the bright flares falling toward them. They sure as hell must have heard our two noisy OV-10s and possibly the jets. Within seconds, I had both "Love Bug" F-4s drop their load of five-hundred-pound bombs on the skyward-gawking NVA troops. Then the last flare went out and the blackness of night intruded. Only small fires of burning grass along a river gave an indication that something had happened there. It was all over within ten minutes. It was now up to recon to body-count in the morning.

Back at the base the next morning, I was going over my plans to determine exactly where I would place my new taxiways, parking aprons, and hangar. I made a discovery. Just about dead center of where my new hangar would be erected by the Seabees was the ROK CO's large bunker on the sand dune. I checked and rechecked, but that was the only place that I could fit something as large as an aircraft hangar. I told my group commander about the situation and then drove over to see the Korean lieutenant colonel.

Having had the problem over the stolen plyboards, the Korean CO was a little edgy when I sat down and sipped some hot tea with him in his massive bunker hootch. Then I dropped it on him. He had to move out of his large, safe bunker home. He couldn't believe it and naturally protested with such statements as, "But Majo, we Koweans go home in one month. Why I have to move now? You wait one month, then you build hangar here."

After a few more words were exchanged, the ROK CO drove himself over to see my group commander. My group commander not only told him that he had to move out of that bunker, since I was going to rip it down, but that our base military police at the main gate had reported that Korean SNCOs were buying excessive liquor at our SNCO club and driving the liquor out through our gate. That meant only one thing: they were selling the liquor at the black market in Da Nang city. When the Korean CO was driving back to his bunker, he stopped his jeep beside me. I was standing next to a deep trench as an army bulldozer was pushing sand over several hundred fifty-five-gallon fuel drums full of sand.

"How'd it go at the group commander's office, Colonel?" I asked him.

"Not so good. He say I must move. But I say I need help to build new bunker. He say you help me."

"Yes sir. I'll help you. I'll start my work force tomorrow

building you a new bunker down next to your hangar. But it won't be as large as your current bunker."

"Why not so large?"

"Because I would need that big lumber that you have. Where would you live if I rip your bunker down first and only then build you a bunker?"

"Okay. I move to smallow bunko. But must have ail conditiono."

"Sorry, Colonel. I have no air conditioners. If you can dig one up, I'll have our utilities section hook it up for you."

"Solly Majo. No ail conditiono, no move."

"Well sir, we'll see. I'm going to start removing that large mound of sand under your bunker tomorrow. Also, our utilities section will start construction of your new bunker home tomorrow next to the hangar. Have a good night in that bunker tonight, Colonel."

Late that night I was sitting in the VMO-2 ready room on an "on call" status as the night flare bird. A call came in for a flare aircraft to go down to support the Korean marines near Hoi An. My AO, Cowpoke Thirty, and I launched and checked in with a ground FAC from 1st ANGLICO who was assigned to the ROK marines. He told me that a large number of NVA were trying to breach their defense line along the southwest corner. When I got over the area, I couldn't miss the extensive firefights in the darkness around that area. I ran several sections of marine A-4 attack aircraft on the NVA lead elements, after dropping my own onboard MK-24 parachute flares to illuminate the NVA. There were one hell of a lot of NVA there. A lot more than I had expected to see until my flares lit up the countryside. After the marine jets departed, I dropped more flares and made several of my own rocket and gun runs. Shortly, "Spooky" checked in and I briefed him on the active situation. Spooky was an air force DC-3 that had its own flares and two miniguns, or Gatling guns. It was also called "Puff the Magic Dragon" or "Skytrain." Spooky, out of Da Nang Airfield, was available every night upon request. As I was low on fuel and had to depart soon, I watched Spooky take over the night mission. He was awesome. He just orbited at two thousand feet over the southwest perimeter of the Korean defense line and dropped flares, followed by a continual steady stream of hot steel bullets. The firepower was so heavy that the volume of tracers descending through the black night gave the illusion of one long yellowish stream from the vintage DC-3. Yet the tracers represented only every tenth bullet traveling down upon the once-attacking NVA. There was no way that the NVA could continue after the bombings and now the firepower of Spooky. I departed, knowing that Spooky, if needed, could stay airborne on station there for the rest of the night until dawn.

The next morning, I was in my office calling all bases in the RVN to see if there still were any prefabricated Butler building hangars in country. Finally, I found out from the Air Force that there still was one left down at Tan Son Nhut Airfield. Shipments of any new prefabricated hangars and buildings had been curtailed seven months ago because of Nixon's withdrawal plan. I was lucky. I don't know where I would have gotten a hangar for the soon-to-arrive CH-53 squadron from closing Phu Bai Airfield. I had just hung up my phone, after discussing the hangar, when my phone rang. I picked it up. It was an army sergeant who was on loan to me as a bulldozer operator.

"Major, you've got to get over here right away. You won't believe this."

"I won't believe what? Where are you?"

"Sir, I'm at the base of the mound of sand that the Korean CO's bunker is sitting on. I've been digging and removing parts of the sand dune as your marines are dismantling the bunker. You'll have to see it to believe it."

"Sarge, I'm on my way."

I hung up without asking him again what it was that I wouldn't believe. I quickly drove across our runway, after our tower flashed a green light, and continued up to the base of the sand dune by the Korean CO's bunker. The army sergeant's bulldozer's engine was not running, and the operator was standing well away from it.

"What's up, Sarge?"

"Hell, Major. Take a look at this, but not too close."

He pointed toward the front of the blade of his Cat.

"Holy shit! Look at that. Old rusty grenades and bands of old M-60 machine-gun bullets."

The dozer operator had removed about a quarter of the south side of the mound of sand that held up the bunker flooring. He had then, fortunately, sighted this old sensitive ammunition. If he had moved his dozer blade just another inch, he could easily have exploded one of those old grenades. That, in turn, would have gotten all the rest exploding and would have had bullets cooking off all over the place. Despite his being behind the big dozer blade, he would probably have been killed by those fireworks. I calmed him down. I told him not to move the dozer and not to let anyone near the area. I ran down to the ROK hangar. I explained the situation to the Korean CO and then called the navy demolition squad located on a base to our immediate north. The demo squad would come down and blow up the old ammo right on the site. I then walked up to the bunker location with the ROK CO. When he saw all of the old ammo located directly below the thin wooden flooring of his big bunker, he turned white. He immediately recognized that while feeling secure in his bunker every night, if a single NVA rocket had come in and impacted ten feet below and to the south of his great bunker, it would have exploded all of this old ammunition directly below his ass. He would have been killed from below his thin floorboards.

He looked at me and said, "I live hele one yeal and feel good. Now I grad I move. Maybe you save my life. We get many mo wocket attacks next fo weeks, befo I go home."

As I stood there and listened to him and looked around, I then realized where that pile of old ammunition was from. This site had been the exact location of our M-60 machine gun defensive bunker that had been installed last at Marble Mountain Airfield during my previous tour here. It was placed here after my final four M-60s belatedly arrived through the supply system from Japan for Lieutenant Grinder's defensive perimeter in 1965. I had a flashback of the gun emplacement here. This was the spot that the NVA had not planned on when they attacked our airfield on the night of October 27–28, 1965. Our newly placed gun here had not been on the mockup model of the base that the NVA and VC had rehearsed their attack on. The gunner here that night had killed nine VC who had run right up in front of the unknown gun position as soon as the mortar barrage had ceased for the VC ground attack.

Sometime over the last four years, the base expanded and this gun emplacement was moved. But all of the ammunition wasn't relocated. Then the normal wind-blown sands at this beach area filled in the bunker hole and covered the ammunition. Somehow the blowing sand created a high mound over the buried explosives. Then three years later the ROK CO arrived and built his comfortable bunker hootch right on top of this part of the history of Marble Mountain Airfield. For a year the ROK CO had a false impression of safety in his bunker, living directly over those volatile explosives.

Now that construction work began, I needed more sheet tin for the new hootch roofs. I also needed something to thicken up the loose sand in the area of the ROK CO's bunker where the new hangar's concrete decking would be poured for the foundation for the prefabricated hangar. The continual blowing sands on this beach played havoc with all of the foundations of our buildings, particularly under the corners of the concrete deckings. There the wind eroded the sand and cracks would start on the concrete slabs. I found out that there was a claylike soil near riverbeds in Vietnam, a soil which engineers called laterite. This laterite soil, when mixed with sand, made much more stable and firm ground to lay the concrete slabs on. And I knew from my previous combat tour here that the only place to get the needed corrugated sheet tin and the laterite would be from Lily Ann in Da Nang city.

I drove down to Da Nang city to see if Lily Ann was still in business. As I drove into downtown Da Nang, I decided to check on my old friend, the old Vietnamese crucifix-carver that Chaplain Roland had put into business with all of the crucifix orders four years ago. The wood-carver's little shop was now operated by someone else, who sold marble vases and marble-chiseled animals. I asked around and nobody remembered the little old wood-carver. I drove down to the old-men's home where Chaplain Roland and I first met the old Buddhist wood-carver. The old-men's home manager informed me that the old man had died a year ago and that his wife went back into the aged-women's home again. I thought, Well, Chaplain Roland did obtain that old man some self-employment and at least three years of the old man living again with his aged wife, after he had started his crucifix-carving business.

I arrived in the center of bustling Da Nang. The store and warehouse of Lily Ann looked the same. Upon entering it, I asked her old store manager if I could meet with her. In a few minutes, Lily Ann and I were upstairs sipping tea like back in '65. We negotiated delivery of the corrugated sheet tin to the Seabees for the roofing of the new SEA huts. The discussions for the laterite were a little more complex, but finally were resolved and specific delivery dates were set. During our discussions, Lily Ann informed me proudly that one of her daughters was now a senior in premed at UCLA. I rapidly, jokingly, informed her that she could certainly afford to send a daughter all the way to UCLA from Da Nang.

I had to fly down in an OV-10 to Tan Son Nhut Airfield to make arrangements for paperwork and shipping of the only available hangar in country. The air force cooperated very well and began shipment of the sections of the prefabricated hangar while I was still at their airfield. If I'd had more time available, I would have loved a ride to nearby Saigon, since I had never been there. In fact, in that heat, it would have been good to have a cold beer at the USO on Nguyen Hue Street in Saigon. But I had to get back for a night mission in the OV-10.

Construction moved at an unbelievably rapid pace. Soon the taxiways and parking aprons were completed along with the living quarters for the new squadrons. As the Seabees erected the prefabricated hangar, I saw that unlike all of our other hangars, this air force hangar had no windows designed into it. The air force probably air-conditioned its hangars, I enviously thought. I had the Seabees simply cut out big squares here and there for ventilation. When heavy rains came we could put tin covers on the openings. Within weeks everything was completed except the construction of the lineal revetments, the concrete wonder arches, and the expansions of the three club houses. I made several trips up to assist in closing Phu Bai Airfield, and then the three helicopter squadrons arrived at Marble Mountain Airfield for operations.

By the time the fall monsoons hit with their rains, the wonder arches, lineal revetments, and clubs were completed. I had more time to fly daytime missions. I still did have a problem with Lily Ann of Da Nang. When her trucks were delivering me my ordered laterite for the mixing with sand, I had posted a young marine at the main gate to count the truckloads of laterite. Lily Ann had charged me for thirty-nine truck loads. My counter's tally was thirty. So we had a little bickering before I paid her for thirty and then showed her the daily count sheet. Her only statement was, "Oh, sorry. My foreman not count correctly."

One night about midnight our alert siren blew and awakened us. Knowing that it was incoming rockets, I grabbed my helmet and flak vest and ran out of my hootch. On the way out of the hootch, I shouted to my roommate, "Benny, get up. We have incoming."

"Why get up? If we get a direct hit, it's all over with in that bunker out there anyway."

Benny Bart always responded that way as he just lay awake in his rack during the rocket attacks. I got into my jeep and drove toward the MAG-16 command bunker. Within seconds, the rockets began impacting upon our flight line. Besides my assignment as the base development officer, I was also the damage assessment and repair officer. This meant that during a rocket attack, when most people were diving into a bunker, I would be driving to the command bunker. At the command bunker, I would call several of my damage-reporting posts to find out exactly where the rockets impacted and where there were possible duds or unexploded rockets. I then would call the group commander at his hootch and report the initial information. After that I would drive to the site of the damage and determine exactly what repairs were needed and how soon. This particular night, with my roomie Benny Bart just lying in the rack ignoring the rockets, I drove from the command bunker to the flight line of HMM-364. I had received a report from our tower watch crew that they had seen a rocket fall into that flight line, though it did not explode. Knowing that there had to be a big dud out there among the CH-46 helicopters, I drove onto the flight line cautiously. As I neared the helicopters, someone shouted, "Where the hell do you think you're going?"

In the dark, except for my jeep's headlights, I answered, "I'm the damage assessment officer and I'm out here looking for duds."

"Well, I'm the XO of this squadron and nobody is going to drive around my helicopters at night unless I'm in the jeep with them," responded Maj. Marty Martin. Marty climbed into my jeep and we slowly toured each parking revetment, looking for an unexploded rocket. On the fifth CH-46 parking area, we saw it. It was about a six-foot-tall rocket and it was sticking at a slight angle into the pierced-steel planking next to a CH-46. Marty's eyes opened widely.

"Goddamn it. That thing can go off any second. Let's get the hell out of here," said Marty, a Silver Star winner from a previous CH-46 helicopter combat tour.

"Marty, I have to get several of your people out here. We must gently pull the chopper forward out of the revetment. Then, I'll have a work party put wooden boxes full of sand all around the rocket. I'll then call navy EOD"—explosive ordnance disposal—"guys up here to blow it in place."

Marty got his maintenance people cautiously to pull the helicopter away from the rocket, and I called our utilities people to bring sand-filled rocket boxes up to build a wall all around the rocket. I then called the navy demolition personnel, who came over and blew the rocket up, filling that revetment with splintered wood and sand. The entire operation was always dangerous because, on occasion, the VC fired a rocket with an acid fuse. In other words, not a dud. It just took some time after impact to explode after the acid ate through and the wiring ignited the rocket. These delayed explosions quite often killed someone.

After the navy EOD personnel exploded the rocket, I made my full report to the group commander and drove back to my hootch.

"Benny, you still awake?"

"Yeah, I'm awake again. You and those late explosions out there always wake me back up. I had just passed out and then, bang, your silly-ass explosion went off."

"Well, Benny, what else can I do with a stinking big dud rocket? And by the way, I keep telling you, one of these nights we're going to get some rockets near or into our hootch here and you're going to eat hot steel. You better get into our bunker during that incoming, not just lie in the rack exposed."

"Look who's talking about exposed. You're a damn fool for driving out there while it's raining rockets."

"Hell, I have no choice. I've got to get to the command bunker immediately. Only other way to do it is to sleep in that command bunker every night."

Three days later, Benny had landed one of our eight new Cobra gunships down at An Hoi to refuel it. It was high noon as he was refueling the AH-1G, and An Hoi began to take incoming NVA rockets. The impacts began hitting on the runway and then came closer to Benny and his Cobra. Benny started to run from his parked Cobra, but it was too late. A rocket came in next to the Cobra, destroying our brand-new toy. Shrapnel tore into Benny. He got a couple of pieces of steel in one arm and a large chunk in an unmentionable area.

When I heard of Benny getting hit, it bugged me. But besides his injury, there was another problem. Benny was scheduled to fly the next day to Hawaii for his R&R week. His wife was probably already there waiting for him. That's the way it turned out. Benny was in the hospital and his wife was waiting for him at Fort DeRussy, Waikiki, after having paid her own airfair to Hawaii from the mainland. It was another day by the time the Marine Corps representatives in Hawaii had been able to track his wife down to tell her the bad news and that he would not meet her there for R&R.

About a week later, Benny was back in our hootch ready for work, but could not fly due to his sore, unmentionable wound. He made new R&R arrangements and communications with his wife, with a promise that this time when she flew into Hawaii, he'd show up.

That night, as we lay in our racks, Benny jokingly said, "Tomorrow, I'm heading to Hawaii to show off my unmentionable wound."

He no sooner said that and our alert siren went off. As I grabbed my helmet and flak vest and ran for the door, the door wasn't there. It was wide open and Benny had beat me through the hootch doorway. As he got down into the bunker, I started up my jeep and headed for the command bunker chuckling. I thought, I guess Benny's not going to lie in the rack during incoming rockets anymore after that close call when he lost the Cobra at An Hoi. It made a believer out of him.

The next week, Maj. Marty Martin was leaving for R&R in Australia. I kidded with him to bring me back a koala bear. He did. It was a small stuffed fake one that I immediately sent to my wife, who just loves koalas.

Next, it was my turn for my R&R. I chose Hawaii and had my entire family meet me there. My wife and three children headed for Waikiki from California as I flew in from Nam.

I arrived at 1000 at Hickam AFB and took a cab to Fort DeRussy at Waikiki, where my wife had made room reservations. At 1100 I was walking with my bag past a group of civilians when I heard, "Dada, Dada." I turned around and there was my youngest son, Ed, who was only twenty months old. He was only twelve months old when I left him in California. Until even this day, I could never figure out how he, at that young an age, could recognize me among those other uniformed marines. It was a good week for the five of us, except when we ran into hippie-type anti–Vietnam War protestors. But then, that's what we in Vietnam were fighting for: freedom of speech, freedom to protest, freedom from dictatorial governments, freedom from

Returning to Vietnam was heartrending. But I only had a matter of months left to go on this tour. The big construction was completed and so I began flying more missions, day and night.

Christmas was coming soon. I received a phone call from Capt. Joe Rock. Joe had been transferred to the wing headquarters and maintenance squadron located over at Da Nang. I was surprised to hear from him.

"Major, how would you like to fly to Udorn, Thailand, for Christmas?" he asked me on the phone.

"Joe, I'd love to spend Christmas in Thailand. I don't know if I can get the group commander's permission to go. What type of aircraft are you flying?"

"I'll be flying a C-117 Hummer. You can be the copilot. I'll ask wing G-1 to send a set of orders to your group so your group commander can't grumble about it."

"Great. I'm looking forward to those orders. I'll go tell the group commander to expect those orders for me. How many days are we staying there?"

"Major, we'll be there only the day before Christmas and Christmas day. It's a spare-parts run to get some F-4 parts from the air force. We'll come back the morning after Christmas."

"Good. I'll do my Christmas shopping on Christmas day. My wife wants one of those large Siam bronzeware sets of knives, forks, and so forth. I should have purchased her a set during my R&R in Bangkok during my last tour out here."

On the afternoon of Christmas eve, 1969, I was flying copilot in a vintage C-117 transport with Joe Rock as the pilot in command. It was a very dull flight at ten thousand feet from Da Nang over the jungles of western Vietnam.

As we approached the Ho Chi Minh Trail to cross into Laos, Joe said, "We'd better climb to fourteen thousand feet over the Ho Chi Minh Trail. We don't have oxygen in this aircraft and it wouldn't matter if we did. The NVA triple-A sites up here could hit us at our max altitude, if we go directly over them. I came this same route last week and didn't get shot at. Good chance we'll be safe crossing at this point. We're a little more south than a straight route to Udorn. Do you see that big turn in the Ho Trail to our northwest?"

"Yeah, Joe. I see the trail and the big bend in the road. This goddamn trail keeps getting wider. It's now a six-lane highway down there. I haven't seen it lately. Anyway, what about that bend in the road?"

"Well, I crossed over that bend in the road three weeks ago and I almost got shot down. There's a hell of a lot of triple A up there. I'll feel more comfortable crossing at this point."

The six-lane-wide swath of road network was coming up under us fast. I looked for trucks or tanks on the road. I saw none. Then looking to my right, I saw a large barrage of antiaircraft flak explosions going off at about eighteen thousand feet directly above that bend in the jungle highway. It was about five miles to our north. Then I saw our silver navy A-7 jets in a steep dive angle, dropping bombs. They must have been attacking a North

Vietnamese truck convoy, but I could not see the trucks because of the trees along the road and the distance. There were four of them in the attack orbit. The flak umbrella began getting darker from the large number of explosions going off at almost the altitude of where the jets were rolling in from.

The nose of our C-117 now was directly over this main North Vietnamese supply highway and began crossing it at fourteen thousand feet. I kept watching the navy attack bombers making their runs despite the antiaircraft fire. Then both Joe and I noticed that the sun above us began to dim. We both instinctively looked up. It wasn't clouds covering the sun. It was about six flak explosions directly over us at about nineteen thousand feet. Joe poured the coal to the engines, as we now crossed into Laos. We both knew that as the black puffs of flak smoke above us increased in numbers, those gunners below, shooting at our slow-flying transport, were rapidly increasing their chances of hitting us. We both were dead silent, just sitting there hoping that we'd be lucky. I kept looking up to see if the flak barrages of the high-altitude explosions were straight above us. If they continued above us, we'd avoid the hot chunks of steel shrapnel descending, since we would always be out in front of the hundreds of falling pieces of steel. Then in a few tense, sweating minutes, the flak puffs were high and behind our tail.

"Shit, Major. I didn't expect any flak this far south of that big bend in the road. Coming back, we'll have to go a few miles farther south."

"I'm all for that. A little farther south, coming home. Joe, we're just lucky we're at fourteen thousand feet. Those gunners are used to aiming at eighteen-thousand-to-twenty-thousand-foot attack roll-in altitudes. Plus, it's obvious that they set their fuses for about eighteen-thousand-foot altitudes, rather than proximity-fuse settings, or we'd been shot down on the very first barrage."

We lumbered along the large mountains of eastern Laos, and then the hills began to appear, followed by rolling green forests. In minutes, we were over low, flat forests, and then open rice paddies appeared ahead. Next to the numerous rice paddies were grass shacks of the farmers. The thatched huts were similar to those in Vietnam, except that all of the homes were built up on tall stilts. This placed the single-story dwellings at about a two-story elevation above the ground. I didn't know if they were built elevated that way to protect them from flatland floodings or to protect them from wild animals. Then came the wide, winding Mekong River, making its way from somewhere in northwestern Laos and Burma and heading south to our left into Cambodia and then on down into the delta region of South Vietnam, below Saigon, before emptying into the South China Sea. We crossed the very muddy Mekong River and switched our UHF radio frequency to Udorn Airfield approach control to listen to any weather reports. The weather was CAVU—clear and visibility unlimited. It would be a nice warm Christmas eve in Thailand tonight.

Upon landing our C-117 and taxiing into the U.S. Air Force side of the Udorn Royal Thai Air Force Base, we were embarrassed to hear ground control call to tell us that our large cargo door on the left rear of the fuselage had dropped off onto the taxiway. Our crew chief went back and confirmed our missing door. Ground control alerted the crash crew to dispatch a truck and crew to pick up the door and deliver it to our parking area. We'd sure as hell have to make sure that it was repaired and hung back on securely before our trip back to Nam.

As soon as Joe, our crew chief, and I climbed out of our C-117, after parking it, we were met by two young Thai girls. They had a small German van parked by flight operations.

"Where you Amelicans go?" asked one of the Thai girls.

Joe said, "The Grand Hotel, downtown Udorn."

"Good. We take you and yul bags there fwee. But foost you must make sholt visit to finest jewey store in Thailand."

"Where is this jewelry store?" I asked.

"It wight here on base. Two blocks away."

"Hell, Joe. If it's a free ride to town, it won't hurt to go look at their jewelry."

So the three of us climbed into the van along with our two female escorts. They drove us down the base street just a short distance to the Royal Thai Air Force side of the field. The van stopped and we followed the girls into what appeared to be a medium-sized base-exchange store. Inside the store it was like a trip through Asia. The counters were filled with hundreds of faceted, colored, precious and semiprecious stones. Most were mounted in eighteen- and twenty-karat gold settings. The best buys were in the corundum species of rubies and sapphires, followed by the beryls of emeralds and aquamarines. There also were many necklaces and bracelets of twenty- and twenty-two karat gold, or almost pure gold. The other Asian items, such as ivory and jade, were in abundance and at prices at about 80 percent less than the American retail store prices. Our self-appointed female guides were right. There were "once in a lifetime" buys here. Then, in the rear of the store, I came across what I really flew to Udorn for. There were many different types of bronzeware dining utensil sets. Each had from twelve to twenty settings of bronze knives, forks, spoons.

The clerk showed me both the rosewood-handled bronze-type utensils and the solid bronzeware. The rosewood handles looked good on the contrasting bronze. However, the clerk cautioned me that the rosewood could crack in the heat of dishwashers, or if improperly handled. I purchased a large solid bronzeware set that came in a large, wooden, three-shelved case with a bronze carrying handle. I then made arrangements to leave the set in the base exchange store until my departure morning. Both our female guides were pleased that we bought something. They drove us to the only decent hotel in Udorn. On the way, I asked one of our guides who it was that owned the base exchange store that we had been in. Was it the Royal Thai Air Force, like our military-operated stores on our bases? No, it was a store personally owned by the Royal Thai chief of the air force. Ironically, he was named General Thai. Apparently, he owned such a retail outlet on every Royal Thai Air Base.

Joe and I were dropped off at the Udorn hotel without any more sales pressures from General Thai's bird-dog salesgirls. They promised to pick us up at the hotel at 0800 the day after Christmas to get us back to the base.

The hotel was a modern four-story building similar to those of Japanese construction design and standards.

I sat down in my personal room on the fourth floor and drank some refreshing Perrier water, which was furnished with the room. I couldn't believe that I was here—away from the war for two days on an official trip. I could sleep this night without fear of a rocket attack and without having to fly a combat mission in the morning.

I enjoyed a very long hot bath. This was the first bath since my R&R, some months before in Hawaii. I then went downstairs to enjoy a Thai dinner in the fine hotel restaurant. It was Christmas eve and I was about nine thousand miles from home. Christmas is naturally a nostalgic time, for people who celebrate it. So I wandered into the cocktail bar next to the restaurant and ordered a scotch and water to set the mood of mentally transcending those nine thousand miles and to imagine what Christmas eve at home in San Juan Capistrano would be like this night with my wife and three children. Being out of Vietnam was great. But still being away from my family hurt particularly on Christmas eve.

Then my private, quiet contemplation was intruded upon by someone saying, "May I join you?"

I looked up to see a tall, curvaceous Caucasian woman with long brunette hair standing next to my table in the semidark cocktail lounge.

"Sure . . . go ahead, make yourself at home," I responded.

As the tall woman sat down and her face was illuminated by the flickering candlelight on my table, I saw that I was wrong. She was not Caucasian. She was Eurasian.

"Will you buy me a drink?" she asked, in flawless English.

"Yes. What'll you have?"

"A gin and tonic will do. Thank you."

I thought, Oh boy, another hooker or bar girl. I sure don't need involvement on Christmas eve. But I'll buy her a Christmas eve drink and send her on her way.

"How long have you been in Udorn?" she asked.

"I just arrived and I'm only staying a very short period."

"You are obviously an American. Where did you come from?"

"Yep. I'm American, but I don't want to get into my personal life tonight. Why don't you tell me about yourself? I certainly didn't expect to see a Eurasian woman in Udorn."

"Fine. We can talk about you later. I am what you call White Russian and Laotian. My father was a Russian from the upper Czarist class, and he escaped Russia during the Bolshevik revolution in 1917. He migrated to Vientiane. Here he married my mother from Laos. That's all there is to my story. What about you?"

"Well that's interesting, but an awful short story. So what are you doing here in from Laos?"

"I came here yesterday to buy clothing and jewelry. It is difficult to buy nice things there."

"When are you going back to Laos?"

"Tomorrow at nine o'clock in the morning. But only to deliver my purchases to my sister. She is staying in Laos. I will return to live here. I like it here. There are many Americans here."

"How can you come and go through the guards on the frontier of Laos, both in Laos and Thailand?"

"No problem. They all know me. I have been crossing that bridge from Vientiane for two years now. Would you like to come with me on the bus in the morning? I'll really show you the sights of Vientiane. It is very different. I have taken many Americans across that border bridge and they all enjoyed the visit."

"No thanks. I'm extremely happy here. Besides, tomorrow is Christmas and I'm going to church, not Laos. You'll have to excuse me. I see a friend of mine."

I got up and left her. I walked over to Joe Rock, who was sitting at the bar.

"Joe, stay the hell away from that pretty Eurasian over there. I think she's a modern-day Mata Hari. Would you believe that she was trying to talk me into going on a bus in the morning with her to visit Vientiane?"

"Laos! You've got to be kidding me."

"I shit you not. I wonder if she's been able to spirit some air force guys out of here to Laos that they never heard from again. On our return to the Thai base, I'll report her statements to the Thai base staff. Maybe she's a spy. Or maybe simply an active person who crosses to and from Laos frequently."

After an early breakfast in the hotel on Christmas morning, I asked the desk clerk where the nearest church was located and the times of the services. I then had to rush to make the eight o'clock service. As I departed the hotel, I looked at the bus stop located in front of the hotel. It would have been interesting to be here at nine o'clock to see if that Eurasian gal had convinced any American to ride on the bus to Vientiane with her. On the way to the church, I noticed that as the people approached the modern-looking church, they were stepping off the dirt sidewalk and walking on the street along a large empty lot about a block from the church. So I followed the group and I walked in the street. At the entrance to the church was a Thai priest. I talked briefly with him and also asked him why everybody left the sidewalk down by that empty lot that was overgrown with elephant grass. He said that there were cobra snakes in that lot.

"Right here in the middle of the city?" I asked.

He assured me that there were cobras in that unused lot.

I was impressed with the modern design of the church. It was built in an amphitheater style, with each semicircular row of seats higher than the row in front. I didn't expect such a modern structure to be in Udorn. (Ironically, sixteen years later, I saw a church in Carlsbad, California, that was designed and then built almost identically to this structure.)

On my way back from Christmas services, I walked on the other side of that empty lot that supposedly had cobras living in it.

The next morning at 0800, the Thai girls and their van arrived on time. We left the hotel for the Royal Thai Air Force Base. I checked in with their headquarters to discuss the Eurasian girl. They knew about her and suspected she was an intelligence gatherer. But they did not have any hard facts on her yet. She was under surveillance.

After picking up my bronzeware set at General Thai's store and carefully checking that our C-117 cargo door was secured, Joe, our crew chief, and I took off for Vietnam. We crossed the Ho Chi Minh Trail about ten miles south of where we had been shot at going to Udorn. We crossed without incident.

Returning to Marble Mountain Airfield after a short Christmas respite in Udorn was depressing.

A day later, on my birthday, I was flying with an OV-10 just north of the Que Son Mountains. I reported in with M Company, 3rd Battalion, 5th Marines, on frequency 35.6 of my FM radio. They had nothing going on in their area, so I told them that I'd fly south from them and check out the Que Son Mountains. As I left their area and told them that I'd stay up on their frequency while

I'm near their area, I heard someone else come up on the same frequency of the FM radio.

"Hostage Uniform, you have come out to die here today. Keep coming in the direction that you are and we will kill you today."

It was Charlie, speaking in perfect English on Mike Company's frequency.

"Hostage, all of you hostages in your OV aircraft will die."

"Keep talking you NVA bastard. I'm getting close to you. We'll see who dies today," I shouted over the FM radio.

"Hostage Uniform, this is Mudpie. Did you call us?"

"That's a negative, Mudpie. I've got some gooner on our frequency who says he's going to kill me today. This ought to be interesting."

"Hostage, I heard that. Keep coming out here to the mountains and I will show you how fast your airplane can come down from the sky."

I headed straight for the Que Son Mountains and flew up the middle of the deep canyon that separates the long eastern mountain range from the long western range. I circled overhead, well out of small-arms-fire range. It was quiet for a few minutes.

"Well, gooner. Here I am. When you going to start firing?"

The silence was broken with a response to my challenge.

"Hostage Uniform, come down a little lower and you will never leave these mountains."

"You keep talking, asshole. I have a good lock on your transmitter now. Keep shooting your mouth off and we'll see who meets his ancestors first."

That did it. He believed that I had homed in on his transmissions and so he shut up. I flew around there for a half hour and nothing developed.

Two weeks later the 7th Marines swept the Que Son Mountains again, and on the central western slope they captured an NVA radio company. Along with the NVAs, they captured many documents. The documents had all of our grunt operating frequencies as they changed each month. They also had a list of all of our squadrons by call signs and FM frequencies. They had meticulously gathered this communications data by daily and nightly listening to all of the helicopters and OV-10s checking in with the ground units. Apparently, they simply scanned their frequencies continuously until they picked up someone and then listened and wrote down the call signs. Soon they were able to associate the specific call sign with the shape of a particular airplane or helicopter. I heard later that one of the NVA communication operators spoke fluent English. He obviously was the guy harassing me that December 27.

New Year's eve was fast upon us. For me, it was a repeat of the New Year's eve of 1965 that I had spent here at Marble Mountain Airfield. The whole countryside started firing into the sky. All kinds of small-arms weapons were shooting. I stepped out of my Quonset hut and saw the sky from our base to Da Nang to the Que Son Mountains full of tracers.

I turned to George Gross and said, "George, what goes up must come down. I'm not going to sit in this Quonset hut and have a bullet come down through the roof on me. Let's take our rum and Coke and go out into the bunker and wait this out."

We did, and weren't the only ones in the bunker. Several other sober pilots had decided that with all of that shooting all over the place in celebration of New Year's eve, it was safer in the bunker. As I sat in the dark bunker listening to machine guns and pistols firing into the sky, I thought that the NVA must have really thought the Americans were crazy.

New Year's day was an agreed-upon cease-fire day between the North Vietnamese, South Vietnamese, and the Americans and allies. The Viet Cong—what was left of them—had not agreed to a cease-fire.

At about noon on New Year's day, I was flying a routine reconnaissance mission of our southern area. Our grunt troops were all enjoying hot turkey dinners flown in by our choppers. The whole battlefield south of Da Nang was extremely quiet. There were no firefights, no emergency calls for chopper medevacs. It was a true cease-fire in effect. I'll never forget it. It was very strange as I flew along at one thousand feet, looking over the scarred countryside. As I was heading northeast from An Hoa, I crossed over the open terrain north of the Que Son Mountains. Directly in the middle of those lowlands is the railroad track built up on mounds of dirt. As I approached the railroad trestle, I couldn't believe my eyes. Right out in the open were about a hundred North Vietnamese troops. Some were up on the railroad track sitting and standing. Most were down along the south side of the elevated tracks. I slowed my aircraft down to 120 knots and circled the NVA at one thousand feet.

"Well, these NVA sure have the word that today is a cease-fire. Look at them out there sunning themselves," I said to my rear-seated AO, Cowpoke Ten.

"Yes sir, Major. Looks like it'll be a quiet day for everybody."

"Let's go down and look these guys over. If they shoot at us, we'll get the hell out of here. I don't want to be the guy to cause failure of the cease-fire."

"Okay with me, Major. I'll take some thirty-five-millimeter photos of these guys close up."

I throttled back and made a gentle descending turn to line up on the south side of the railroad track. There was no attack roll-in or high-power engine noise to disturb the large number of NVA down there. So the NVA just stood there as we came along side of them at about a hundred feet of altitude. They were all waving at us. None of them held any weapons. Some had their shirts off. As we drifted by, my AO said, "Major, will you look at all of those caves along that railroad berm?"

"I see those caves. I've seen some of them before. I didn't realize that there were so many. We'll report them to intelligence on our return."

I gave the waving NVA a tail shake good-bye as I passed them and added power, climbing north for home base.

Two days later, when the normal warfare had fully resumed, I returned to that railroad area. The night before, we had been rocketed at Marble Mountain Airfield. I was as pissed off at the NVA as ever. I knew exactly where and how to get back at them. I ran three flights of F-4 attack bombers onto the numerous caves along that railroad track. Everything was back to normal. The cease-fire was a distant memory.

A few more routine reconnaissance missions and it was time to quit flying and go home to the real world. I had sent a letter to Headquarters Marine Corps asking them to send me back to Southern California where my family lived in our home in San Juan Capistrano. My orders arrived: Report to New River, North Carolina . . . MAG-26.

* * *

At the end of January 1970, I packed up my B-4 bag. I told my new roommate he could keep my souvenir Chinese AK-47 assault rifle that I had mounted on the Quonset-hut wall behind my homemade bar. I got a Vietnamese to help me pack up two wooden boxes of a couple of two-foot-tall enamel elephants that I had gotten from Tan Son Nhut Airfield base exchange and the large bronzeware set that I had purchased in Udorn. After mailing the wooden boxes home, I turned my survival .38 pistol in to the armory. A jeep ride from Marble Mountain Airfield, across the rusty Da Nang bridge to Freedom Hill on the west side of Da Nang Airfield was nostalgic, but apprehensive. As we drove the streets, young Vietnamese children tried to sell us everything, including whiskey bottles full of water with reattached bottoms glued back on to make the appearance that the whiskey bottles had never been open.

I still had to survive one more night at Freedom Hill while awaiting my Freedom Bird flight out the next morning. There was no way that I could sleep. I sat outside wearing my jungle fatigues, or utilities, that night. I sat on a pile of sandbags directly in front of a bunker. I don't know how many cigars I smoked that night out there under the moonlight. But there was no way that an NVA rocket was going to get me my last night in Nam. I could hear the occasional artillery impacts well to the south of Da Nang and the periodic popping of small-arms weapons just to Da Nang's southwest. As dawn broke through the eastern skies, I saw an OV-10A climbing out southward from Marble Mountain Airfield, three miles to my east. "Good luck and good hunting, VMO-2," I found myself whispering.

In two hours, I was in a contracted Flying Tiger airliner heading home to a country deeply divided and confused by riots and protests of what we were doing in South Vietnam. I again had that feeling that I was a Foreign Legionnaire, not the defender of freedom. Knowing what I would confront back in the States, I wondered if it was worth the sweat, blood, and family separations to have stood up to the united communists, rather than simply let them take what they so strongly wanted. After all, I was returning to a country where most people didn't care.

* * *

During my next year operating out of North Carolina, I made two trips to the Caribbean. I was operating out of Gitmo, Cuba, Vieques, and the Naval Air Station in Puerto Rico, when I received orders to return to the war in Vietnam a third time.

These orders were different. They had me reporting as a staff officer of the Seventh Fleet commander on board the Seventh Fleet flagship, the guided-missile-cruiser USS *Oklahoma City*. These unique orders, aboard a ship, technically allowed me to move my family from Jacksonville, North Carolina, to Yokosuka, Japan, where the USS *Oklahoma City* was home-ported. I quickly flew back from the Caribbean, packed up my family, and headed for Japan. Another mid-year school change for my children.

This third combat tour was entirely different from the previous flying tours and resulted in my participating in some exciting events having to do with mining Haiphong and getting our POWs home. But that is the subject for another book.

Suffice it to say that I worked aboard the *Oklahoma City* participating in the war as the amphibious warfare officer and marine air officer on Admiral Holloway's Seventh Fleet staff for two years, until the end of the hostilities in Vietnam, Laos, and finally the halt of the bombings in Cambodia on August 14, 1973.

Returning to the States, I spent several more years in the Marine Corps serving as a squadron commander and air group commander.

While serving as the Marine Air Reserve Group commander in Detroit, Michigan, the war in South Vietnam seemed distant and remote. However, I was rudely reminded of it when the North Vietnamese broke their promises made to President Nixon and Dr. Kissinger some years before, and again fully invaded South Vietnam. The fall of Saigon was rapid, and the hasty evacuation of Americans from the embassy was demeaning. All freedoms in South Vietnam were removed, and another curtain fell down to lead eventually to another communist country, which would lead their peoples into poverty beyond their expectations.

Some years later, after retiring from the Marine Corps, and working as a sales manager for one of the divisions of Rockwell International, I experienced a reminder of it all.

Rain was falling lightly as I was about to drive onto the

highway en route to a customer in San Diego, California. I saw a clean-cut-looking young man hitching a ride and getting wet. I stopped for him, and as we drove southward, I asked him, "Where are you headed?"

"Thanks for getting me out of the rain. I'm starting a new job today in Del Mar. Obviously, I don't own a car yet. But I will buy one as soon as I work a while on this new job."

We small-talked for a few miles and then he said, "I notice you have a Marine Corps officer's base sticker on your windshield."

"Yes, I'm a retired pilot," I responded.

He answered, "My father was a marine. He was killed in Vietnam."

"What was his name?" I asked.

"Master Sergeant Navine."

I was shocked, and overcome with mixed emotions. This young guy was the son of my platoon sergeant from my preflight training days as a naval aviation student in Pensacola, Florida. This was the son of what we flight students used to call the Navine Machine. I also had a flashback to that hot and dusty day in Vietnam when I landed my helicopter in a battlefield near Cam Ne village. For a fleeting second, my mind vividly saw the dead Navine Machine, his piercing blue eyes staring skyward and finally so peaceful. I remembered my emotions when flying his body to the Da Nang morgue.

I could not turn and face this young man in the rain-pelted car for fear he would see my eyes blurred with tears. I choked up a little and said, "I knew your father. He was a hell of a marine. He taught me my left foot from my right foot in my early stages of pilot training at Pensacola, Florida. He was a tough drill sergeant. I saw your father again . . . in Vietnam. He was a real marine, a hero. He died fighting the communists, who were then trying to extinguish the flames of freedom in South Vietnam. He did his job well."

"I wish I knew more about what happened in Vietnam," the young man responded.

"You know, someday I might write a little something about that war. After all, I was there a long four years."

Glossary

AAA	Antiaircraft Artillery, whether guns or missiles.
Affirmative	Military term for *yes* or *okay*.
AGL	Above Ground Level.
Angels	Aviators' term for altitude in thousands of feet. "Angels one zero" means ten thousand feet of altitude.
AO	Aerial Observer. An infantry or artillery officer trained to fly in an observation airplane or helicopter. The first AOs flew in hot-air balloons during the American Civil War.
Ao Dai	Pronounced *Ow zai'* A tight-fitting long dress with long sleeves and slit up the sides revealing silk pajama pants. Worn by the women of Vietnam.
ARC LIGHT	A B-52 bombing raid.
ARVN	The Army of the Republic of Vietnam (South Vietnam).
BDA	Bomb Damage Assessment. The results of damage caused by bombing. Usually assessed by a forward air controller or flight leader.
Berm	A dirt wall for protecting ammunition or a fuel-storage site.
Bunker	Cover protection against incoming explosives or bullets.

Cantonment	A military base or camp site.
CBU	Canister Bomblet Unit or cluster bomb. When dropped from an aircraft, the canister opens and hundreds of small bomblets with fléchettes and explosives disperse.
Charlie	Name given to the Viet Cong and North Vietnamese soldiers by the American troops.
Chopper	Another term for helicopter.
Close Air Support	Direct support of ground forces by attack aircraft close to friendly troops.
Concertina	Barbed wire for placing a fence without poles.
DASC	Direct Air Support Control. A radar center that controls attack aircraft in an area for mission control.
DME	Distance Measuring Equipment of the aviation TACAN or visual omni range navigational system.
EGT	Exhaust Gas Temperature. A turbojet engine thrust factor. Increase in engine performance results in increased EGT and increased fuel consumption.
FAC	Forward Air Controller.
FACA	Forward Air Controller Airborne.
Flak	Exploding antiaircraft shells.
Formation	Two or more aircraft flying together. Two aircraft constitute a section. Four aircraft form a division.
Frag Order	Fragmentation Order, or an add-on order to an operation plan or operation order, or a stand-alone order.
G	Gravity. A unit of force equal to the gravitational attraction of the earth at the earth's surface. In an aircraft, changes in apparent Gs are caused by acceleration or by centrifugal force (the latter occurring when an aircraft changes direction at high speed).
GCA	Ground-Controlled Approach. Military approach control of an aircraft to an airfield under the verbal control of the radar operator.
GCI	Ground-Controlled Intercept. A shipboard- or ground-based radar control system for vectoring friendly defensive aircraft to attack enemy aircraft.
Gooner	Name given to the Viet Cong by Americans. Similar to the term *gooks* given to the North Korean soldiers by American troops during the Korean War.
Ground effect	A cushion of air developed under helicopters and airplanes. Under helicopters it is created by the downwash of the air from the rotating rotor blades, while hovering and below the airspeed of about fifteen knots. It is also developed by fixed-wing aircraft when the airplane is traveling slowly close to the ground or water. It is an extra beneficial lift for the aircraft.

G Suit	Pilot's waist and leg covering that is inflated with the pneumatic pumping of the aircraft engine bleed air into the covering worn on the body.
Hootch	Commonly used word for home, hut, or tent by U.S. troops in Vietnam.
ICS	Aircraft Intercommunications System. A communications system within the aircraft for the crew to speak and listen to each other.
KBA	Killed by air. The number of enemy killed by air attack.
LZ	Landing Zone. Usually a landing site for helicopters.
Malayan Whip	A booby trap consisting of a large board with sharp spikes. When the tripwire is sprung, the board swings out and the victim is impaled.
MARLOG	Marine Air Logistics. A MARLOG flight moves supplies by air.
Nape	A napalm bomb.
Ordnance	Military weapons, primarily related to the types of bullets, shells, rockets, or bombs.
Rendezvous	To join up aircraft to form a formation.
RTB	Return To Base.
Snakeye	A snakeye bomb, or a bomb with fins that extend to retard the drop of the bomb. A snakeye allows the dropping aircraft to be very low over the target and yet avoid the explosion of the dropped bomb.
TACA	Tactical Air Controller Airborne. A pilot who controls other pilots in a tactical situation.
Tallyho	A pilot's statement that he has the other aircraft or a target in sight.
Tracer	A special round of ammunition. Usually loaded in about every eighth round of a ground-fired automatic weapon and about every tenth round of aircraft-fired ordnance, the tracer glows in flight and helps the gunner direct his shooting.
UHF	Ultrahigh Frequency. A kind of radio used by military pilots and military air traffic controllers.
VC	Viet Cong. The South Vietnamese Communist guerrilla forces. This name was given to them by their enemy, the South Vietnamese government.
VHF	Very High Frequency. Radio frequencies used by commercial and general aviation pilots and controllers.
Viet Minh	The name of Ho Chi Minh's insurgent forces. Called this before the term *Viet Cong* was applied to them.
Winchester	Aviator's term indicating that he is out of bombs, rockets, or bullets.
WP	White Phosphorus. A compound used in certain artillery, naval gunfire or aircraft target-marking rockets. Often

called "Willie Peter," "Willie Pete," or "WP" by the combatants.

Zuni
An air-to-ground rocket that measures five inches in diameter. It is very accurate and carries much more of an explosive punch than the 2.75-inch aircraft rocket.

Index

DISCARD

About the Author

Col. Bob Stoffey was born in Coaldale, Pennsylvania, and graduated from Pennsylvania State University. He served as a Marine Corps pilot for twenty-five years, having flown twenty-four different types of aircraft worldwide. His many military decorations include the Marine Corps Medal for Personal Heroism, two Distinguished Flying Crosses, and twenty-five Air Medals. He retired in 1979 and now lives in Carlsbad, California, with his wife.